DON'T BET ON THE PRINCE!

DR. GILDA CARLE

DON'T BET ON THE PRINCE!

How to Have the Man
You Want by Betting
on Yourself

NEW YORK

Golden Books®
888 Seventh Avenue
New York, NY 10106

Designed by Molly Leach

Manufactured in the United States of America

10 9 8 7 6 5 4 3 2 1

Grateful acknowledgment is made for permission
to republish two quotes from the "Jake: A Man's Opinion"
column in *Glamour* magazine:
    for the November 1995 quote on page 15: Courtesy *Glamour*. Copyright © 1995
by the Condé Nast Publications Inc.
    for the March 1996 quote on page 114: Courtesy *Glamour.* Copyright © 1996
by the Condé Nast Publications Inc.

Individuals depicted in this book are composites.
To protect privacy interests, all names and identifying details
have been changed and letters have been paraphrased.

Gilda-Gram is a trademark and service mark owned by Dr. Gilda Carle.

Library of Congress Cataloging-in-Publication Data
Carle, Gilda.
    Don't bet on the prince! : how to have the man you want by
betting on yourself / Gilda Carle.
    p. cm.
    ISBN 0-307-44000-1
    1. Self-esteem in women.   2. Single women—Psychology.
3. Mate selection.   4. Man-woman relationships.   I. Title.
HQ1206.C266 1997
646.7'7'082—dc21   97-14460
                                                      CIP

FOR

Mom, Kathi, Lauren, and Erin
—with all my love

Acknowledgments

I could never have achieved all that I have without the help of the angels in my life. Elizabeth Hepburn with her golden singing voice has been my spiritual guide and closest friend. Isabel Barnard Biederman has been my "sister" and confidante. I also owe so much to my "family" in the television industry. Geraldo Rivera was the first host I worked with, and I am grateful for his generosity. Sally Jessy Raphaël has been my greatest inspiration. I am indebted to her and her entire staff. Coordinating producer Christina Pane Deyo originally discovered me as I did some public service announcements on Home Shopping. She and associate producer Melissa Costello both initially advanced my daytime television presence. Amy Rosenblum, Sally's genius co-executive producer, pushed it over the edge by continuing to trust my on-air judgment before the worldwide public. Executive producer Maurice Tunick has been a supportive friend. I also thank Richard Bey, David Sittenfeld, and Mark Lipinski for believing in me during my earliest beginnings.

Other angels who have illuminated my path are Sue Kovach, Laura Marini, Lee Fryd, Lara Asher, Lauren Thierry, Robert McGarvey, Judy Lederman, Susan Sandler, Cindy Schneider, Linda Barbanel, Susan Jacoby, Liz Gassett, Warren Berger, Wayne Cioffari, George Tunick, Regan Solmo, Maxine and Seymour Lifschitz, Andy and Marcia Goldstein, Harlan Daman, Mercy College, and countless journalists and television and radio producers who were in my corner.

As these people encouraged and nurtured me, my agent, David Vigliano, and his then assistant, Noah Lukeman, insightfully paired me with my *golden* editor, Laura Yorke, the brilliant driving force behind this work. Finally, my attorney and friend, Bill Liebowitz, offered his wise and humorous words that kept me laughing.

Thank you all. But especially I want to thank my viewers and listeners, the people on the street, the folks who stopped me in stores and at airports, the men and women at my keynote speeches and workshops, my audiences—my greatest angels, who often urged, "Why don't you have a book?" For all of you who probed, finally, here is the information I've learned from you as you spilled your souls. Thank you for your continued support. I feel truly blessed.

Contents

Introduction

👑 **Gilda-Gram** *Ask "I am who?" before saying "I do."*

What did Princess Di have in common with the rest of us less-than-royal women in the world? At one time or another, most of us have bet on a prince, and at one time or another, most of us were duped! Like it or not, relationships are the mainstay for women, whether lover/beloved, mother/child, boss/employee, or girlfriend/girlfriend. Sadly, finding a "good man" seems to be the aim of young women as soon as they reach puberty. And after puberty, the process of single females searching for Mr. Right becomes a career of its own. Yet as soon as we find him and marry him, something amazing occurs: research shows that we, as married women, often become more depressed than single women! Why? Throughout time we have observed this direct correlation between a woman saying "I do" and her almost immediate transformation to "I am *who*?" A woman's capacity to love would not result in her loss of self if her self-esteem were well entrenched *before* she chose a mate. We need not feel that "single bookends" count as nothing. In fact, at certain times, being single is the best choice a woman can make.

Don't get me wrong. I love men. This book is not a male-bashing treatise that accuses men of ruining women's lives. There are plenty of other books on the market for that purpose. *Don't Bet on the Prince!* is a step-by-step manual for women to succeed in love by establishing their personal power, projecting it, and attracting partners who respect it and reflect it. Although the World Health Organization finds that women globally suffer higher depression rates than men, there is a group of married women who are *not* affected by marital blues. These are women who have a supportive partner and outside goals. Ultimately, the way they feel about themselves determines the message they send about whom they attract and how they expect to be treated. Simply, what women project, men will reflect. However, it all starts not with them, but with us.

The basic premise of projecting and reflecting is not new. But the context of this book is. With these principles, women will no longer *attract* the fearful, commitment-phobic, abusive, or negative partners they have magnetized and/or married. With this book, a woman can develop skills to reel in men who think the world of her because she thinks the world of herself. She will learn to exchange the bottom of the barrel for the top of the heap. The premise is simple: The love we give to a partner is secondhand; *our first and primary love is the love we give ourselves.* We are the ones we must share our best and most loving relationship with. Now that's a switch for women: to put ourselves first for a change, before our men, our children, our friends, our bosses. For those who fear being called "selfish" because of it, this book shows how to let others' assessments go unheeded, only to be replaced by strong and clear assessments of yourself. In short, you will never be used as a doormat again.

When we love ourselves, we look better, we walk taller, we laugh heartier, and we enjoy life's spontaneous adventures and passions. When we love ourselves we can *be* ourselves with abandon. We no longer have to worry about our impressions or regressions. Ultimately, we have fun with life—and our optimism is contagious. Every man with an IQ above room temperature knows what attracts him most. Evolved guys enjoy being inspired by stimulating women.

Don't Bet on the Prince! shows a woman how to hook and hug and hold a mate not by tiresome and manipulative game playing, but through natural power, definite purpose, and eternal zest for play. We've done enough contriving, jockeying, and power plays. For women who want to succeed at love, this book can serve as the current-day Koran by which anyone can happily live her life.

GILDA-GRAM
FROM INTRODUCTION

▶ *Ask "I am who?" before saying "I do."*

PART I

Happily Ever After Begins and Ends with You

1

When We Dream of Princes,
We Wake Up with Toads

👑 **Gilda-Gram** *Make yourself the prize before you prize a partner.*

I bet on the prince. In fact, I must have been a very slow learner because I bet on a lot of princes. One after another, for a large part of my life, I put all my faith in men: my husbands to love me, my lawyers to protect me, my clients to support me, my employers to benefit me, my partners to enrich me. So many princes, so little time. . . . I married them, I hired them, I laid them, I paid them. Over and over again, I banked on each one keeping what he often didn't even know was his promise: to take care of me. For one reason or another, I was always disappointed. Each time I bet on a prince, we both lost.

Why did I keep repeating my mistakes? Because I learned my lessons well. Based on the nursery rhymes and fairy tales I was taught as a child, I concluded that men were kings who belonged on thrones and that someday my prince would come, and he would have one, and only one, objective in life—to save me from whatever lay ahead.

For most women, when we were growing up, fairy-tale characters impressed us with their simplicity. These tales taught that being bland and idle would reward us with partners of princely proportions who would deliver us from our doldrums. Rapunzel was locked in a tower until her savior climbed beyond the thorns. Snow White lived with seven sexually dwarfed men until her hero carried her off in her coffin. Sleeping Beauty slept for a century until reactivated by an arousing kiss. Cinderella sat by dirty cinders until her prince stuck her foot in a shoe. While we might have learned that little ladies transform frogs to princes, we also understood that a gal must be frozen to be chosen. And the only real way to gain access to the kingdom was to wake up and screw the prince . . . (un)happily ever after. Did any of us little girls ever ask what happened to the happy couple after they retired to the castle?

Today, most women still search hard and wide for Mr. Charming. Pity that what we often end up with instead is Mr. Cheap, Mr. Bad-

Mannered, Mr. Ill-Tempered, Mr. My-Children-Come-First, or Mr. My-Wife-Doesn't-Understand-Me. Never a Charming Prince.

Unfortunately, none of my princes ever began as royalty. Just as in the fairy tales, they usually emerged as tadpoles, straight from the lily pad, pond scum and all. But not to worry. I knew what to do. If we don't meet him, we manufacture him. We say, "Eventually, he'll change." I told myself that in time love would transform even those who start out squat, warty, ugly, clammy. Like all the women I knew, I pursued my mission of transmission. At worst, maybe I'd end up with a kindly Kermit. Truth is, when you kiss a toad, you don't get a prince at all, just a lot of slime in your mouth.

But the myth remains, the belief that frogs can transform into princes. And in our convictions, we pinch, we pull, we press . . . and when he gets to where we momentarily want him, we quit. That is, we may take a slight breather, but we never fully quit altering him. What we do quit is initiating life for ourselves. Isn't it odd? He couples with us hoping we'll never change, but we couple with him hoping he will! "What does she look like?" he asks before meeting us for the first time, while we ask, "What does he *do?*" foreseeing his earning *potential*.

For most women, finding even an almost princely, charming mate is the beginning of our end. As though we were babbling idiots before our partner appeared, we entrust this guy to take total charge. Though not a mechanic, he knows *better* how to service the car. Though not an attorney, he knows *better* how to advise us legally. Though not an accountant, he knows *better* how to compute the taxes, write the checks, pay the bills. We don't merely delegate; we blindly pass the power plate. And as we do, we unconsciously drive the first nail into our coffin. What follows is worse. Knowing well that the relationship has problems, we often remain in it anyway for many more years. In one such relationship, while I remained, I chose not to upset the apple cart. To be loved, I silenced my needs, wants, feelings, and passions, as many women do once they become part of a pair. We shut down the things that used to turn us on. By doing that, we extinguish our souls.

It is hard to believe that it was so long ago, 1981, when Colette Dowling thwacked women's consciousness with *The Cinderella Complex*. Its subtitle, *Women's Hidden Fear of Independence*, squarely socked it to the women who begged for salvation, retreated from life, and became hapless and helpless to a man. Dowling motivated women worldwide to renew their dreams, pursue their challenges, and, in short, *get a life*. Unfortunately, as it turns out, women's determination to be independent back then was short-lived, their vows vacuous, their promises empty. Today, almost two decades later, on talk show after talk show, on-line, in college and graduate school classrooms, in private therapy sessions, in worldwide workshops and seminars, I continue to meet women who fantasize the *rescue*, the dream that "someday my prince will *still* come." They've been educated well by the romance movies of our time. *Sabrina's* hero rescues her from lower classism, while she in turn rescues him from emotional despair. To the tune of a $178.4 million box office hit, *Pretty Woman's* hero rescues the whore-with-a-heart and off they go to live happily ever after. In the movies the hero says something witty, the laugh track commands our own desire for him, we watch the heroine crumple into his arms, and the music swells. As the credits roll, we emerge from the theater convinced that life as such can happen to us mere mortals. And so it is, at the start of the millennium, the romantic rescue is still alive and well. Some things never change.

Not only do today's women dream about this guy's coming and what he will do for them, they boldly enunciate their *need* for him as though they are merely treading water in the sea of employment, dating, and life's other mundane rituals until they get the kiss that counts. And it starts earlier and earlier in adolescent girls:

> *Dear Dr. Gilda:*
> *I'm 12 and in the 7th grade. I've never been in love, never had*
> *a boyfriend, and never been kissed. Is this normal? How do I*
> *snag a boyfriend who will love me and take care of me?*

This at age twelve! This despite the fact that studies indicate that throughout elementary school, girls consistently achieve higher reading scores than boys, take more academic courses, and are more likely to complete college. Not only do women constitute the bulk of college students, they also receive the majority of master's degrees. Yet eleven-year-old Rebecca, creatively composing words to her own song, writes:

> *When I'm asleep I dream of you, when I'm awake I think of*
> *you. In my fantasies you're my prince, my hero, the key that*
> *unlocks the door to my daydreams.*

And a thirteen-year-old *weenager,* Slater, writes me:

> *Dr. Gilda, I wrote you about the guy at school that I liked but*
> *couldn't tell if he liked me. Well I found out that he does sorta*
> *like me. Should I confront him about it? How long should I*
> *wait before an actual relationship?*

For little girls, as well as for grown-up women, the promise of awakening through the relationship still looms.

Perhaps we can forgive the young girls for their innocence. We'd like to think they'll grow wiser in time. But what about the woman in her mid-thirties with the Internet screen name "Take Cr Of Me"? And the commercial for a popular fragrance with a beautiful woman boldly boasting, "He said he would take care of me." Nor can I ever forget the sickly, overweight welfare recipient with five out-of-wedlock kids I met on a talk show whose future life plans I asked about and who nonchalantly replied, "I'm gonna find a rich guy to take care of us." Mae West put it bluntly: *It's better to be looked over than overlooked.* Some guy to *take care of us* and do what we're too lame to do ourselves? From all walks of life, millions of women *still* search for salvation—not within themselves, but in some yet-to-be-created prince. A man to "take care of us"—when he's barely able to care for himself?

Look at what this power passing is doing to us. Throughout the years that I have collated data about the pain women inflict on themselves, the points that stand out most are that *twice the number of women as men suffer from panic attacks, women are the largest consumers of antacids,* and *we become three times more depressed than men when our marriages fail.* The 1993 Year of the Woman has come and gone. Are we happier, more successful, feeling more beautiful? Do we have more control over our lives?

If anything, our natural power seems to scare even ourselves. Highly paid married women, fearful of intimidating their husbands, lie about their earnings. While many of their mates were originally attracted to these women's independence, as their relationship unfolded, the women sensed a need to protect their men from competitive disappointment. They learned to play down their virtues and play up his. The motto has been "Make your man feel comfortable as you discomfort yourself." This notion has been supported by Catalyst, the women's professional support organization. They found that the women who successfully push through the glass ceiling of corporate America are the ones whose styles make men feel *comfortable* rather than intimidated. Once again, being the "nice girl," placing your own desires on hold, wins out.

Penny dated a wealthy physician several times. When they saw each other for the second time, he complained how the women he dated often tried to assess his finances. He accused them of treating him like a walking wallet and said that he avoided these women at all costs. On their third date, Penny had been elated over a new business contract she had just negotiated. The physician said, "That's great. How much will you earn from it?" Penny replied, "Almost a million dollars." The physician stuttered, "Wow! You're really wealthy." Although they proceeded to have a great time that evening, he never called Penny for another date. In her heart she knew that her date deal *breaker* was precisely her own deal *maker.* Obviously it was okay for this guy to laud his big bucks over the heads of admiring females and complain about their positive impressions of his wealth. But when the roles were reversed, he became the intimidated Road Runner.

While today's women no longer look to burn bras, their desire to manufacture and market them comes with a steep price. Deep in the bosoms of many women lies the fear that their man will abandon them if they make more money than he. A well-paid married client of mine thought she would outsmart the odds. When the $90,000-a-year earner relayed the salary secret she kept well guarded from her husband, I suggested that her marriage could be on shaky ground. No good relationship can be based on lies—whether through omission or commission. My client shuddered and admitted she was in the throes of divorce.

The Great Divide

What I finally gleaned from my experiences and from those of the women I have known is that princes have their own problems—and they sure don't need ours. For one thing, the princes themselves have had a history of betting on their own kind of prince. Theirs was once their corporate job, and they bet that it would care for them forever, from womb to tomb. But suddenly and shockingly they were pink-slipped. The false protection their company membership once bought turned on them. Now they wonder if they'll ever find another setting where they can be cared for as well.

Yet historically, cross-culturally, and among animals and birds, males are set up to protect females. Male birds display colorful plumage so their predators will notice and eat them first. Similarly, women want men to protect us physically, financially, emotionally, and even mechanically. We want our men to hold on to us in the street as we hobble on high heels. We want to put their authoritative voices on our answering machines to ward off would-be intruders. We want them to speak to our professional and service people, to shield us from unscrupulous business practices.

Not surprisingly, there are gaping differences between our expectations and men's abilities to meet them. The reasons are (1) today's men want to be nurtured themselves, but (2) they feel insecure about their own needs and measuring up to ours, and (3) they fear intimacy and commitment too much to get the nurturing they desire.

Men Want Nurturing Themselves

While women continue to fantasize about a prince to take care of them, with life's latest disappointments, today's prince generally wants someone to take care of *him*. It may start with "Can I buy you a drink?" As the courtship progresses, it transforms to "We were meant for each other; you have this great apartment, and I need a place to stay." But at curtain time, the plea is "Will you be my mommy—or at least my dominatrix?"

Although they kick and scream, men know that married guys outlive their single counterparts. Each year millions of Americans continue to tie the knot. According to a government survey in the United Kingdom, 51 percent of divorced men who do not remarry wish they had stayed with their original wives. Men seem to need the warmth and caretaking women provide.

> **Is it better to be single or married?**
> *It's better for girls to be single, but not boys. Boys need*
> *somebody to clean up after them.*
>
> —*Wanda, age 9*

Little Wanda must be on to something. When it was learned that American astronaut Shannon Lucid would be stranded for months aboard the Russian space station Mir, her two male Russian orbiters welcomed her because "we know women love to clean." With their comment came a suggestion from *The Washington Post* that she superglue the toilet seat in the down position.

Yes, because of their learned helplessness over domestic chores, men need our nurturing. But they also require our nurturing to fill the loss of job promises and the need for love they won't admit they have. In an effort to get our attention and keep it, droves of men are now running off to princify themselves to make us want them more.

Men Feel Insecure About Their Own Needs and Measuring Up to Ours

Although they want to be wanted, men are afraid of putting themselves out on a limb and falling off. Just like women, they fear abandonment, rejection, and now, in light of the ever-ready vibrator and the single-parent adoption, the possibility of being dispensed with altogether. Lurking in their minds is always "What if she refuses my advances?" Jerry Seinfeld, the modern-day finger-on-the-pulse-of-life commentator, found the solution to keeping the sperm bank at bay. He named it a "dating loophole." In one episode from his TV show, he relays to Elaine that instead of a guy asking a woman out and possibly getting rebuffed, he can set up a bet with her whereby if he loses, he buys her dinner. The guy makes sure to lose and thus gets a date without having to ask for one. This gets him off the possible rejection hook while still getting the girl.

Single guys really do have a lot of pressures. Alcoholism, unemployment, depression, illness, and suicide are reported to be significantly higher among single men than married ones (while single women fare better than those who marry these guys). So to win a woman's heart, men focus on "measuring up" for the bedroom while packaging themselves for the boardroom. Besides the usual suit jacket that puffs out the male chest, they supplement their bottom lines with "super shaper briefs" and pack their privates with the new "endowment pad." Back from a marathon workout, they glob Rogaine on their head to thicken their hair, and alphahydroxy is sloshed on their face to smooth their wrinkly skin. Even the American Academy of Cosmetic Surgery boasts increased numbers of male patients. From hair regrowth centers, men even go to penile augmenters. Ouch! The price of princehood.

A *Glamour* magazine poll questioned one thousand men about what concerns them more: the size of the national debt or the size of their penis. While 55 percent of the respondents named the national debt, a whopping 44 percent named their penis size. A few letters to me from some men concur:

> *Dear Dr. Gilda:*
> *My penis is 4 inches long and on the skinny side. Does this impact on how I can perform sexually? My girlfriend says that her last boyfriend was 8 inches and a lot wider and he felt better. . . .*

> *Dear Dr. Gilda:*
> *I'm 39 years old and my sex drive is sky high. My physician referred me to a neurologist. He ordered an EEG and an MRI to check for brain tumors. Both tests came up normal. . . .*

> *Dear Dr. Gilda:*
> *I'm a 24-year-old male. I sit on a couch with a woman and get hard, but once I get her in bed, Stanley heads south. . . .*

With America's sweeping ab-session, we watch our guys wrestle to transform their wash*tub* midsections into chiseled, wash*board* stomach stereotypes. But the ultimate driving machine is just a few inches down. Most men think their penises come in only one size—too small. While the average is five to seven inches in its erect state (and three to five inches flaccid), research by Bernice Kanner finds that men claim the average to be ten inches. Since Casanova could allegedly keep an erection for seven hours (!), fear of the Lilliputian levitation has accelerated the demand for Mandelay Climax Control Gel to help a guy "stay in control." Of course, it comes in "Maximum Strength."

It is no wonder men are increasingly unhappy with their bodies and performance. Their role models are Hollywood's three S-men: Schwarzenegger, Stallone, and Seagal. Hal Ketchum stands in a boxing ring and croons his country music video "Hang in There, Superman," as cowboys, fishermen, athletes, fliers, jazz singers, even stuntmen shot from cannons all flash across our TV screen. *Hang in there, Superman!* Fear of sexual failure is so pervasive that the National Institutes of Health recommends replacing the term "impotence" with "erectile dysfunction." With all the pressure to be Superman, according to the American Urological Association, impotence—uh, erectile dysfunction—strikes some thirty million American men. Generation X–ers are pressed to use their apparatus before their angle of turgidity droops below the horizon and they need a forklift to rise to the occasion. How depressing for aging baby boomers who brush away middle-age malaise with "natural" color, who dump their *First Wives* for newfound "trophies," who substitute one symbol of constraint, the jockstrap, for another, Depends. But there is no way to avoid the creeping decrepitude of life moving on. From inner plumbing to outer housing, men have done everything possible to maintain their edge. But the hair from their head seeps through their ears and nose faster than the proverbial speeding bullet. *Hang in there, Superman!*

Are all his machinations a waste of energy? A *McCall's* survey found that the sort of man women fantasized about most was the teddy bear type, not the strong-stomached mantelpiece. Maybe cuddling with Quasimodo wouldn't be so bad after all. Are these guys missing the point in their zealous pruning and grooming? That's *their* issue. *And that's precisely my point.*

We have our own problems. In particular, as soon as we become an official "couple," a once trailblazing woman transforms into retiring soldier to her colonel. At first our man may encourage our reticent demeanor, coupled with our eagerness to "help him." Thanks to us, his own importance shines. While he fears workplace downsizing, thanks to us at home, he now feels *upsized*. Achieving sudden security, we willingly settle into the r-e-l-a-t-i-o-n-s-h-i-p. Ohhh . . . Ahhh . . . Bliiiiss. But not for long. Before we know it, he feels trapped and resentful about the exact behavior he elicited from us in the first place. But we have only ourselves to blame.

Men Fear Intimacy and Commitment

Far from home on the range, the word on the street is still *"Hasta la vista, baby!"* as our men often distance themselves even from the women they love. Their training in separation tactics has been long present. Don't forget the first words in our *Dick and Jane* readers: "Run, Dick, run." The Marlboro Man rode solo into the setting sun. Even the Lone Ranger, occasionally inviting Tonto to join him, never commingled with Ton*ta*. The simple fact of human life is that men are threatened by women's need for intimacy, and we are threatened by men's need for separation. Men feel *invaded*, while their partner feels *evaded*. These differences do not make for happy times.

Women use intimacy to establish their identity: "Someone loves me, so I must be all right." In contrast, men's identity precedes their need to be intimate: "I have to know who I am and where I'm going before I commit." Male isolation is especially evident after the heat of entanglement. We wonder if he'll call again as we often bemoan that sex ruins everything. Reminiscent of the image of the creepy crawler, many guys fear that women will engulf or "devour" them after they become close. Actually, most women can't understand why guys fear this connection. Even Orkin Exterminating Company notes that the female black widow spider is usually unsuccessful in her attempts to eat her mate after sex!

After a man's distancing, some women exercise their misplaced aggression and kick Cupid square in the bow. Their feelings of rejection catapult them into degrading obsession. This pathological passion is so strong, even Calvin Klein can't differentiate between the imagined and the real as he asks, "Is it love or is it obsession?" Fatally fixated, these women try to net their elusive butterfly. Now the man who moved like a tortoise toward commitment darts like a cheetah toward the cave. The fear of evisceration looms larger. No wonder popular male fragrances have names like Safari, Wings, and Escape.

Sure, men press for sex. When a woman receives and accepts a man's offer, adding a new notch to his belt makes him feel wanted. Yet although most women fantasize sex as the first step to the altar, men's fear of engulfment begins to take over. One man, about to sleep at his girlfriend's house, looked at her pink-and-white bedroom with inflated pillows and gasped, "It's so pink and puffy in here, I'm afraid I'll wake up gay." Another, who had spent twenty-five years after his divorce successfully avoiding the melding of love and sex, walked into his new lady's bedroom for the first time and imagined the odor of mothballs in her closed closet. He said, "I can't sleep here," and used the excuse to sleep on the living room sofa while his woman slept in her bedroom *alone*.

We want closeness, they want separation. Our past behaviors have led us nowhere. So what do we do now?

....

 👑 **Gilda-Gram** *If we always do what we've always done, we'll always go where we've always gone.*

....

Snap out of your former habits and remember this: Most men will hold on to their power at any cost. A smart woman knows that the closeness she values is precisely what her lover fears. She understands and accepts her guy's inevitable distancing, does not take it personally, and invests in *her own life* so she doesn't feel abandoned. No matter what, there is only one way to remain in charge of who you are:

👑 **Gilda-Gram** *Choose, rather than be chosen.*

How and where do we begin?

Make Love Happen!

Women must cease emptying their own potency into the hands of someone else. How? For starters, let's revisit our fairy tales with a different interpretation than we derived from our first reads. There's a better rendition and a clearer guide for women to succeed in love.

To begin with, the tales taught us that finding love takes time. They asked us to relinquish the rash reach for immediate pleasure and substitute waiting for when we can better handle our consequences. Scheherazade showed every girl-in-a-hurry how to take her time, save her neck (literally), and win a lifetime partner. In this tale, the king partook of a different virgin by night and beheaded her afterward by day, predating Lorena Bobbitt's carvings by centuries. When it was Scheherazade's turn to titillate the king, she decided instead to seduce him in a different way. Unraveling exciting stories that captivated his continued attention, she'd feign fatigue each time she'd get to the climax and suggest continuing on the following evening. Not only did her scheme guarantee her a steady date for three long years, the king found that he could not live without either his suspenseful entertainment or his captivating lady. In the vernacular, this couple did manage to live "happily ever after"—but that was only after three years of ardent seduction by one very smart young woman. Good advice for today's bed-hopping hopefuls who rush to give sex to get love.

Second, the fairy tales taught that pain must be endured and risks taken for us to grow at anything. No woman rises in the morning, acknowledges her perfect mate, and risks exchanging him for the other side of midnight. It is the torture of sickness and sorrow and boredom and love lost that pushes our buttons to grow in a different direction. Rapunzel was locked in a tower, Snow White remained deadened in a coma, and Cinderella sat soiled by the cinders. Each maiden had to experience suffering before she could find salvation. Too bad for women who mistake life for some carefree magic carpet ride and who become disappointed when they discover otherwise. Truth be told, despite all the happily-ever-afters, there are no happy endings without a lot of turmoil and hard work. Pain is a needed lesson for all the women pushing for quick commitment. Distress management tells a lot about how people will cope with life's necessary future losses. Navigate the ebbs and flows before you drown in waters over your head.

Finally, deeply hidden in some distant interlinear fairy-tale translations, we learned that victory would be measured not by the power we have over others, but by the power we have in ourselves. Although Snow White's apple was poisonous, it was *she* who coughed it up and awakened herself from her seven sexless servants. Rapunzel, too, drew from her natural body parts as her tresses became her ladder and her tears healed the prince's thorn-blinded eyes. Finally, despite all our Cinderella bashing, we've got to admit this woman was no dummy. She sure didn't look *east* for the sunset! She knew the ball was approaching, and *she* strategized a way to get there. *She* arranged assistance from her fairy godmother, found the best transportation in town, and dressed to impress. Although she never consciously considered herself "entrepreneurial," she knew exactly what to do to make love happen. Once face-to-face with the prince, she talked, danced, flirted, and romanced. And despite the fact that she was having the time of her life, at the stroke of midnight she disappeared. The story might have ended there, but this woman has to be admired for her creativity. As she departed, since she didn't have a business card, she left one of her shoes. Fortunate for her the prince had a foot fetish!

Love is a paradox. Those women desperate for it are the women who lack it. Those who could care less are the ones who attract it. Since today's real catch is a guy who doesn't want the dead weight of dependence around his purse strings, a woman's power is a *real* man's aphrodisiac. And who doesn't want a *real* man? Like our male counterparts, we all seek someone who, when found, we consider a prize well sought, well won.

> *Look, you can fish for bluegill, and they'll just about jump on your line. When you fish for trout, they tease you, you tease them, until they take the fly. Then they fight you. I cannot remember a single bluegill, though I've hooked hundreds. But I can remember every trout I have ever caught.*
> —Jake, A Man's Opinion
> *Glamour* magazine

There is only one rule that all women must follow:

👑 **Gilda-Gram** *Make yourself the prize before you prize a partner.*

Unfortunately, nice girls that we are, we continue to be shocked each time a prince tells his princess: "With this castle, I thee dump." Before our amazed eyes, the alleged Rambo transforms to graceless Dumbo. What went wrong? At one time or another, most of us have bet on the wrong person, *another person*, rather than the one reflected in the mirror.

I've appeared on hundreds of TV shows where women's issues center around loving and being loved. The major mistake our gender makes is concentrating almost exclusively on our men instead of striving first to better our own lives. Instead of examining what's wrong with him, discover what's best in *you*. Rather than searching for love, seek to be lovable. This is the key to your success in love. When you act from the heart, it's not a manipulative means of playing hard to get. You are simply into your own life, thereby making yourself a better prize. The consequence of taking care of yourself first is that although you'll never change your man, you may help him transform himself, if he is a willing participant, or you may end up with someone far more worthy. It's a simple spinoff of making yourself the trophy: when you throw a pebble in the ocean, there is a rippling effect. Similarly, when you make yourself the best that you can be, all your relationships will reflect the enhanced you.

In short, don't bet on the prince. Bet on yourself. The more you have to offer, the grander the guy you'll get. You'll hook him, hug him, hold him . . . and he'll never stray. Because you'll project the message that you're worth it.

👑 Gilda-Gram *Don't bet on the prince. Bet on yourself. Self-love is never unrequited.*

GILDA-GRAMS
FROM CHAPTER 1
When We Dream of Princes, We Wake Up with Toads

▶ *If we always do what we've always done,
we'll always go where we've always gone.*

▶ *Choose, rather than be chosen.*

▶ *Make yourself the prize before you prize a partner.*

▶ *Don't bet on the prince. Bet on yourself.
Self-love is never unrequited.*

2

Women Who Bet on the Prince: We're All in Good Company

👑 **Gilda-Gram** *Commit to yourself instead of waiting for a prince to commit to you.*

Not long ago, I watched a group of eight businesswomen sitting at a large round table in a Chinese restaurant. They were joking and laughing loudly as they ate their lunch. Their conversation was punctuated with workplace gossip and personal intimacies. They were having a wonderful time. Suddenly a man they knew joined them. As they made a place for him at the table, the atmosphere turned quiet and reserved. The mirth had disappeared from their party. There were no longer sounds of spontaneity and genuine enjoyment. Because of a man.

What is it with women? Why can't we enjoy life for itself without a man and enhance our life with one after we have already established ourselves as whole people? Why don't we supplant the desperation with a desire for enhancement? In short, why does it take so long for women to learn to bet on ourselves?

Rich, poor, sick, healthy, white, black, young, old, clerical worker, company president, every one of us was raised to bet on some prince. From the Ozarks to Scarsdale, from trailer park to castle, from the heartland to Hollywood, women were raised to believe there's a soulmate somewhere who was put on this earth to romance us, slay our dragons, mend our wounds, and protect our assets for as long as we live. We may come from different oceans, but we all wind up in the same boat, the one labeled "I'm Less of a Sailor Without a First Mate." To secure a first mate, many of us finagle our way into coupledom without scrutinizing our partner and why we've paired with him. Consequently the partner we attract out of desperation is often less a "soulmate" and more a "fill-a-hole mate." This match can be lethal.

Why do we attract whom we attract? Two distinct forces operate when we attract a potential partner:

1. *We attract our opposite.* We typically choose mates with traits complementary to our own. Unconsciously we mistakenly believe two halves are required to make us whole. So I, as a dancer, with fluid, "feminine" body

movements and a dramatic personality, typically chose an organized, directed, "masculine" type of man with a more conservative personality. At first we found each other captivating. Our differences were refreshing as we "fit" together like a perfect puzzle and became a single "whole."

2. *We seek traits, both good and bad, that we unconsciously recognize from our parents.* Usually the bad traits are more influential in our attraction, because this gives us the opportunity to relive and heal old wounds inflicted on us during childhood. So I, whose father was very devoted to my mother, yet who communicated with her through angry Archie Bunker–like put-downs, unconsciously sought a man whose negative words toward me provided comforting familiarity. Unconsciously I intended to make *my* relationship with *my* man better than what my mother allowed for herself.

In short, we "fall" passionately in love with our *complementary opposite*, who also reflects the *worst traits* from our parents. The general length of elation is eighteen months to three years. Regardless of the length of time, it seems that as soon as we go from love to commitment, the romance screeches to a halt. Then the opposite and negative traits we at first found so attractive begin to irritate us. I become frustrated that my partner won't go dancing with me and be more emotionally demonstrative. He becomes frustrated that I am so flashy and not more logically grounded. He begins putting me down as his means of getting me to comply with his behavioral standards. I accept his coarse tone, looking to avoid his angst, mirroring the way my accepting mother compromised herself with my father. We enter into the same power struggle patterns we learned at birth, each convinced our partner doesn't love us enough.

While each partner began in search of a committed relationship (despite moans to the contrary from the male species), having a committed relationship should not be the goal at all:

👑 Gilda-Gram *A relationship's real objective is to provide the journey for our own personal growth.*

Harville Hendrix says that commitment to a partner can match or exceed any of our other personal growth therapies. John Bradshaw testifies that his own committed relationships provided him with more understanding than any of his other experiences. I must concur that the same has happened in my own life, painful as the passages seemed at the time. If not for having experienced and pushed through the ghosts of my past, I would never have evolved to the point I am at today.

Unfortunately, most women are fixated on *getting* the relationship instead of *growing* it. They are unaware that a relationship is like a variegated garden with multicolored flowers and even assorted weeds. Each aspect of the landscape is always at a different stage of bloom. But before the flora and fauna can be part of the entire vista, each must be implanted firmly in the earth with its own roots.

Traditionally, women have viewed just getting into the garden, or being part of a relationship, as their sole goal. They have not learned that to stay there they must water their roots, nurture their stems, and grow their stalk strong. In short, to be a vital part of a partnership, and to maintain their connection in it, women must commit themselves to themselves first. This is the only way they can deal with the differences between themselves and the men they naturally attract. It is also their best means for maintaining their power amid these differences.

So with unwavering self-commitment, and esteem about my personal worth, I will not be swayed if my partner criticizes my light-hearted humor about life. I will not accept his angry put-downs, however familiar they may sound. I will firmly uphold my right to my behavior and personality and let slide my partner's efforts to over-power me with his preferences. He, in turn, will respect my unwillingness to oscillate at his attempted domination. I can feel safe with this man because of our deeply established respect, and also because of my ability to shine through our differences. But I feel even safer with him, knowing that I will never lose myself in his company. Our committed relationship provides the path for my journey. My roots are firmly grounded, and with him I can continue my personal growth.

One woman who was unable to contain her own identity in love was the legendary opera star Maria Callas. When she met Aristotle Onassis, she stopped singing. She devoted her life to her lover. But her lover grew restless, abused her, then married not her, but Jacqueline Kennedy. Like so many women, Callas expected to find new meaning in her life when she fell in love. When she committed herself to her man and dismantled her personal passions, her career became a shambles. She died at age fifty-three.

Losing ourselves to someone we love is a surefire way for us to lose our selves. When we lose our selves, we lose our lives. Sometimes we actually do die. Other times we die in spirit and merely mark the motions of living, but we are nonetheless dead. Maria Callas was physically alive for a time, but she had lost the very elements that first attracted Onassis to her: her talent, her career, her power to intrigue and influence audiences.

It is up to every woman herself to provide the means to rise from the ashes of dependence. For one thing, a partner can never make a woman whole. Despite what she might think, he will never become her *womb mate*. For another, love is not an all-or-nothing proposition that will fulfill all our needs or none of them. No one thing or person can ever do that for us. Finally, acquiring love is only part of the challenge; maintaining it over time is the test. And what a test it is!

> *Life is a school room, hardships are lessons, upheaval is growth, pain is transformation, tears are healing, and the meaning of love is the test question that decides your final grade. Do you ever remember signing up for any of these courses?*
>
> —*Anonymous*

Here are the sad but true stories of eight real women of varying ages, socioeconomic levels, and educational backgrounds. Unlike the fairy tales we patterned our lives after, these are no childhood myths. Although each saga is unique, every woman's conclusion is the same. Each began her romance by believing in, loving, and betting on a prince. In the end, each woman was doomed—not necessarily because her prince was such an awful character, but because she assigned him superhuman expectations and allowed him privileges with her power that she should have reserved for herself.

Finally, in the last part of this chapter you will have the opportunity to become true story number nine. You will describe your own love experiences as they have actually unfolded. By documenting on paper occurrences in our lives, we can stand back and observe the players from afar. We can also analyze our own participation in situations as though our behaviors belonged to someone else. This enables us to drop our own emotional involvement and become more objective about the choices we have made and the consequences we have endured.

Whether you are a searching single or are already married, this exercise will also give you guidelines to assess your mate selection. As you review your interactions with the men you have bet on, you will notice certain behavior patterns you continued to follow. After you have reviewed your most recent love patterns, you will have the opportunity to rewrite your "HerStory." As you do, you will be able to re-create the "facts" in the way you wished they had evolved. By evaluating the path you have already taken, and re-creating the path you prefer, you will begin to assess your choices. This assessment process is the start in changing the problematic love you now have, or the one you had that didn't work, into one that suits you better. By going through this assessment process, you will be able to make subtle changes day after day while you are living your life. Note that this love assessment is never about changing your man. Rather, it is about enhancing your own personal qualities so that you alter the kind of man you will attract. To start, let's look at the woman who literally bet on the prince.

Princess Di: The Realest Princess of Us All

Little girls the world over have patterned their dreams of love after the fictitious fairy tales which taught them that someday their prince would come. Grown-up women were assured that such dreams could really come true when we watched the splendid marriage ceremony of a conventional nursery school teacher to a real live prince. Women everywhere wondered, "How did she get him?" as we wished we were she. We emulated her "look," her hairdo, her skirt length. Maybe if we discovered her "secrets," we, too, could hook a prince. But as we cataloged the daily comings and goings of the new royal couple, it soon became obvious that the princess's life was one of dashed promises and unhappy endings, not what dreams are made of.

We have heard the *less-than-fairy* tales of Diana's eating disorders and of her attempts at suicide. In fact, as early as their honeymoon, Prince Charles demeaned his svelte new wife for being too chubby. Diana wanted to please her man, remake herself in his image, and gain his love. So she began her long struggle with bulimia, the dangerous and possibly deadly disease that strikes many beautiful young women. Here is the story of a real princess who, in fact, was willing to sacrifice her life for the love of a man who boldly admitted he did not even care.

Diana was a woman who bet on a prince to fill the role of absentee parent, companion, lover, and friend. When she was five years old, her mother deserted the family. To compensate for her sorry upbringing, not unlike any typical woman, she dreamed of a man who would be there for her, available both physically and emotionally. What she got instead was a stiff-upper-lipped cold fish who dispassionately announced that he had never really loved her and admitted to having had sons purely out of a sense of duty to the throne. In public, stuffy and aloof Charles disrespectfully displayed greater affection toward his mistress than toward his wife. When the fairy-tale kiss became the royal diss, the sad princess was Di-sected daily by the entire world.

While Princess Diana's life was miles apart from those of the ordinary people we see on America's talk shows, her reaction to the "other woman" matched what we continue to view on daytime TV. The cuckolded wife usually indicts her husband's lover far more than she charges her husband. On air, before a live audience, I have intervened in hundreds of such triangles: the husband, the wife, and the other woman. The wife gets into a verbal and/or physical battle with her husband's lover as the husband sits in the middle, immobile, like an innocent bystander. I have commented that most of these men seem to enjoy being fought over. I ask the women why they want to stroke their men's egos this way. They can offer no answer; there is none that is rational.

Like the talk show guests, a brooding Diana scorned Camilla Parker Bowles as "the bitch," "a Rottweiler," while being perfectly cordial to the man who used her as an heir factory. Surely the princess was not too fond of the prince, either, as her affairs with other married men would attest. But she mostly blamed Camilla. And, like most women who believe the relationship is *their* sole responsibility, she blamed herself. She rationalized that she had expected too much of Charles and of marriage in general. Who doesn't commit to marriage expecting a lot?

Before we ever met Diana, we saw thousands of fairy-tale romances gone bad. There were the Hollywood stars, our next-door neighbors, our own relatives. Yet for some reason we expected more from Charles and Diana. Real royalty. Real wishes. Anything but the usual "irreconcilable differences." How can two people with *everything* end up with *nothing*? In a way, we, too, were duped. We thought *everything* consisted of riches, servants, fame. Not for one moment did we consider self-respect as the basis for a couple's lasting love. Diana bet on a dream, and so did we, as curious spectators in the bleachers. But the glass slipper shattered before our eyes. Knowing this, why do we commoners continue to long for some makeshift prince? Some of us, in fact, go to some desperate extremes to seek him out.

Desperate Clerical Worker

When I met Selena, she was a panelist on a TV dating show on which I appeared. She toiled as an entry-level clerical worker, hoping to move up in time. Earlier in the year, she had met a Jewish doctor, a Ph.D. scientist, gone out with him, but never heard from him after four wonderful dates. Like most women, Selena wondered, "Why hasn't he called?" after such good times. She revealed that she had had her hopes set on marrying a Jewish doctor, with all his princely income and status, and Roger fit the bill. She felt that they had shared a special spark and there was great potential in their future.

Perhaps it should have been obvious that he did not share the same feeling; otherwise he would already have beaten a path to her door. However, Selena decided to be the aggressor in this romance, so she called the show in hopes of being reunited with her former friend. Roger was told that he would have a surprise date with someone from his past, and he gladly agreed to go along with the adventure.

When Selena appeared on stage with a bouquet of roses, Roger looked genuinely happy to see her. She had brought along some meaningful memorabilia that the two had shared. After the show, the couple agreed to rekindle their former romance. With overwhelming excitement, Selena whispered invitations to the show's staff to what she planned to be their eventual wedding.

Things seemed ideal, but there was one hitch. Roger had spent so much time in school that he was somewhat backward in his social finesse. He told Selena that his parents were perfectionists and they'd accept no woman into his life who was in any way flawed.

Several weeks after the pair had resparked the flame, an agitated Selena called me. She said that she was a diabetic and had developed a dangerous infection on her foot. Her doctor had told her to stop walking around for a while, but that would have meant her not attending the TV show. On the day of the taping, contrary to her doctor's warnings, she pushed a very swollen, infected foot into her shoe, aching terribly each time she bore down on it to walk. No one knew that this was happening, as she somehow managed to hide her horrible pain. Whatever the cost, she refused to give up what she saw as her once-in-a-lifetime chance at love. Selena wanted desperately to be married, and she would have done anything to become Roger's wife, although she really knew little about this man.

Unfortunately, Selena's plan backfired. Her foot became gangrenous and she had to have it amputated, a condition diabetics often fear. From the hospital Selena called me again. This time she asked, "Should I tell Roger the truth about my condition? I haven't called him in over a week now because I'm afraid he'll discover my imperfections." Why hadn't he called her during that stretch of time? Although I was flabbergasted, I felt sorry for a woman who would sacrifice her own health to hook an alleged prince. I questioned, "How do you expect to be in a relationship based on dishonesty?" Sadly, but with greater insight, she agreed that she must come clean and accept the consequences of her truth telling, whatever they were.

Too bad Selena never got to tell Roger the truth. When they finally did speak again, he broke off their renewed friendship with the excuse that he had found someone else his parents preferred as his marriage partner. Selena realized the pain she had endured, both physically and emotionally, for a guy who never really wanted her after all. Was her bet on this prince's heart ultimately worth sacrificing her limb? Yes, Selena's story sounds crazy from our perspective. But the world watched as a royal princess might have died from real-life starvation to become more appealing to her prince. And there are too many other women out there who continue to suffer anorexia, bulimia, emotional pain, and physical abuse just to be loved. In short, love is not supposed to damage and hurt us. The objective for all women today must be to reinterpret love, not as a condition of suffering, but as an act of extending an already en-riched self that will never put *up* with any man's put-*downs*.

Middle-Class Teacher

While some women may go to extremes to get love, others just follow the patterns of loving they observed in their homes. Caitlin grew up with two parents in a traditional middle-class neighborhood. Her father held two jobs while her college-educated mother stayed home to raise her and her older sister. Throughout her upbringing, Caitlin observed her father's emotional blowups and verbal put-downs of her mother. She noticed how her mom walked on eggshells to avoid verbal onslaught. On some level Caitlin decided early on that she'd get out of that house as soon as she could.

The young girl was barely nineteen when she met Lou at a party. He was twenty-two. Although she saw him lose his temper frequently at the begin-ning of their romance, she felt comfortable with him and the middle-class values he demonstrated that were so similar to her own. From what she had learned in her home, she assumed that all men lost their temper when they became frustrated, angry, tired, disappointed. Caitlin fell in love with Lou, and within a year they were married.

As soon as they cohabited, Caitlin happily surrendered control of the money and household chores to her new husband. Lou was delighted to cook, clean, and shop, and Caitlin believed she had found nirvana in this unusual husband who helped out at home while she was free to complete college. After she graduated, the couple moved to a suburban community, where Caitlin used public transportation to get to and from her new teach-ing job. Lou protectively insisted that Caitlin was too nearsighted to drive, and she didn't need to get either a driver's license or a car because he would gladly drive her wherever she had to go. Since she had heard her fa-ther tell her nearsighted mother the same exact thing years earlier (!), Caitlin unknowingly bought into the familiar excuse that kept her depen-dent. She believed that she was not only in love, but that she had now been *saved* from living amid her parents' screaming bouts.

Soon one child came along . . . then another, each necessitating an ex-tended maternity leave from work, until she finally quit altogether. But as time went on, and the children got older, Caitlin became increasingly aware that she needed to have more freedom than wheeling baby carriages by day and waiting for hubby to return from work by night. She wanted to learn to drive. She wanted to buy a car. She wanted to return to her teach-ing career. She wanted to get a master's degree. On all counts, Lou gave her a hard time. He liked their life the way it was, and he was not about to "let" her change it.

Caitlin and Lou began to get into heated arguments about her burgeoning need to be more independent. Clearly he felt threatened by her "demanding" requests, and he got involved in an affair with one of the women who worked in the restaurant he managed. Although Caitlin found out and they presumably "worked through" their difficulties, she found it hard to forgive him for straying. Their fights became louder and their words became nastier. Caitlin was beginning to fight back. On some level she knew that she needed to be more self-sufficient, and to her husband's chagrin, she did eventually get her driver's license, her own car, her master's, and an elevated teaching position with a high salary. Rather than being supportive and encouraging of his wife's new achievements, however, Lou became increasingly more angry and sullen. When he was home he sat immobile before the TV. He began to drink heavily, take drugs, and gamble away the family's small savings.

For many years Caitlin buried her head along with her emotions as she found solace in going to sleep at 8:00 P.M. and awakening after her husband had gone to work at 6:00 A.M. She focused on her job and her children. Similar to her father, Lou continued to lose his temper and direct verbal epithets at her. But unlike her father, Lou began to strike his wife physically, sending her to the hospital on more than one occasion. Sometimes she took the kids and ran to her older sister's house to escape. But these were temporary measures at best, and finally, after twenty-five years of fear and control, Caitlin filed for divorce.

If Lou had demonstrated anger during their marriage, now he raged. He told the children horrible things about their mother, their aunt, and everyone else close to Caitlin. When he picked up the kids on weekends, he dangerously and drunkenly sped off in his car. The children, too, lived in fear of their father's irrational temper. Unfortunately, another generation of little girls quickly learned the kind of behavior to expect from men who don't get their way.

During the split, Caitlin discovered that Lou had gambled away their last $10,000. At the time of her divorce, the woman did not know how to balance a checkbook. Although this forty-seven-year-old had fought for and won some autonomy through the years, her basic survival skills were sorely lacking. She had recently lost her father. She mournfully watched her own mother struggle with not knowing how to balance her checkbook or drive to get around. Despite her lifelong attempts to be different, Caitlin sadly acknowledged how much like her mother she had become. This was the beginning of recognizing the choices she had made, clearly following in the footsteps of her heritage.

Not unlike Princess Di and Selena, Caitlin did not even know she had agreed to the sacred covenant of betting on a prince to give her security and self-worth. In such a bet, a woman's loss of self diminishes subtly, day by day, each time she agrees to something that goes against her grain. Caitlin was no different. It would be nice to think her daughters will know better, but they lack a role model to teach them otherwise. When one was twenty-four, she was partnering with young men who were emotionally unavailable and were causing her pain. When the other was eighteen, she was having hopeless crushes on boys who treated her badly. The cycle cannot be broken until Caitlin retakes her life and enunciates her power, giving her girls a model to emulate.

This is not an impossible task. As she becomes more aware of how she has imprinted her own mother's behaviors, Caitlin will assess the choices she has made and the necessity for her to change past scripts. Then she will be able to re-create new and bolder versions of who she is yet to become. She has already taken the first step by divorcing the man in whom she had put her faith.

Lonely Secretary

While divorced Caitlin is on her way to enhancing her power, Karla is a woman resistant to learning from past mistakes. I met Karla on a TV talk show. She had been a fifty-two-year-old unmarried secretary when she met John at a singles club one lonely Sunday night. Immediately she felt the physical attraction between them. "He was the man I had always dreamed of," she revealed to the audience. He wined her and dined her and often sent cards and roses for no occasion. Karla admitted that until she had met John, she had never really believed that any man would love her, and she'd practically resigned herself to spending the rest of her life miserable and alone.

John and Karla quickly became intimate. He was living in a trailer park, working at a trucking company, and didn't have much money, an obvious contrast to Karla, who was supporting herself nicely. But despite their earning and lifestyle differences, to the surprise of her friends and family, the two married after only a few months of being together.

John told his bride that he wanted to set up a private consulting business. Practically right after the wedding ceremony, his alleged business took off and they were rolling in money. They bought a new house, a new car, fancy clothes, and a lot of jewelry. For Karla, things couldn't be better. She never asked questions.

About a year into their marriage, John announced that he had been called to Thailand to expand his business in another direction. Karla drove him to the airport and made plans to meet him abroad within a few weeks. Only two days after he left, however, the police came to Karla's door. They announced that John had embezzled almost $500,000 from the trucking company where he worked and there was a warrant out for his arrest. As if this weren't bad enough, Karla discovered that all their possessions were in her name. The company sued Karla for everything she owned, and she suddenly found herself penniless. She also discovered that John had run up $600 bills with prostitutes in Nevada on their jointly held credit card and $200 in charges to sex lines on their family phone line.

John continued to escape the law for a while, but eventually he turned himself in. He went to jail for a year, and Karla got an annulment.

Pathetically, the story doesn't end there. Although Karla had been emotionally and financially devastated by this ordeal, John had the gall to seek her out again. He appealed to her sense of decency and reminded her that she had vowed to marry him "for better or for worse." When he got out of jail, he started a new job, committed himself to therapy, and became a regular churchgoer. He convinced his former wife that he had changed and begged for a second chance. Still desperate to be loved, Karla decided to trust him once more. She married him for a second time against the wishes of family and friends.

It was six months into their second marriage when John said that he had to leave for an important business meeting. Completely trusting of his turnaround, Karla thought nothing of it. So she was shocked to find that her husband had now disappeared with her new car and money. He left no note, nothing. Karla called the police, but she was told that since they were married, his absconding with property they owned jointly was not considered a crime. Again Karla was broke. Borrowing money from her few remaining friends, she hired a private detective, but all roads led nowhere.

Seven months later Karla received a call from police in a distant state, informing her that John had been found living there and using her Social Security number. They further informed her that although he was not divorced from Karla, he had married another woman. After he stole that woman's money, cars, and credit cards, he ran off for another several months. Finally the police caught him, and he was sentenced to ten more years in prison.

Karla said that meeting and marrying John twice had been the most damaging experience of her life. But now her former husband was starting to write to her from prison. She was ashamed to admit that she took pity on him and actually sent him money. On a remote TV screen from his cell, during the show, she confronted him about why he had lied to her. Did he ever really love her? she wanted to know. Of course, he could not offer answers.

At fifty-two, Karla had been so needy to find a man that any man would do. And any man would have been able to feel this woman's desperation and use it to his own advantage. She barely knew John when she agreed to marry him. Then, even after being proved a fool time and time again, she did the deed for a second time . . . and now fantasized doing it a third! When America last saw Karla, her family voiced fear that she would be seduced again by this Casanova con artist. Karla was a woman so desperate to be loved that she would relinquish even her last thread of dignity. Despite all the abuse, poverty, and embarrassment she underwent, Karla continued to bet on her prince. For her, *a* man was better than *no* man.

Karla looked like Anywoman USA, attractive enough, intelligent enough, but also willing enough to be walked upon. Her body language projected the obvious roar of "I need love!" When a woman wears her heart on a sleeve on which a man can wipe his sniveling nose, that's an open invitation for disaster. We all take love detours, and that's how we learn to develop our power. But a woman who thinks well of herself understands that her *next* mistakes will be *new* mistakes, not reruns of the old scenarios.

A Baby Having a Baby

What about our younger generation? Wouldn't we like to think that they are more assertive and independent than we had been? Fifteen-year-old Shimeika lived with her mother, four sisters, and two brothers in a public housing project on Chicago's south side. The family had been receiving welfare for the past ten years. To her struggling mother's chagrin, Shimeika had been having unprotected sex with her fourteen-year-old boyfriend, Lloyd, for a year. Lloyd didn't like using condoms and he said he loved her anyway, so what did she have to worry about? Around the projects, they were known as a "couple."

Shimeika was a high school sophomore when she dropped out of school. She was now pregnant. As she sat on a TV show beside her mother and boyfriend, Shimeika boasted no remorse about her situation. Now at fifteen, she and fourteen-year-old Lloyd would get married. He had promised.

During the show, Shimeika's mother tried to drum some sense into her daughter. She pleaded with her, offering some viable alternatives: Get an abortion and finish school. Or at least give up the idea of running off and marrying Lloyd, have the baby on her own, and continue her education. The young girl stubbornly would hear nothing of it. She and Lloyd were in love. They were ready to begin their lives together, leave school, and live as husband and wife.

We all asked how the couple intended to support the baby. Shimeika named as their means of support Lloyd's job at McDonald's and her own yet-to-be-found job with whoever would hire her. The audience asked if she knew the cost of diapers, food, child care, and housing. The woman-child came up blank. But the audience would not give up. They proceeded to badger Lloyd about his financial commitments to Shimeika, the baby, and their impending marriage. They asked about the amount of money Lloyd had in his paycheck after taxes. Slowly he began to balk. For the young man, reality was suddenly beginning to set in. He said that during the show he had begun to reconsider the whole idea of lifelong commitment. After all, he was only fourteen. Now he boldly declared that he decided not to get married after all. There was silence on the stage.

Shimeika was visibly crushed. She cried uncontrollably. Fortunately her mother was there to hold her young teenager in her arms. The older woman promised they'd raise the child together. And Shimeika would continue high school, go on to college, and make something of her life.

I spoke to Shimeika after she gave birth. She said she sees Lloyd hanging out around the neighborhood with his friends. He barely greets her in the street when they pass. He has become a drug dealer and is high most of the time. He pays no money toward the support of his infant son. Shimeika is just glad she didn't run off with Lloyd and get herself and their baby into a life of poverty, crime, and hopelessness. She knows it won't be easy to work, study, and mother her child at the same time. It would have been better had she not been taken in by her boyfriend's promises at such an early age. She says the projects are filled with girls in the same predicament. They don't know how they will handle their overwhelming responsibilities and also prepare a future away from the life they have.

Unfortunately, our young women have learned our lessons all too well. It is not only girls from lower-income families who believe that their way out of loneliness is through a guy. Affiliation with a male continues to offer girls from every walk of life the status of being wanted. "Look at me," it says to their impressionable peers. "Someone loves me. I am loved." On TV show after TV show, I warn these girls, "The sooner you open your legs, the quicker your guys will close their hearts." Many of us who are older and wiser have been there. We know that the only way to keep a man coming around is to keep him intrigued with who we *are*. Not just with our bodies, but with our *selves*, for carnal delights fade quickly. Feeling good about her *self*, however, ensures a young woman the right to control her destiny in the face of peer pressure. It also ensures her ability to say "No" when these pressures seem to get out of control.

High School Dropout

Sometimes we think that all it takes for a woman to exercise her power is for her to be beautiful, as this letter suggests:

> *Dear Dr. Gilda:*
>   *As an aspiring actress and ex-ballet dancer, I was a very confident person. Most people in high school hated me because I did what I said I was going to do. Until I met Mike. . . .*
>   *At 19, I can say that Mike totally destroyed my self-esteem.*

He is a frat boy and he is absolutely gorgeous. But he used me for 6 months and now he acts like he had nothing to do with it.

He lied to me and told me that he didn't like any other girls. Of course, I slept with him because he was awesome! I loved holding him and caring about him. I'd look at him and swear that I had never seen anyone more attractive.

Well, it's a known fact that he treats girls like shit. So it's not like I'm denying the truth. I was depressed because he'd take other girls to his functions and then call me for sex after their date.

We had great sex!!! He was the first guy who fulfilled my needs. I grew dependent on him. I became jealous and I asked for a commitment. He freaked. He took off, but would come back on occasion when he wanted sex.

I feel so guilty and impure and used. I wanted to have a relationship with him. He makes me laugh and he is a strong person. He fell in love with my body. I had a nice body and he'd go crazy. But then I got fat and gained 20 lbs. and he lost interest. That's when I dropped out of high school.

My plan now is to concentrate on myself, lose weight, and start working as an actress and model again. When the new and improved me comes out I'm going to call him and he'll gladly come back. But how can you really get an asshole to change? I know what you are going to say: "You can't change people, why do you want an asshole, revenge doesn't work." But he is the type of asshole who, if I lost weight and looked really good, would try to have sex with me again and hang out. So all I have to do is not have sex with him and make him want me more. I want him to realize how stupid he was to leave me and treat me like shit. Will it work?

Jacqueline

Here is a supposedly beautiful young woman who offered sex for love and ended up bartering her body for a large dose of disrespect. Knowing that he'd come to her privately for sexual servicing after attending parties publicly with other women, Jacqueline willingly welcomed this lopsided arrangement. In fact, she thought her carnal offerings would not only lure Mike, but keep him hooked. But sex can go only so far, especially when body-beautiful balloons to body-blimp. If their sexcapades had been based on more than physiology, their interaction might have had a chance. Instead the couple became enmeshed in an emotional tug-of-war when Jacqueline demanded the C-word. What did she think a commitment would be based on, her new and improved dress size?

Sadly, this woman knew the answers I would offer, yet she discounted my responses. Jacqueline *accepted* Mike's lying, cheating, and general poor treatment of her. Then she blamed *him* for destroying her self-esteem and her life.

Come on. Unless a woman is bound, chained, and kept against her will, she cannot blame her man for anything that she has consented to do with him. In reality, Jacqueline's self-esteem had to be pretty shabby to begin with, otherwise she would never have put up with her doormat treatment. Her own impression of herself, not the one that Mike held of her, was the reason for her increasing weight. The moment a woman relinquishes her decision-making powers to a man is the moment she wears thin her own self-image.

And now Jacqueline's intention to expend more time and energy getting him to want her again makes one wonder. Why won't she let go and seek someone she need not *make* want her? Jacqueline bet on Mike to make her feel good about herself. When he hadn't complied with the pact he didn't even realize he had made, she got angry with "the asshole." A woman who feels good about herself will exercise her option of walking away from Mike look-alikes. A woman who feels good about herself probably won't even give her phone number to versions of this guy in the first place.

College-Educated Corporate Manager

It would be grand if we could say that the sole solution to a woman's power taking is for her to mature and get a good education. Unfortunately, maturity and a college degree have nothing to do with a woman's empowerment. Christine was completing college when she landed a management internship at a Fortune 500 company. She was excited over that accomplishment, but she was sadly getting over an affair with a stud who had maintained a steady girlfriend the whole time she and he were an item. Christine was a recovering dumpee still upset over having been had.

One night, not feeling too attractive after learning the truth about her cheating boyfriend, Christine acquiesced to two of her friends who insisted she accompany them to a singles event. All she could think was that she'd be no competition for any of the pretty girls in the room. But her friends dismissed her protestations and insisted she go.

The party was held in the hot, smoky room of a basement apartment teeming with sweaty bodies. Christine at once assessed the guys to be nerds, one of whom immediately sought her out. Clearly she was not interested. Out of nowhere, someone named Howard appeared. Sensing Christine's annoyance, he rescued her from the clutches of the little irritant. Christine said gratefully, "Ahhh . . . my hero!" When she asked Howard what he did for a living, his reply, "CPA," spelled "p-o-t-e-n-t-i-a-l." All the necessary ingredients quickly flashed: not only had he saved her from the clutches of a creep, but his promising career counted him as husband material. Dashing, dizzying hormones abounded. In a Hallmark moment, the woman was in love.

Howard courted Christine for a year, and then they married. Since he was such a financial wizard, he said he would take over the responsibility for all her college loans. Now that's really being *saved*, she thought. He assured her that since she now took on his new name and was no longer living in her parents' house, the state government would have no way of tracking her for repayment of the tuition loan. Christine reasoned, "Whom could I believe if not my own CPA husband?"

For three or so years the couple was free and clear of the money Christine had borrowed for college. But suddenly her parents began to receive official threatening letters and phone calls from collection agencies demanding their money back. Still following her husband's advice, she told her parents to ignore the "intrusions." But her parents could take the harassment no longer, and Christine was caught in the middle. Against Howard's wishes (he still believed they could get away with not repaying the loans, and he was furious that Christine's parents stood in their way), she contacted the government and told them she was ready to repay the school loan in installments. But it was too late for her credit rating. Even though Christine now had a good job, she soon learned that she would not be allowed to get her own credit card for seven years. In addition, the couple was applying for a home mortgage, and she discovered that the deed could not include her name. Everything the couple owned jointly now legally belonged to Howard. Thus, for a long seven years Christine was totally financially dependent on her husband, and resigning herself to that fact, she dutifully handed over her paychecks to him. Since money is a symbol of power in relationships, she often felt the need to grovel for it even for such necessities as tampons. Meanwhile, it seemed that Howard was enjoying his role as benevolent despot, because he occasionally exercised his right to say "No" to his wife's requests. For seven long years Christine suffered as subordinate in a marriage that had presumably begun with two equal working partners.

Christine was a typical trusting young wife who believed in the man she had married. She had confidence in his ability as a CPA, she took stock in his integrity as an honest human being, and she had every faith that he would "take care" of her and her finances. After the whole incident blew up in her face, she learned the need to take more responsibility for her personal affairs. In one nation under plastic, today that translates to her having three credit cards of her own. Yet after fifteen years of being married, and four children to support, she still totally entrusts the family's financial well-being to CPA Howard. Some women never learn.

There are two words that *can* provide the means for a woman to map her path to self-respect. They are "economic freedom." When she has her own money, a woman *can* be free to decide how she wants to live her life—whether she chooses to keep a controlling male around or not. Yet in our society we see even economically independent women who wholesale their power to a man.

Brilliant Corporate President

Although a woman may have achieved phenomenal credentials, have a job that allows her economic independence, and exercise all kinds of organizational power on the job, she may still lose her power when it comes to being in a love relationship with a man. Alice was an M.D. who had worked her way up to president of a large HMO. She met Mark at a fund-raising dinner while he was campaigning for a seat on the city council. Mark went for airbrushed women whose features were porcelain perfect and whose siren looks attracted attention. Alice's appearance was not reflective of his usual taste. She was quietly simple and plainly attractive, usually wearing little makeup and loose-fitting clothes. But unlike most of the model-type females Mark escorted around town, Alice was unusually quick-witted, bright, and articulate. In fact, Mark came to depend on the intellectual stimulation they shared, and whenever he met with a crisis in his life, she was the one with whom he found comfort.

Alice had been divorced from an engineer years earlier, and now she was ready to settle into a committed relationship again. The problem was that she had little time to invest in meeting and dating, as her very public job not only required twelve-hour days, but also kept her inside a fishbowl where the media enjoyed taking potshots at her personal life. Consequently Mark would be a satisfying partner who was respected politically and who would make an appropriate squire for Alice in public.

Mark had been married earlier and often had custody of his rambunctious fourteen-year-old daughter during weekends. Since he did not want to give the adolescent an impression of wanton sexuality, whenever Alice stayed at Mark's home, she was cast to sleep on the lumpy living room sofa. Alice put up with this arrangement because she loved Mark and believed that they would eventually move to the next step, marriage.

The relationship endured for four years. During its time, it was rumored that Mark had been flitting about town with several other women whom he kept on the side. Alice had heard many of the rumors but chose to ignore them for the sake of keeping intact what she believed she and Mark lovingly shared. She reasoned that the man would eventually come to his senses, cease his cheating, and ask her to make their relationship permanent.

Unexpectedly, Mark was invited to accept a higher political position in a distant city. He would now have to move much farther away, and he despised traveling. With his new role, he was determined never to trek to Alice's home again; he gave her the remaining toll bridge tokens he had bought when he was routinely making the round trip to her home. Now Alice was left to commute three hours back and forth to spend time with him. On weekends when his daughter stayed over, Alice remained on the creaky couch. Still, she took the situation in stride because of her lack of time and access to new alliances.

Finally Mark was linked publicly with a not too bright runway model. Their photos appeared in the local newspapers. It was when one of Alice's aides brought in the clipping of the happy new couple that Alice accepted the truth. She was destroyed. She had patiently invested years waiting for Mark to commit. She had done more than her share of the emotional work, as well as the physical travel. In the end, the man selected an airbrushed mannequin as his bride. Alice took a job in South America to escape her pain.

Where did this brilliant, credentialed woman go wrong in betting on her prince? Alice expected little from her man, so that's what he ultimately gave her. For one thing, Alice knew of Mark's transgressions, but she preferred to ignore them, believing his behavior would simply go away. She also never confronted him about being treated like a second-class citizen in front of his daughter. Surely any self-respecting lady would not want to flaunt her lover's sexuality before an impressionable teenager. But eventually the young girl could have been told about her father's commitment to Alice—if it had been that at all. Then the sleeping arrangements, uncomfortable for Alice, would have taken care of themselves. Obviously Alice had chosen not to push that, either, hoping that Mark would come to his "senses" by himself. Finally Alice also continued to make the long trek to Mark's new abode, while she allowed him the luxury of making no overtures to get to her. She invested years of her life in this too kind and accepting manner, and when reality did hit, it hit her and hurt her, hard. A woman who loves herself would have stopped hoping—and started walking—in the direction of someone who returned her love.

We have met eight women, each from different walks of life, each believing that a prince was worth her wait. But each learned instead that a bet on a prince never got her to Mecca.

Self-Assessment #1 is going to be the final story you read. It is your story. You know your life better than anyone. Imagine you are writing your autobiography for publication. This assessment may take a few days to complete. You may want to put it down and return to it later. Complete Items 1–3 with as many details as you can recall. After you finish, sit in a quiet place without interruption and read what you have written. Read it as though you are reading about someone else's experiences.

In Item 4 you will happily have the luxury of reinventing your life *as you want it to turn out.* This is your most vital challenge. It's your chance to change the rules you once felt compelled to follow. How differently are you willing to paint your new life? You will compare the differences between the real and the retold versions in Item 5. And in Item 6 you will examine your feelings about the differences. Be honest with yourself, yet enjoy your fantasies. They can be the start of your *new* realities.

SELF-ASSESSMENT #1

MY STORY

1. Describe your personal story. How did you bet on a man? When did you know you were disappointed?

2. Describe other men you bet on in the past. Describe your disappointments with them.

3. What patterns keep reappearing in all your interactions with the men you have bet on?

4. Retell your most recent story, but re-create your actions to make your story end in a happier way. Even if you don't feel as though this is how you'd behave in real life, make believe, and have fun with your boldness. There is one catch: You may not do or think anything evil, even toward the man who has hurt you. Evildoing is a waste of energy, and you are worthy of much more. Your two choices, then, are either to confront him or walk away. Within those limitations, rewrite your story and make it magnificent. Make it turn out as *you* want. You are now in total control. Enjoy.

5. Compare the differences between the real and the retold versions of your life.

6. How do you feel about what you learned?

It took the corporate president, Alice, four days to complete Self-Assessment #1. Through her tears and reminiscences, she detected her pattern of finding men she misconstrued as being worthier than they actually were. She recognized how she tended to put these guys first, even before her own pressing career needs. She noted how they initially enjoyed her attentions. But after a while they felt smothered. Each went on to find a woman *he* could care for more than the other way around. From this exercise Alice vowed to focus on the professional dreams she enjoyed. The next man in her future would come second to her caring for herself. He would have to understand.

Using this self-assessment, teacher Caitlin realized that she would never again accept the horrible put-downs she had endured from her husband. She is now engaged to a loving, respectful professor who serves as a terrific role model for the daughters who, until recently, knew men only to be angry and tantrum prone.

Corporate manager Christine has finally recognized the anger she feels toward Howard. He continues to control not only her finances, but her entire life. After completing Self-Assessment #1, she discovered she has no friends because Howard doesn't want anyone around her but him. Her insight is a start. Her actions are yet to be seen. We will follow them throughout this book.

If your self-assessment didn't depict an idyllic life, don't be disheartened. We have all been there. On some level we will probably continue to attract someone with complementary and opposite traits whose parents' worst qualities would present the setting for our life's drama. But our relationships can still work. Like all of us, you must:

👑 Gilda-Gram *Commit to yourself instead of waiting for a prince to commit to you.*

Nothing in life that has any value can be created without this absolute commitment. Only when we are self-accepting can we begin to see our partner as he really is.

👑 Gilda-Gram *Happiness begins when we recognize reality.*

Once we recognize where we are, as you did in Items 1–3 of Self-Assessment #1, we can create a more hopeful, but realistic, dream. This is a very important step, because you can't go forth if you do not know where you are heading. That is why you re-created your story in Item 4.

Finally, in Item 5 you compared the glaring differences between the reality and the make-believe. Sometimes the make-believe is where we conjure up what seems to be impossible at first, but what serves as the healthy impetus to our future risk taking. We can dream about our goals before we set out to meet them. We can fantasize about our future however we wish. Item 6 asked you to express your feelings about what you learned. After this self-assessment, most women question why they took so long to see the truth. They also often berate themselves for not escaping sooner from their problematic princes. While these feelings are often natural for someone who has just seen the light, a woman's beating up on herself is needless and deenergizing. Use this assessment as a starting point to begin your commitment to take action, however small it might appear at first. This commitment is an agreement with yourself to start making the changes you need to enhance your life.

Now that you are on your way, part 2 of this book will teach you the fundamental tools to self-empowerment that most women would never think to use in searching for the "prince." For starters, you'll learn to ask for what you need and believe you deserve to get it.

GILDA-GRAMS
FROM CHAPTER 2
Women Who Bet on the Prince: We're All in Good Company

▶ *A relationship's real objective is to provide the journey for our own personal growth.*

▶ *Commit to yourself instead of waiting for a prince to commit to you.*

▶ *Happiness begins when we recognize reality.*

PART II

How to Get the Man You Want

3

Ask for What You Need and Believe You Deserve to Get It

Remember the Archie comics? Betty and Veronica reflected the either/or extremes of our fairy-tale characters. On the one hand was Veronica, the femme fatale. She forever enticed Archie simply by believing she deserved to have him as her lover and by projecting her power in his direction. Veronica was a Will-Be Woman, always knowing that she *will be getting exactly what she wants*.

> **ANATOMY OF A WILL-BE WOMAN**
> *Will Be's are the women who seem to have it all. They use their hard times to reinvest in themselves. They are directed by their personal goals and refuse to be affected by others' attitudes about them. In winter, Will-Be's don't sit around shivering; they go skiing.* Men of quality love Will-Be Women.

On the other end of the spectrum was Betty. Since she was six years old she had held a torch for Archie, but she forever jockeyed with Veronica for the number one place in his heart. In one comic strip episode, even when Archie asked Betty to be his prom date, she thought he was kidding because she didn't believe she deserved his love. Betty is a Wanna-Be Woman, always *wanting to be like someone else* and never believing she deserved a man of her own.

> **ANATOMY OF A WANNA-BE WOMAN**
> *Wanna Be's want to be like the girl who "has it all." Yet instead of working toward self-improvement, they complain and remain as they are. Lacking self-esteem, they feel helpless in controlling their own lives. Envy and jealousy often permeate their character as they dispense cynicism, pessimism, or hopelessness to everyone they meet.* Men with little to offer want Wanna-Be Women.

Unfortunately, many women start out like Betty. This type of woman may meet a boyfriend of one of her friends, then give him a dozen of her business cards to distribute to his male acquaintances. She *needs* to meet a great new guy, she says. Her friends' boyfriends will disparagingly throw the cards in the garbage, disgusted by her desperation. Despite what they say, on some level deep beneath the surface, needy women believe that they either don't deserve any love at all or, at least, they don't deserve quality love from a quality guy. Often these "believers of nondeserve" attract men who are abusive, distant, or unavailable. No guy of value wants a gal so emotionally broke. Just as women yield to their intuitive senses, men heed the need to run from the woman whose radar flashes "Help! I'm needy for love!!"

While the women may ultimately blame their guys for the paltry attention they get, it is the women themselves who, first, invite these men into their lives, and, second, allow them to continue to stay. Ultimately, what we believe we deserve is what we receive—nothing more, nothing less.

Are You a Will-Be Woman or a Wanna-Be Woman?

We often believe that we have two separate, segmented existences, personal and professional, and we can be strong in one even while the other crumbles. But the reality is that we act out the image we have of ourselves in every arena of our lives, both at work and at play. And the behaviors we attract in others match our own belief system about ourselves because:

👑 **Gilda-Gram** *People attract people like themselves.*

I was a "believer of nondeserve" myself. I stayed in a public school teaching job for eighteen long years with abusive bosses. Similarly, I remained in disrespectful relationships, one after another, probably for just as long. I remained and complained, like everyone else I knew, but I did not get out. Many women stay in dead-end jobs because they're afraid they can't do better—or can't risk the lack of security. They come up with endless reasons to remain stuck. In the same way, many more women stay in toxic relationships and blame their staying on the children, the finances, the roof over their head, and other convenient circumstances. These are our crutches, each of us holding a different one dear, as we sob to our best friends who think they're doing us well by listening.

Although I kept fantasizing that someone—anyone—would find me and rescue me from my nasty mates and my awful job, my phantom saviors came and went. As I know now, I didn't feel good enough about myself then to attract bona fide "charmers." I left one guy after another, none of whom could provide salvation. No one can save us. Peculiarly enough, what rescued me from both my love and work woes was crippling back pain that landed me in a thick, painful brace. Yes, the pain was unbearable, and yes, it also became my reason to change, because:

....

👑 **Gilda-Gram** *When something happens* to *us, it really happens* for *us.*

....

Pain pushes us to open our eyes, and I found that my crisis made me aware that something in my life had to go. When I examined my unhappiness, I knew I needed to let go of the "secure" things that weren't so secure after all, but that instead had made me sick. Fortunately, only one of my many personalities got tenure, while the others were free to expand their natural talents. I left that horrible job in the face of my parents' disapproval. They begged me to remain in the school system for just two more years to earn the "security" of a twenty-year pension. But I could not stay. I knew I would be financially strapped for a while, and I felt very, very scared about no longer having a steady paycheck. But I was in too much physical agony. I didn't know what my future held when I left, but almost instantly something special occurred. In place of the "security" I thought I had known, I discovered freedom, independence, and a belief that I deserved to be happy.

When we're pushed to the brink, we draw from strengths we never knew we had. Needing to earn a living, I expanded the management consulting I had casually begun while teaching public school. To my surprise, I created a wonderful business, I made more money than I could have imagined, and I discovered that I loved making a difference in the lives of large groups of people. I created and conducted corporate workshops, and I also became a full-time college professor at night for adults returning to school. My motivational speaking led to many TV appearances, to my own show on MTV Online as "the Love Doc," and to my being a spokesperson for Hallmark's humorous Valentine's Day Shoebox Greeting cards to discuss the necessity for play in relationships. I began to refuse offers I did not want. What a change for someone who clocked in and out for eighteen years, someone so stuck, miserable, and crippled that she didn't think she could survive without her "security."

Finally, there was one last change that had to come. I now had enough insight to jump ship from Noah's Ark of twosomes. At last I realized that I didn't need a man to take me where my soul was hiding. My new life was an expedition I'd have to make alone. After I learned to stand on my own two feet, I would see about coupling again. But next time I would be a far better partner, and, as such, I would attract a far better prince.

Women have indeed begun to make major strides in the world, especially as they become more aware of how to succeed in the workplace. Many more than in the past appear as Will-Be Women in their jobs. Yet since the average woman *still* makes only about $.72 compared with a man's $1, something continues to be dreadfully wrong. Might it be the way women really feel about themselves and how they project these feelings? In study after study, when it comes to their future incomes, women consistently see the glass as half-empty. In desperation they find partners who they presume know more than they do about taking care of them. Obviously, no matter how they strive toward workplace greatness, most women remain stuck as Wanna-Be Women when it comes to men.

In chapter 2 we observed eight women at different socioeconomic, educational, attractiveness, and success levels. No matter whether their assets were mediocre or superb, their negative self-images propelled them to *need* a constant sidekick—even when he didn't serve them. I remember one reason I got married was that I felt I *needed* a man to help care for my car. (I know, I know; this sounds horrendous. Unfortunately, it was my sad and dependent truthful past!) While I can attest today to how pitiful I once was, I wonder what would have happened had I taken the time to differentiate between *needing* a man and *wanting* a man. Had I recognized the pure convenience of having a man in my life to perform such minor rituals—a *want*, but far from a *need*—I would never have married in exchange for a thirty-thousand-mile tune-up.

Will-Be Women differentiate *needs* from *wants*, and when we've set our priorities, we project that we *deserve to receive* whichever of these we should have. Veronica projected her *want*. Betty projected her *need*. There is no question which is the greater turn-on to a worthy man. When we project our deserve level as a matter of *want* rather than *need*, it shows both professionally and personally. But to do that requires that we know the difference between the two words.

Distinguishing Between Our Needs and Wants

Before we seek our soulmate, we must first unearth our soul. There are three parts to soul finding. First, we must discover what we need. Second, we must determine what we want and learn how to ask for it. Third, we must project that we deserve to get what we believe we should have.

Our needs are the most basic forces that motivate us. They are distinctively different from our wants. Wants are less pressing desires that we may crave but that do not require our immediate attention and satisfaction. As human beings, we primarily *need* to survive, so our most essential requirements are our (1) physiological and (2) security needs. In other words, we must feel that we are fed, clothed, protected from bodily harm, and safely earning enough money to sustain us.

After our physiological and security needs are satisfied, we climb the ladder toward three more advanced essentials: (3) love and belonging; (4) feeling good about our status in life (self-esteem); and (5) fulfilling our goals and dreams (self-actualization). According to behaviorists, until each level is at least somewhat satisfied, we cannot seek gratification on the next higher rung. At which needs level are you functioning now? Take Self-Assessment #2 and find out.

There is one note about all the self-assessments that follow in this book. The questions are specifically meant to be broad and open-ended. As an educator, I use these types of questions in my workshops. The kinds of questions and statements you see here motivate people to think long and hard about their responses, especially regarding things they have never considered before. Such probing queries prompt respondents to enter into lengthy discussions with friends and family, where more insights can be unearthed. There are no right or wrong answers. The questions should guide you through personal introspection that will remain with you for some time. Most important of all, since we all get to pattern our lives according to our own specs, your reactions will begin to form the blueprint of the empowered woman you will soon become.

S E L F - A S S E S S M E N T   # 2

DISCOVERING YOUR NEEDS LEVEL

List the following statements in their order of importance to you, starting with the most important (1) and going to the least important (5).

_____**1.** When I'm hungry, I stop whatever I'm doing to eat.
(PHYSIOLOGICAL NEEDS)

_____**2.** A steady job with good money is extremely important to me. (SECURITY NEEDS)

_____**3.** Being happy is one of my main goals.
(SELF-ACTUALIZATION NEEDS)

_____**4.** I feel comfortable promoting myself.
(SELF-ESTEEM NEEDS)

_____**5.** I would do almost anything for my friends.
(LOVE AND BELONGING NEEDS)

On which needs level do you tend to place the most emphasis? the least?

Noting His Needs, but Meeting Your Own

Clarice was dating Craig for six months. Throughout this time she could not understand why he was not showing her more affection and attention. She knew he was going through a difficult divorce, but she assumed that their hot sexual passion was powerful enough to make him forget his pain. Craig was in heat all right, but his heat consisted of his ongoing debates with his soon-to-be-ex-wife and their lawyers. For him, each day meant another kick-butt, drag-out argument.

I explained to Clarice that even if she were Queen of the Nile, Craig was still functioning at his first- and second-level needs, physiological (concern over how he would afford to eat) and security (concern over where he could afford to live). These two needs are basic to everyone's survival, and Craig was expending all his energies fighting for his future. Sure, their relationship was pleasant, and the sex was invigorating, but no matter what Clarice did at this time, it *would not matter* because:

👑 **Gilda-Gram** *A man in the "ing" position—divorcing, separating, losing, grieving—is at his two lowest needs levels: physiological and security. While struggling for his survival, he is unable to rise to the third needs level of love.*

I told Clarice that her choices were to take a more nonchalant approach to her relationship with Craig, or, if she insisted that she *needs* a close relationship now, she should find someone else who had already earned his *emotional* divorce decree. Craig was not toting baggage at this time, he was hauling steamer trunks. He was definitely not ready to give Clarice what she said she *needed*. But our discussion got Clarice to question why she would want a man who was in Craig's "ing" position when she said that she *needed* more.

Ah . . . This is the point. Many women think they *need* a close relationship when they really only *want* a close relationship.

👑 **Gilda-Gram** *If you don't know what you need, you won't get what you want.*

If Clarice really *needed*, rather than *wanted*, intimacy leading to marriage, she would not have chosen Craig. Or was it just a case of uneducated choosing on her part? Clarice began to question why she was pursuing someone who was not emotionally available.

She completed Self-Assessment #2 and deemed Item 5, love and belonging, her most important need. She recognized that at this time Craig did not share her same needs level. It was simply a case of not being aware of her own needs before choosing her prospective partner. She decided that since her needs level was at love and belonging, and Craig's at this time was more at security, she would begin dating other, more available partners. Clarice was on her way to taking care of herself as she noted her lover's needs but decided that it was up to her to fulfill her own.

Many of us tend to confuse our needs with our wants. Our needs program what we require to sustain ourselves, and they produce tensions that demand fulfillment. For example, when we are hungry our bodies alert us that we *need* to eat. But what kind of food will we choose? Our discriminating taste is our want. In actuality, if a steak were not available, perhaps a bag of pretzels would suffice. Our most desired want would not be fulfilled, but our bodily need to eat would be. We'd still go on.

Do you *need* or *want* to drive a flashy car? If you *need* a car to get you to work, any dependable set of wheels would suffice, but it need not be flashy to do the job. Similarly, do you *need* or *want* a man to listen to the travails of your day? You may enjoy having someone to listen to you, sometimes you may even *need* a shoulder to cry on or a person to share an exceptionally great event with. But must it be a *man*? Actually, a good friend or neighbor could serve the same purpose. Before we can know what it is that we are really after, we must first distinguish between our needs and wants. To do so, complete Self-Assessment #3, and remember to take your time in responding. The point is to learn some things about yourself.

S E L F - A S S E S S M E N T   # 3

DISTINGUISHING BETWEEN
OUR NEEDS AND WANTS

- My *needs* are what I <u>MUST HAVE</u> to SURVIVE.

- My *wants* are what I <u>PREFER TO HAVE</u> to FEEL GOOD.

  - My greatest *needs* are . . .

  - My greatest *wants* are . . .

- If I did not fulfill my needs, I would . . .

- If I did not fulfill my wants, I would . . .

After completing Self-Assessment #3, most people have a better sense of what is *really* necessary to their lives. They often discover that while their needs are limited, their wants can be great. For example, a woman starved for love and affection may find herself sleeping aimlessly with many men to fill the basic physiological void. She may tell herself she *needs* sex, but in actuality she *wants* to be wanted. *Want* can often be so strong that it does indeed mimic *need*. So the distinction is far from simple. Many women act out years of their lives without being able to differentiate between the two. It is precisely because this process is so difficult that we must be aware of it—and conquer it. If we could truly identify them, most of us could satisfy our own needs more often than we believe.

As naive as I had been to marry to get car service, I could easily have counted on myself to get the car to mechanics when needed. Depending on a man for things we can do for ourselves gives women a false sense of security. It also makes us needy. The problem with being needy is that such women communicate desperation that usually turns off the very souls they want to attract. A woman must understand that she can survive without being in a relationship. Yes, for most of us it's easier and more fun to have a partner to share our daily doings and undoings. But having a man is more a luxury than a necessity. And, of course, having the *wrong* man is a total debilitator.

When her *need* behavior is converted from grubbing and grabbing to *want* behavior of lighthearted humor, a woman becomes more appealing. This applies to all aspects of life, whether a woman is being interviewed for a job, negotiating to buy something, or flirting with a man. The connotation of *wanting*, rather than *needing*, suggests that if someone or something is not available, we will live just fine.

Asking for What We Need—and Want

Once we determine what we want, we must take the next step and ask for it. Until we request the seat by the window, we will continue to get the one by the kitchen. Asking for what we want is a problem for most people. Sales training courses specifically teach salespeople to *ask* for the order. But women seem most afflicted by this inability to articulate their desires—and the consequences of such inaction. We may be afraid our requests will be denied, or that we'll appear too aggressive, or that, even worse, we won't be liked. But unless we ask for what we want, we project that we don't believe we *deserve* to get it.

> *Dear Dr. Gilda:*
> *I am a twenty-five-year-old liberated woman who has been on the pill for the two years I've been with my boyfriend. It's getting expensive and I think he should share the cost. The problem is that I don't know him well enough to discuss money with him.*

At first this may seem funny, but this woman is far from liberated and her communication far from direct. Being intimate with a guy she's known for two years, yet feeling uncomfortable about discussing birth control with him? Really! I hear about this quandary often from women too insecure to take responsibility for their own sexuality. Nevertheless, their moaning after an accidental pregnancy is terribly sad. On the less extreme side of the spectrum, I often hear about a woman's unwillingness to speak up when she's hit with half the dinner bill because she felt too intimidated to say, "But you asked *me* to dinner." These are our fears. We fear speaking up and making that fateful faux pas that will lose us this man we believe we *need* to weather life's storms. So we hold our tongues about things ranging from a trivial dinner bill issue to a far more important one about birth control. The point is, if we allow our fears to hold us back in small ways, they will certainly contain us from expressing our desires about the big issues. These women unwilling to ask for what they deserve are the women I tell to *get a life*. I should know. Until I began to speak up, I was without one myself.

Every woman, before an extended relationship ensues, is responsible to share her wants, and especially her needs, with her partner. If she doesn't, she is setting herself up for continued disappointment, and especially for getting him what *he* needs and wants rather than what's on her own separate agenda.

In Self-Assessment #4 you will practice asking for what you *need*, then asking for what you *want*. The objective here is three-pronged: to get you to practice asking for what you believe you deserve (whether it's a need or a want); to listen to the difference in the way you use your voice for a *want* as opposed to a *need*; and to check the response of your listener. For example, when we *need* something, there is an urgency in our voice that alerts our listener to be alarmed and act immediately. However, if he senses that we use this same seriousness with everything (including our wants), we are quickly labeled needy and whiny, demanding things he does not deem to be grave and pressing. This is a sure way to turn off any worthy man.

SELF-ASSESSMENT #4

ASKING FOR WHAT YOU NEED AND WANT

Ask each of the following people for something you have neglected requesting in the past. First ask as if you want this thing. Then ask as if you need this thing. Even if your requests seem foolish, remember that they are important to you. And if you do not ask, you will not get.

> **1.** Ask your mate.
> **2.** Ask your boss.
> **3.** Ask a stranger.
>
> ---
>
> • How did you feel about asking?
> • Did the tone of your voice sound urgent? too urgent?
> • What were your listeners' reactions?

Did you have trouble with Self-Assessment #4? It was important for you first to differentiate between your needs and wants in Self-Assessment #3 to determine your immediate and dire requirements. Ultimately you realized that your needs are few. But in case you misjudged a *want* for a *need*, in Self-Assessment #4 you got to assess the way you requested each of the two, which should have helped you distinguish one from the other. Then you heard your listeners' feedback. If you asked for a want in the same manner as you asked for a need, did you sense that your listener was becoming turned off? Did you become more aware of toning down a voice of urgency and substituting a calmer one when you requested something to simply make you feel better? When you can communicate unagitated composure, your listener is more prone to satisfy your wants.

A woman who had taken one of my workshops described how she was now passing along to her daughter the information about asking for what you want. As they neared the counter of the child's favorite fast-food restaurant, the girl selected her lunch and placed the order herself. After the pair found a table, the girl whined, "I think I'm supposed to get a free mug with lunch." Her mother really didn't know, but she told her child to return to the cashier and ask for it. The child shyly refused. The mother said, "Do you *need* this mug?" Her daughter replied, "No." But she clearly felt cheated. Evidently she *wanted* it.

My student could easily have gone to the counter herself, but she knew it was necessary for her daughter to request what she wanted on her own. Finally the girl rose from her seat and crept to the front of the order line. She whispered her request so quietly that the cashier had to ask her to re-peat it. Although she learned that her size lunch portion was not entitled to a mug after all, as the youngster returned to the table, her mother noted that she was walking quicker and taller. She said with a smile, "Mom, next time, to get the free gift I have to order more food." The two laughed as my student realized the valuable lesson her daughter had learned about asking for what she wanted—and it had nothing to do with getting a free mug. It is never too late—or too early—to learn the lessons of asking for what you need and want.

If you are not open in expressing your needs and wants, you are not communicating honestly. Buried feelings don't just disappear, and they eventually show up in other ways, perhaps by losing your temper over some entirely different argument or by stuffing your anger into your body and overeating or overdrinking. From chapter 2, corporate manager Christine is a woman guilty of not asking. She continues to try to keep the peace at any price by refusing to request from husband Howard what is rightly hers—her personal freedom. She recently quit her well-paying job to become more available for her four unruly children and her complaining husband, further ensuring her economic servitude and adding another barrier to developing healthy self-esteem. She has ballooned to a hundred pounds beyond her healthy weight. She incarcerates herself in a body reflecting her dismal marriage. But she is afraid to rock the boat because Howard often threatens to leave. She is under the impression that she and the children *need* him, and she will have to observe his commands to keep him coming home. In an effort to gain some pocket money, she has now begun to do freelance work servicing other Fortune 500 companies like the one she quit.

Christine described a typical conversation with her husband:

> Howard told me today that he plans to take Monday off. "Can we do something together?" he asked.
>
> I said, "Monday is when Johnny Jr. is in school till three-fifteen, so Ellie comes to work with me all day. Even if I could take time off, I have no baby-sitter, so we'd have to take Ellie along with us." I asked, "Actually, I was wondering if you would watch the kids at three-thirty while I meet one of my few paying clients."
>
> Howard replied, "I'm not going to waste my vacation baby-sitting so you can fulfill your client obligations."

Throughout their marriage, Christine's requests of her husband were usually like this one, *wondering* and wishy-washy. Never would she indicate her own needs and wants. Consequently the support system she needed from her mate was nonexistent. She didn't ask for it because she didn't believe she deserved it. Similarly, when she did work, her business crumbled as clients refused to pay, because her demeanor with them was no different from the way it was with Howard.

As her husband continuously rejected her requests with put-downs about the importance of her work (and her possible economic independence), Christine simply stopped asking. Instead she stuffed her requests—and her anger—into her body.

One night one of Christine's few girlfriends called, exhausted from a long day at work, and suggested they meet for coffee while Howard watched the kids. Christine was in the middle of making dinner. She whispered into the phone that she'd get back to her friend in an hour. When she did return the call, she said, "Sorry, I'd love to meet you, but boss man said no."

The next day her friend brought over Self-Assessments #3 and #4. While completing the assessments, Christine realized how *selfless* she was feeling. She recognized she was in trouble. She reviewed her hesitancy about asking for a mere night off. Her overweight condition was now exhausting her. Her constant bickering with Howard was draining her. A few hours away from the family, she realized, might once have been a *want*, but it had now become a *need*. She recalled the seven years of suffering without a financial identity. More than that, she realized that most things had not changed in her marriage since that time. And she also understood that her life was getting worse, rather than better, as the years began to build. That night she asked her controlling husband for a brief break of a few hours, but this time her request was different from anything she had ever communicated to him before. Suddenly her voice lacked its usual needy and predictable whine. She remained calm and focused, but *very* firm. She *told* Howard of her need to change the scenery in her life for a bit. She *told* him she'd return before midnight. Yes, it was still a request, because she needed his compliance to remain at home with the children. But her request was offered with such strength that it sounded as though her decision had already been made. It had been. When she left after dinner that evening to meet her friend, for the first time in a long time she closed the door to her home with a smile. Also for the first time in a long time, Howard stood there dumbfounded. It's miraculous how a quickly a man *gets it* as soon as a woman claims her power and sets the stage for grown-up standards. Regardless of whether it was a need—as it was in this instance—or simply a want, Christine was beginning to ask for what she finally realized she *deserved*.

We Get What We Believe We Deserve

Deep down many people believe they just don't deserve to get what they need or want. Each person has his or her own unique deserve level, and it is this measure that determines what he or she ultimately gets from life. I first discovered the significance of deserve levels while training salespeople at a seminar. On an index card, I asked them to write the earnings they believed they *deserved* in the next year. We sealed the cards into envelopes, I collected them, and when the year was up we reconvened. Most of the group had forgotten they had even performed this activity. But after I redistributed the cards, they were amazed that with few exceptions, each person had earned what she or he had predicted within a few thousand dollars of his or her deserve level.

I continued to incorporate this exercise into all my workshops worldwide, especially when the subject matter dealt with personal goals. The results were always the same. We create for ourselves exactly what we believe we *deserve* to get, nothing more, nothing less.

👑 Gilda-Gram *What we believe we deserve is what we receive.*

Your deserve level is the electrical wiring that delineates your boundaries and commands respect. It lets people know where *you* stand so that *they* can determine where they stand in relation to you. When you send messages that you are deserving, people unwittingly treat you as you are "telling" them to.

Therefore, what you believe you deserve determines how you'll live your life. Complete Self-Assessment #5 and find out how your deserve level predicts your future.

SELF-ASSESSMENT #5

EVALUATING MY DESERVE LEVEL

List everything you spend more than ten minutes doing over the course of one week.

1. Underline *one time* everything you do for YOU.

2. Underline *two times* everything you do for YOUR MATE.

3. Underline *three times* everything you do for YOUR CHILDREN.

4. *Circle* everything you do for your HOUSEHOLD.

5. X everything you do for OTHER PEOPLE.

- On which of the five items do you spend the most time?
- Is this how you *need* to spend your time?
- Is this how you *want* to spend your time?
- How do you believe you *deserve* to spend your time?

This assessment is important so that you evaluate how you apportion your time, because your time management trumpets how you value your self. Does this sound surprising? When I was running time-management classes in corporate America, the executives were amazed to learn that the way they scheduled their lives told more about them than did their own self-descriptions. For example, after completing this self-assessment, Christine discovered that she spent the majority of her time performing chores for her children, her home, and for Howard. Obviously time was allocated for everyone else's *needs*. In managing a home, some of this behavior is mandatory. But there was never time left for the activities from which Christine derived pleasure. By eliminating herself from the equation, she projected the message that she was unimportant, that she did not count, and that she deserved little when it came to others devoting time to her.

A strong deserve level is necessary in seeking a soulmate and sustaining a relationship. We can observe how Christine's questionable deserve level set the stage for Howard's disrespect from the outset. As a bright woman, she was aware that her mate devalued her, and she had been furious at him for years. Yet she lacked a strong deserve level, so her anger wasn't empowering, as it might have been for some other woman who could have taken her distress as a sign that she needed to make some changes. Instead Christine's fury only got her to stuff herself with food and distend her body. She might have been looking to punish Howard by becoming less attractive to him. Or her weight might have been protecting her from further frustration and hurt. Either way, her self-esteem was in the gutter.

Like Christine, many women live at home as somebody's daughter, then become somebody's wife, never having discovered they are *somebody*, first and foremost. When a woman has not firmly defined herself as *somebody*, she will never know, first, *that* she deserves, and then, *what* she deserves. As she bounces from one unhappy relationship to another, she either asks tentatively for what she wants or she does not ask at all. The consequence is that she doesn't get what she might have, had she only made the firm request.

Each emotionally abused and physically battered woman I've worked with has had a deficit in deserve level. Each of these women somehow learned that she *deserved* no more than this kind of treatment from a man—and that's exactly what she got. I sat with one woman on a talk show who was learning for the first time that her husband had committed adultery. After this woebegone woman heard the news and cried, she was quick to rationalize, "All men cheat." Because of her original belief about "all men," she clearly manifested a cheater as a mate. So although she was upset about her discovery, she figured love—and men—are like this. She had obviously settled for what she felt worthy of attracting. We always get what we believe we *deserve*.

Unfortunately, this woman is not alone in dropping her own needs and wants because she never learned that she deserved more. But we as role models have an obligation to set new standards. When we understand why we attract the men we attract, we realize that our old patterns must not be repeated before those who witness our dismay. The only way to break our negative behavior styles is to substitute more positive designs. Thus while Christine mirrored her parents' own unhappy union (a do-it-all mom with a constantly complaining and emotionally absent father), she recognized that her children must now get to see a brighter side of love.

Though still doubting her lovability, with the guides of the self-assessments Christine is beginning to question not only her motives for overeating, but what and who she really needs in her life. She is beginning to discriminate between her *needs* and her *wants*. She is learning that when we consider our own requirements as least important, everyone follows our lead. In reality:

👑 **Gilda-Gram** *What we accept, we teach.*

Becoming a Will-Be Woman

Here's a flash: Not only do you deserve to attract good things into your life, *you* determine which good things you attract. After you assess your deserve level, it is time to evaluate your willingness to place yourself as *numero uno*. When you feel you *deserve* to devote special time to meet your needs and wants, you should also feel comfortable putting your needs and wants first when necessary. This is often difficult for many women who feel that when they put their own priorities before those of other people, they are being *selfish*. That is not a pretty word in a society that stresses women as *nurturers*, as being there for others above all else. Are you comfortable in occasionally meeting your own needs and wants before others'? In Self-Assessment #6, examine a list of your daily chores and find out.

Learning to Put Yourself First

SELF-ASSESSMENT #6

DO I PUT MYSELF FIRST?

Divide a piece of paper into two columns. Do each of the following four steps, one after the other.

1. In the left-hand column, with your dominant hand, write, "I put myself first."

2. In the right-hand column, with your nondominant hand, write whatever response comes to mind.

3. In the left-hand column, with your dominant hand, write, "I put myself first."

4. In the right-hand column, with your nondominant hand, write whatever response comes to mind.

Do this exercise until you run out of right-hand column responses.

> *Your **dominant hand** represents your **conscious** mind.*
> *Your **nondominant hand** represents your **unconscious** mind.*
>
> • What is your unconscious mind telling you on the right side
>   of the page?
> • Do you put yourself first?

What did you learn about how you treat yourself? What are your reservations about placing your priorities before those of others you love?

Christine's responses for Self-Assessment #6 were as follows:

LEFT-HAND COLUMN (Conscious Voice)	RIGHT-HAND COLUMN (Unconscious Voice)
"I put myself first."	"No, I can't do that."
"I put myself first."	"That's not fair to my family."
"I put myself first."	"I would be selfish."
"I put myself first."	"Howard would kill me."
"I put myself first."	"Howard would leave me."

From this exercise, Christine saw how she felt deep down about putting her own needs before her family's. She admitted she thought it was "selfish." On the right side of her page, her nondominant hand reminded her that her children and husband must be her priorities. Forget about her own needs and wants. Because she had always been there for everyone at all times, no one had dared call her "selfish" in the past. But during this exercise, her unconscious fear loomed loud and clear that if she did make any changes, someone would use this awful word to describe her. What she had learned during her upbringing, and modeled in her life, was that if women don't play down their personal needs, they won't be loved. In fact, they will be *left*. She rationalized that this must be true as Howard continued to threaten leaving if she voiced her needs and wants.

Now that Christine knew the underlying reasons for her behavior, she was left to deal with the consequences of changing it. Change is one of the toughest parts of life. No one looks to change the "security" they think they have. The continued fear of abandonment was going to poke its ugly head into Christine's affairs, and she would have to learn to cast out these demons. She had to be reminded constantly that she had spent thirty-something years building this sort of life for herself. It would now take some time to undo it. She needed to have some patience. This is where many women often lose heart. In our sanitized and homogenized world, we are often under the impression that our stains and wrinkles can be quickly dry-cleaned and pressed. Then off we could go, a new and improved person. Unfortunately, change takes time.

Christine completed the self-assessments many times and began to see changes in her responses. She was finally feeling better about herself. But as she was beginning to grow, she came face-to-face with the fear that she had not yet encountered.

One night, as her family sat around the dinner table, she announced to Howard that she needed him to baby-sit. She had to attend an important cocktail party where a potential client for her freelance work had agreed to meet her. Without warning, her husband threw his fork across the table. He stammered, "Christine, I—I've kept quiet as you went off on your half-cocked dreams with your nonsensical business. But lately, I don't know what's gotten into you. You've become the most *selfish* woman I know."

Oops! That ugly word—"selfish"—now being issued by her husband. For most women, this word is a hot button. When we hear it, most of us are immediately put on the defensive. Then we tend to *react* defensively. Our reaction is destructive because it then validates what our name-caller has said. The cycle goes round and round, and we often find ourself as frustrated as we were before we asked for what we needed. In reality, by dismissing her own needs and wants, Christine had become more self*less* than self*ish*. Accepting the word "selfish" might not be so bad for her after all.

There's another point to be highlighted in Christine and Howard's interchange: Just as we get what we believe we deserve, the behavior we *accept* from others is the way we train them to continue to behave toward us. Many women accept angry put-downs from their mates, figuring the guy is in the midst of losing his temper and his emotional outburst will soon pass. One man actually told his new fiancée that his mother had once instructed his ex-wife to ignore his tantrums until they were over—and now his future wife should do the same. By not putting their foot down immediately upon being slighted, however, these women unintentionally teach their men that they can continue their foul behavior. The men, in turn, believe their actions are all right because their women do not communicate otherwise. What we are saying here is that a woman must *not* accept, and thereby teach, that disrespect in any form or at any time in the relationship is okay. It must be nipped in the bud as soon as she senses it. It is entirely up to you to make your life wonderful. It is entirely up to you to take a starring role in it!

Here I Am, World—Starring Me!

To project your deserve level, *star in your own commercial*. I instruct women around the world to do a commercial that boasts what they believe they deserve. Boasting is a message most of us were never taught. In fact, we probably learned the opposite, to deny and dismiss positive and complimentary feedback whenever we are lucky enough to get it. No wonder we complain about its short supply when we become adults. I felt this poignantly when I told a three-year-old girl, "You are so pretty." Boldly yet innocently, she responded, "I know." Her mother jumped in to scold her for "sounding conceited." The mother-to-child message was to play down her shining star. The child looked perplexed. Not to contradict the mother in front of her offspring, I winked and told the child, "All you have to do is smile and say, 'Thank you.' Everyone will know that you know you're special."

As adults, how do we project we know we're special? How do we project that we "deserve" without it appearing that we "demand"? The trick is to boast your assets without batting your listener on the head with them. Projecting your deserve level is easy once you learn to:

👑 **Gilda-Gram** *Project a strong shell with a soft sell.*

Now it's time to project the skills you have developed during this chapter. Complete Self-Assessment #7 and star in your own commercial. All you need are thirty seconds. In truth, it is harder to do a thirty-second commercial selling yourself than it is to do a one-hour presentation on an aspect of your work. Yet in this short time span, you will project your essence. As in media commercials, thirty seconds is ample time to make a case for your wares. In a sparse thirty seconds, you can appeal to someone to like you, and maybe even love you in time. Practice this often until you feel comfortable. It is the real expression of your soul, the genuine and authentic representation of who you really are. Even if this seems uncomfortable at first, act "as if" until you feel it. The nervous system cannot tell the difference between what is real and what is imagined. So fake it till you make it.

👑 **Gilda-Gram** *Eventually your outer mask becomes your inner soul.*

SELF-ASSESSMENT #7

STAR IN YOUR OWN COMMERCIAL

Use a stopwatch. In thirty seconds, the length of most commercials, hook our attention with something positive about yourself. Your objective is to be remembered and referred. Have someone assess you, or assess yourself on video.

1. How did you feel about this commercial?
2. Was thirty seconds enough time? too much time?
3. How do you feel about promoting yourself?
4. If you were the listener, would you remember and refer yourself?

Enact Self-Assessment #7 as often as possible until it becomes your second skin. The more often you sell yourself, the more you will raise your deserve level, and the more comfortable you will be in stating your needs and wants. From the popular movie *Field of Dreams,* we learned that if we build it, *he* will come. But *he'll* never know we're out there if we don't advertise.

One day I gave Christine the assignment of promoting herself to three different people she spoke to. This felt very awkward to her at first, and she resisted the very thought of raising her own flag, fearful of being called vain and egotistic. I actually had to begin by telling her exactly which words to say: To her five-year-old daughter, she was to boast, "I am attractive." To a new client, "I can improve your customer relations better than anyone because I possess the necessary skill of following through." And to her husband, "I will tell you when you have hurt my feelings." After she used these statements with the three people, I asked her to tape them, then watch herself. This process was even more painful, as it is for most of us who are unfamiliar with how we come across to others. However, I insisted that she state these sentences again and again. And I had her tape whole fantasy conversations as springboards to the statements. In just several hours she began to grow more comfortable in saying kind and positive things about herself and in viewing herself on tape.

Self-promotion is a skill that can be learned. All it requires is the risk of self-revelation. But as we age, we become more cautious about revealing ourselves and being vulnerable. From our previous years of hurt, we fear abandonment should a new man discover the "real me." So we protect, we hide, we put on added weight, we wear dark glasses, we bury our faces behind fabulous hair or makeup, we disrobe, we overrobe, and we ultimately run from our honesty. When we hide, we attract hiding men, men who aren't honest about themselves. Aren't you fed up with the losers in your life? Now that you've learned your needs and your wants, now that you recognize that you deserve to get what you ask for, it's time to project who you really are. It's time to project your power.

GILDA-GRAMS

FROM CHAPTER 3

Ask for What You Need and
Believe You Deserve to Get It

▶ *People attract people like themselves.*

▶ *When something happens to us, it really happens for us.*

▶ *A man in the "ing" position—divorcing, separating, losing, grieving—is at his two lowest needs levels: physiological and security. While struggling for his survival, he is unable to rise to the third needs level of love.*

▶ *If you don't know what you need, you won't get what you want.*

▶ *What we believe we deserve is what we receive.*

▶ *What we accept, we teach.*

▶ *Project a strong shell with a soft sell.*

▶ *Eventually your outer mask becomes your inner soul.*

4

Project a Power Image

The beautiful mannequin peers at you from behind the sparkling glass of a department store window. Her perfect plastic body is devoid of feeling, vacant of vitality. As magnificent as she may look, she is merely the rendition of a woman. She lacks both depth and dynamism. She is a figure with no power. A woman without power is a woman without pulse. She remains a mannequin forever—unless someone installs a circuit board to ignite her with thinking, feeling energy.

Many women live mannequin lives. They say "Yes" when they really mean "No," their opinions mirror those of everyone but themselves, their life's role is to manipulate a man to marry them, their mission is to serve and service, and then, once they have exchanged their independent souls for a pittance of approval, their overriding emotion becomes depression. These are the mannequin women, the women without power, the women short-circuiting a connection to life. They can't buy power, they can't borrow it. Men who have it won't give it to them. To get power, they must develop it themselves. For many women, power development and maintenance is a mystery, especially since it connotes a negative spin that promises to ward off the very gender they long to attract.

> *Men don't want to share power. Why should they? Power is fun. It's an aphrodisiac.*
> —*Cathleen Black, president of Hearst Magazines and former publisher of* USA Today

SO . . .

> *The thing women have to learn is that nobody gives you power. You just take it.*
> —*Roseanne*

Quite a predicament we find ourselves in. Men don't want to part with their power. For women to get power, they must create it themselves. But if men think they are the only ones entitled to it, and women go off to establish it anyway, beware the fallen male ego. The 1980 romantic movie

The Competition depicts rival classical pianists who fall in love before their musical match. She wins, he loses. He tells her they must part. Her winning would contaminate his life and their lovemaking, he says. Her mentor wisely advises that it will take centuries to find a man who can accept a woman's stardom. Almost two decades after this movie was filmed, men and women still debate this conflict.

Who is most eligible for power? And must it be an either/or, male/female contest? When your man isn't the great attention getter, watch out: divorce could be the future tense of your marriage. Anthropologist Helen Fischer suggests that the two words that most account for today's high divorce rate in America are "working woman." No doubt economic independence allows a woman to pursue her own power and thereby sets her up as "difficult" or, even worse, a "bitch." Remember the teacher Caitlin? When she began to take back her power and divorce her husband, he, too, called her a "bitch," along with those who supported her decision. His name-calling, especially in front of their children, upset her terribly, as well it should. Indeed, "bitch" is the name assigned to most women, including Roseanne, who have taken a powerful stance. Imagine if the roles had been reversed in *Gone with the Wind* and Scarlett O'Hara had said to Rhett Butler, "Frankly, Rhett, I don't give a damn." A whole generation of women who felt free to be bitchy might have changed the course of "HerStory." As it stands, the fictional movie character Dolores Claiborne rationalized, "Sometimes being a bitch is the only thing a woman has to hold on to."

Ina was barraged with continuous phone calls from an ex-girlfriend of her husband. The girlfriend would call at 8:00 A.M. on weekends to speak with Max about her personal problems, obviously considering Max a good "friend." Max was evidently flattered and refused to tell his ex to cease her calls despite Ina's requests. As most wives in this situation would do, Ina beseeched her husband to exercise his power and get his ex-girlfriend to stop her early morning calls. But whatever his logic, he refused. Finally Ina took charge. She called the woman and *told* her not to call their house again. In the predicted parlance, the woman called Ina a *bitch*. So be it; Ina was in control.

> *Our deepest fear is not that we are inadequate.*
> *Our deepest fear is that we are powerful beyond measure.*
> —*Marianne Williamson*

Too bad many women today fear projecting who they really are.

I had just filled my car's tank with gasoline, and while I was paying the greasy, toothless attendant, I nicely asked him to check one of my tires. He looked at the wheel in question, nonchalantly said the tire looked "fine" to him, and proceeded to take my money and walk away. The price of nice! Annoyed at being summarily dismissed, I opened the window and in unladylike fashion growled that the tire didn't look "fine" to me. *Bitch!* He continued to walk on. Now furious, I swung open the car door, jumped out, and demanded that he check that tire. *Super Bitch!* I was seething. Seeing the commotion, the owner of the gas station appeared and said that the attendant would "gladly check *all* your tires"—which he reluctantly did. The tire in question needed air after all. Because of my emotional exhaustion over a mere tire, I hardly thought of this as a victory. But I was proud that I had stuck to my guns and taken care of myself even when the guy in charge said I didn't need such caretaking.

As I drove off, I thought of the days when I would happily have taken a man's word for something as important as my personal safety. I remembered years earlier telling my ex-boyfriend that our car felt "strange" and how he disregarded my concerns. But because of my persistence, and thankfully not too late, I discovered that we had been driving dangerously on two bald tires that could have blown at any time. That could have cost us our lives!

I took my power and was at first shot down. So what? It may not be a matter of life or death, but women must never depend on a man to hand us power. And for those less courageous, who fear his banishing you altogether from his life:

....

♕ Gilda-Gram *If he doesn't want you on his team, form your own.*

....

It is probably no accident that many women (myself included) have felt able to enunciate their greatest power in the small, enclosed space of an auto. For one thing, when we are behind the wheel ourselves, we feel mighty and in total control. For another, we are free to pump up our power with self-affirming thoughts that can't be negated by anyone around us. Finally, if we are sitting in this confined space with a man, we feel he has no choice but to hear us without interruption. Yet, as I think about it, this last notion of power might be a *false* one. My own persistence in driving home a point while my ex drove the car caused his loss of temper—and a cracked steering wheel in every car we owned. While this experience affected my willingness later on to join car pools, I learned to reconsider how much power I really have when I'm in that particular arena.

Yes, Roseanne is right. Nobody gives a woman power. Yes, Cathleen Black is right, too. Men enjoy their power too much to share it. Even Henry Kissinger named power an aphrodisiac. Of course, he was referring to *male* power. For women to get power, we must take it, we must project it, we must command that others respect it. If we are criticized, so be it.

Without dependence on anyone for it, a man's assessment of our assertiveness will not matter. At least we will always have ourselves. When you appreciate yourself, that's a great start. Sure there's a price we must pay for taking charge. But in the long run, most of us would agree that it's worth it.

Why don't we take control when we need to, before our blood begins to boil? Sometimes it takes being pushed beyond our limits to get us to recognize that there is even a problem. It would be healthier if we women would take our power before we become emotionally heated so that we could calmly, yet strongly, project our power with finesse. However, most of us really don't know how to craft a power balance. Instead we find ourselves running from one extreme to the other, from being devoid of power (or what I call being a Toastmaster) to becoming too controlling (or becoming what I call a Taskmaster). Each of these alone has merit. But neither of these as a constant behavior pattern serves us well.

Taskmasters and Toastmasters

All evolved women eventually discover that there is nobody out there but us. So if we know we have to take charge of our lives anyway sooner or later, why are we so meek about empowering ourselves now? Perhaps we are paralyzed by watching our men worry that they can never be powerful *enough*. We see them strive forward and stress out—to perform in shining armor and become the official **Taskmaster**.

The Traditional Taskmaster Male

Both in their professional and personal lives, men are trained to project their power in the form of strong exteriors and well-executed tasks. As human *doings*, they define who they are by what they *do* for a living. What they perceive as power translates into obligation and responsibility. At the top of the heap are the brilliant, remorseless men with icy intelligence and aggressive designs on the world. Freud names these organized and obstinate characters "anal" types. They are the left-brained list makers. These are the guys who tell women what to do and how. Their dictates often include "You wouldn't understand," "That's none of your business," and "I'm doing this for your own good," as parents would talk to children.

Some Taskmaster anals channel dormant violent tendencies into their work. They may be corporate raiders and legitimately murder companies instead of people. Or they may be just your average everyday narcissist, whose major objective is not to love anyone as much as he loves himself and his tasks. Taskmasters depend on their external accomplishments to define their (questionable) sense of worth. They shield their sensitivities from their significant others for fear they may appear weak. In fact, most Taskmasters have low self-esteem. High-level power seats at work no longer provide the foam cushion they once did. Consequently, when they suddenly lose their jobs, they shockingly feel their definition of self has died. The drive of striving toward *Who's Who* is now replaced by the fear of becoming *Who's He?* What will they ever do now?

The Taskmaster's expression of love often shows itself as keeping vigil over his partner. He feels that it is his birthright to dominate his woman. He may mold her in his desired image, as Professor Henry Higgins did to Eliza Doolittle in order to establish ownership in *My Fair Lady*. Or he may place her on a pedestal, the perfect platform to possess her, far removed from other mortals. In his mind, he's won the heart of a "perfect" woman. This idealization can be very flattering to a woman at first. But it is a subverted attempt of a dependent, fearful man to feel great by bolstering his own shaky self-esteem. Joseph guided his thirty-five-year-old fiancée around a large convention center, where he spoke for her and asked the vendors to explain their wares "to this young lady." His fiancée already had a successful entrepreneurial track record, but in Joseph's company she was treated as his child. When she felt sure enough about herself to stand up to her bully boyfriend, she rebelled and their relationship ended. Peter controlled his wife in another way. Whenever they were at a party, he would visibly hold on to her belt loop to prevent her from talking to other men. He also often criticized her raucous laughter and scolded her in full view of other people when she didn't "behave like the professor" she had worked as. This woman felt jailed. During the raging portion of their divorce, she chanted: "Peter, Peter, pumpkin eater, had a wife and couldn't keep her. Put her in a pumpkin shell, and there he kept her very well. *Not on your life, Peter dear!*"

As soon as the Taskmaster's "perfect woman"—or Stepford wife—shows some human flaw, he becomes angry at her for having ruined his fantasy. The relationship's demise is inevitable, since no woman can keep her footing on a skimpy, slippery pedestal. Eventually a strong woman gets fed up with all the needed coddling these men demand. Turned off at the need to change his pin-striped Pampers, she may also exhibit anger over being "let down." The Taskmaster, however, will replace her out of desperation. *Any woman* can take on the same significance as the *right woman*. Poor Taskmaster! It must be a burden to have such a monopoly on power.

The Nontraditional Taskmaster Female

Men's power levers certainly topple to the side of performing and achieving. But what about a woman's thrust toward control? Yes, when we think of control in our culture, we generally think of the male gender. But some women display Taskmaster behaviors that can rival those of any man. On the positive side, the Taskmaster female is the quintessential caretaker, the reliable list maker, the perennial party planner. This woman is so dependable, everyone comes to her without fail to fulfill their task obligations. But the negative side of the Taskmaster woman can be most unattractive. It seems that people can accept the notion of "controlling male" because our culture accepts that a *Taskmaster* is synonymous with *testosterone*. But the idea of being a "controlling female" is tantamount to being—back to that word—a "bitch" to other women and, worse, a *castrating* bitch to men.

Arleen was a bright lady with a highly visible job in her wealthy community. However, she felt quite insecure that everyone knew that she had grown up on the poor side of town. While most men define themselves by their jobs, it doesn't matter when they marry women of lesser socioeconomic status. But women tend to marry up, and they use their "catch" to make them feel better about who they are—usually. Not so for Arleen. Her husband was a successful attorney in the town they lived and worked in. Unfortunately, the popularity enjoyed by this charming, mild-mannered chap only goaded her. Worse, he commanded a hefty salary, as local residents often sought his expertise. He made at least four times the money Arleen did, which was another source of insecurity for his wife. She was desperate to equalize everyone's perception of the power imbalance. Her neediness took on a controlling aspect. She offended him with disrespectful put-downs in front of their friends. To outsiders, he accepted what she dished him. However, the paradox of "women most needy are the ones who don't get" was about to reveal itself. Without warning, Arleen's husband told her he was in love with another woman, someone, he confessed, who made him feel "special." No "I'm sorry to do this to you" or "Hope you have a nice life" good-byes. He simply packed and left.

Now desperate and dateless, Arleen pressured everyone she knew to fix her up with a potential new mate. Her ambition was to be a desirable woman once again, and she was determined to stop at nothing. She was so fierce in her neediness, in fact, that at a prestigious singles function, she berated a newly engaged couple for attending the event when tickets for the singles were scarce. Meanwhile, behind her back, the entire community shook their heads in pity and described her as a hungry barracuda.

But to everyone's amazement, she bulldozed a naive and similarly needy acquaintance to become husband number two. Their subsequent relationship was predictably rocky: the couple barely knew each other, Arleen never sought reasons for husband number one's abrupt departure, and she had not done any therapeutic work on herself to prevent the same power plays from recurring in her new marriage. But now at last the young woman's honor was resurrected, and that was all that mattered.

Further bolstering her newly found security in the eyes of others, she got elected to the presidency of a local women's organization. Yet despite her new relationship and new presidency, Arleen still suffered from the trauma of abandonment. She wondered if she could ever really depend on anyone again. Could she ever be sure enough of a man's love? Subconsciously she was determined to make up for in her professional life what she had been unable to control in her personal life. Arleen reigned like an autocratic queen. Once boasting a coterie of powerful and dedicated members, the organization began to splinter. Finally Arleen was asked to resign.

Not all female Taskmasters seem as domineering as Arleen. They may sometimes be clothed as schemers and screamers, redeeming exactly what they want, like the fictitious and wacky Lucy Ricardo. Or they may appear as helpless and selfless, with a perfected "I can't do *this*" routine, soliciting pity while getting the upper hand, like Marilyn Monroe and her bevy of solicitous men. Nonetheless, the Taskmaster is a controller, and whether she is soft-spoken or strident, she'll do almost anything to get her way—and rationalize that what she gets is in the name of love.

Do you exhibit Taskmaster tendencies? Complete Self-Assessment #8 and find out.

SELF-ASSESSMENT #8

TASKMASTER'S CHECKLIST

Are you a Taskmaster? Check the items below that apply to you:

- Do you need to have a hand in everything?
- Do you hold on to issues?
- Must you be right?
- Do you lay blame on others?
- Are you short-tempered and impatient?
- Are you a poor listener?

If you checked even one item, you may have some Taskmaster tendencies.

The issues of power and control go hand in hand. The question, however, is how we demonstrate our power and over whom we wield control. We are most comfortable when we feel we exercise choice over our own circumstances. Those of us who feel we have lost our right to choose—whether real or imagined—sense a loss of personal power. When we feel that our power is depleted, we become unbalanced and attempt to regain equilibrium however we can. For instance, a woman may find it artificially comforting to hold a dominating work role such as boss, cop, teacher, doctor—even parent—to compensate for her low status as a wife. Indeed, a Taskmaster personality is drawn to such power positions to perpetuate the role of top dog. Unfortunately, although Arleen had the luxury of distinguished employment, it wasn't enough to compensate her for feeling that she stood in the shadow of her husband. She felt imbalance between her husband's upbringing and her own, and now between his salary and hers. She also felt that while he had successfully ingratiated himself with their community, she was performing a less prestigious role. It all reminded her of the lowly status she had on the "other side of the tracks" while she was growing up. To regain balance, she now found herself in competition with her husband for who could garner the greatest approval. Her insecurities forced her to look outward, rather than inward, at what made her feel needy in the first place and, then, at what she could do to feel better. As we see, marital competition can be dangerous as one person tries to upstage the other.

One upstaging technique used by overbearing Taskmasters is to denigrate another person. We observe the nasty cashier, the greedy maid, the irate neighbor, the abusive spouse, as unempowered people. They attempt to control their lives by controlling the lives of others. Arleen clearly tried to dominate her husband by humiliating him publicly, falsely assuming that her vacuous superiority would impress onlookers. Often, however, the Taskmaster ploy backfires. Browbeating is nothing more than bullying, and power abuses don't always go unchecked. Finally, Arleen's beaten-down mate sought solace in someone who made him feel "special" rather than oppressed.

....

Gilda-Gram *The Taskmaster who feels her own life is out of control often tries to control others, but few people are willing to withstand such domination for long.*

....

As much as the Taskmaster may try to control other people, the problem is that no grown-up or even child does exactly what we want all the time. So the Taskmaster whose goal is to control finds herself constantly miserable, *herself out of control*. She cannot indefinitely continue her dominating role, whether it is mother, mother-in-law, wife, or boss. Eventually her subjects feel unduly suppressed, regain their backbone, and leave. Sometimes the controlling Taskmaster finds someone else to replace the loss, but not for long. Growing and developing people will not withstand such governance over time.

It is possible for women to feel power within, without feeling the need to exercise external control over someone else. These women are the only *real* powerful women. We'll discuss how to accomplish this inner power later in the chapter. But first we need to look at other women who, feeling insecure and powerless, drop the whole power notion altogether, in preference of the saccharine realm of being "nice." Surely they think this behavior will gain them acceptance, security, and inner control. As you will see, this extreme is not the answer any more than the wielding of power over another.

The Traditional Female Toastmaster

Women know that power is not a kind and gentle term for us. In this either/or world, to uphold our image of the "weaker" sex, most women choose to be power*less* instead of power*ful*. So that they don't rock anyone's boat, they find it far more praiseworthy to take on the role of **Toastmaster**. While Taskmaster men are the doers, Toastmaster women are the dreamers. The Toastmaster suffers from the "smiley-face syndrome." She commissions herself to make people happy, not make waves, and accept the wisdom of the Taskmaster men in charge. These men may be her bosses or her significant other. Whoever they are, the Toastmaster trusts that *Father* Knows Best. In her view, man's mission is to be the meat of the sandwich while hers is to act like (milque)toast.

Do you exhibit Toastmaster tendencies? Complete Self-Assessment #9 and find out.

SELF-ASSESSMENT #9

TOASTMASTER'S CHECKLIST

Are you a Toastmaster? Check the items below that apply to you:

- When something goes wrong in the relationship, do you blame yourself?
- Do you walk on eggshells so as not to upset him?
- Have you relinquished your own opinions?
- Have you ditched the activities you love?
- Have you altered your appearance and behaviors according to his taste?
- Have you separated yourself from your friends and family?

- Have you allowed him decision-making rights over your life?
- Do you keep your feelings under wraps?
- Do you yield to others' demands at the expense of taking care of yourself?

If you checked even one item, you may have some Toastmaster tendencies.

Toastmasters manifest themselves by scurrying to meet everyone else's demands on them and ignoring their own needs. Certainly a Toastmaster yields most often to her mate. But this trait can extend to all of her relationships. This was evident at a seminar I was conducting for nurses, "Caring for Yourself While Caring for Others." The room was filled with tired female nurses of all ages, shapes, and sizes. Many were overweight, most requested "smoking breaks," and all admitted to being stressed beyond repair. In this group sat one particularly shining star, Caroline, a short, round, jovial woman in her forties. If anyone could have won an award for "Woman Who Cares Too Much," it was she. As the other women in the room slouched in exhaustion, Caroline nodded her head with a smirk, as though she knew her results before she completed the assessment. She immediately volunteered to address the group with her findings: "Okay, I'm guilty. Yes, I feel hurt when you criticize me." She was getting emotional and she rose as she continued, "Yes, my goal is to please you. Yes, when hard-pressed, I'll change my opinions to yours. Yes, I'll put off my own stuff if you call for help. Yes, I care what you say about me behind my back. Yes, yes, yes. *I care too much and I'm burned out.* So I sit on my car horn in traffic, I'm pissed off when things aren't done to perfection, and I'd rather do everything myself than see them screwed up by someone else. I checked all ten items in both the Taskmaster and the Toastmaster categories. I'm in a constant state of panic and stress! Heeeeeelp!"

Being both Taskmaster and Toastmaster is very common for women. Indeed, it seems that extreme behavior in one realm often catapults us to extreme behavior in the other, in a never-ending cycle.

The audience roared at Caroline's response. Sadly, the laughter exploded not so much because she was funny, but because the nurses in their chairs could identify with her issues. Their role as second-class subordinates to the doctors and as endless caregivers to the patients made for all-encompassing pressure that they were unable to turn off when they returned home. I asked, "Did you become nurses because you wanted to serve others, or did you serve others first because that's what you were taught to do, then later decide to become nurses?" The same question can be asked of other traditionally female, caregiving roles like teachers, social workers, mothers, and wives. The nurses did not know how to respond to a question that examined motives seemingly so inbred. There could be no answer.

Here I am, accomplished TV personality, author, college professor, motivational speaker, holder of a Ph.D., and the nation's love doc, *and from time to time I, too, still fall into the trap of "He must know better."* It's the veterinarian I dated who professed to be a computer expert and then wiped my most important document off my system after *I allowed him to use it against my better judgment.* It's the art framer who insisted I not use glareless glass *despite my continued requests,* and now I stare at pictures in my office that glare from the incoming sunlight. It's the painter I hired who disregarded *my instructions* to patch the holes in my wall. I wanted him to finally complete the job and get out of my home, so I didn't push it; now it galls me each time I note the crevices. These three events occurred in the course of only one weekend. On each occasion, disregarding my own gut feelings, I had bet on a prince, surrendered my power to him, and subsequently paid, sometimes in dollars and always in self-respect. These men didn't grab control; I *gave* it to them. Just as it is in love, I, the woman, had had the upper hand. Then, for some reason, I handed over the keys. After each incident I felt bad that I hadn't stuck by my gut and gotten what I really wanted and in some cases paid for. What makes us think that men know better, or *best*?

In thirty-seven cultures studied around the world by psychologist David Buss, it was found that the woman is the one who holds the cards at the beginning of every relationship. Evolutionary psychologists explore the male impulse to propagate at the mere thought of sex with anyone handy. They tell us a gene's gotta do what a gene's gotta do, and people behave according to their lineage. But the power of the female, pejoratively named "pussy power" by our terrified men, can put the kibosh on whoever she thinks won't stick around for her and the kids. While men may *want* sex, it is women who decide to *have* sex. Women are the gatekeepers.

However, once a couple is into a sexual mambo, something remarkable occurs. She begins to adjust her schedule to meet his, she adopts his personal tastes as her own, she assumes his political posture as the gospel. In short, although she had once gatekept—and joyfully challenged—this man, now he ends up in a relationship with a mirror image of himself. It had been their fascinating differences that titillated him at first. Now he's bored. This smiley-faced Toastmaster person has abdicated her decision-making and problem-solving powers to her man. When given a woman's power as his own, a guy runs with it as far as he can take it. But that is at the beginning. Soon the monotony finds him running *from* it as far as he can go.

What happened to the woman's evolved mind? Why don't we get, and keep, a life of our own? Why do we abdicate our power? Unlike the men who are certain that the task is the major goal that matters, we remain insecure about how much power is too much power. The sparse selection of available choices paints us either as bitches in britches or docile doormats. There is no in-between. Onlookers often confuse assertive women with aggressive women, while anything short of that remains the wilted lily. Despite the fact that we're nearing the millennium, no woman is taught power projection at birth. We are trained by our mothers, who were instructed by their mothers, who in turn imprinted the habits of theirs. As enlightened as we think we have become, the truth is that change takes time, and it's certainly never going to occur if generations continue to mirror the behaviors of those who preceded them. We still equate subservience with acceptance—and we want our princes to love us and take care of us.

A joint study of personal ads by researchers at the University of New Mexico and the University of Liverpool, England, found that women were nearly five times more likely than men to advertise requests for wealthy prospective partners.

> *When is it okay to kiss someone?*
> *"When he's rich."*
> —*Gerrilyn, age 7*

Men know the score as well as we do. They up their appeal by flaunting their toys. Personal ads in a large city listed one man boasting of his own StairMaster, another offering to share his lottery winnings, and still another celebrating his "Steinway" (when just the word "piano" would have done fine). Women young and old are apparently impressed. Just like their ancestors, today's women look for a big strong guy with status and *money*, while men still seek the same things their forefathers did—youth, fertility, and *honey*.

In the face of Toastmaster behavior, it's still our life and we know it. Feeling as though we've lost our "voice," our ability to be heard, we repress and suppress who we really are. As a result, we naturally become depressed and/or angry. Depression is anger turned inward, and it is more acceptable for a woman to be depressed than it is for her to be angry. Why? Because in our society being an angry woman is just plain ugly.

....

👑 **Gilda-Gram** *The Toastmaster who feels without control often becomes depressed and/or angry that she has surrendered her voice.*

....

For some women, depression and anger are not enough. Two-thirds of all divorces are initiated by women, even though we tend to lose more economically. Some women don't see splitting from just their husband as enough of a break from their Wonder Woman lives. Women-on-the-verge sometimes bolt from their entire family, including small children. *Watch the fabulous Esmeralda raise three kids single-handedly, organize and maintain a home, run a small business out of her basement, oversee the cooking, ironing, and laundry, heal the physical and emotional wounds of everyone under the roof, including the cat, who just got into a spat with a raccoon. . . . See her today, for this is her final performance.* Most bolters view only two alternatives: to leave or to die. This is serious business. Could anyone have predicted a Toastmaster's price of nice? All predicated on a woman's desperate desire to be liked.

Choosing Task or Toast in Order to Be Liked

At the height of laughter with Caroline at my nurses' seminar, I went to the chalkboard at the front of the room and wrote the word "NO." Contrary to what we've been taught, the issue for women is not our ability to say this word. Certainly by now most of us have gleaned that it is to our benefit to avoid the word "yes" at least at times. But the real issue is our inability to say "No" *without guilt*. We live our lives with Catholic guilt, Jewish guilt, Protestant guilt, and even guilt about guilt. One of my friends confesses she has taken on guilt over Chernobyl. Another relays her guilt over eating red meat. And my own guilt occasionally gets so out of hand, I jokingly re-cast my first name to "Guilt-a." But beyond the Catholic, Jewish, Protestant, Chernobyl, or even guilt-over-guilt guilt, there is one guilt that stands far above the rest: women's guilt. In a Penn State University study of re-cently divorced or separated adults, it was found that women who had ex-tramarital affairs took them more seriously but had greater guilt than their male counterparts. Since we figure that relationships are women's sole re-sponsibility, when they get off the mark, it *must be our fault*, and as a result *no one will like us anymore*.

As I write these words, they appear so foolish, like a page from the ele-mentary school yard where the girls formed cliques that did not include me. The need to be liked. While men vie for *respect*, little girls, then women, settle for smiles and group admission. The need to be liked was the force behind Caroline's Toastmaster yielding as much as it was the drive behind Arleen's overbearing Taskmaster aggression. My own desire to please and my reluctance to make waves have created my own occa-sional power surrenders throughout my life. Some women go to greater extremes.

After an angry and painful divorce, Brenda typically began to question her worth as a woman. A usually aggressive Taskmaster, she now went to the opposite extreme of displaying Toastmaster traits in the arms of as-

sorted and often sordid men. As is often the case during this time of deple-
tion, these characters were called upon to satisfy Brenda's desperate need
to once again feel loved. She rationalized that since they all wanted to sleep
with her, she must be desirable.

On a more positive track, Brenda enrolled in a Ph.D. program in one of
the most prestigious universities in New York. Without a doubt, the woman
was brilliant, and she was right to focus on honing her talents. But as intelligent as she was, since her marital breakup, her self-esteem was shaky.
Sadly, she proceeded to compensate for its lack even further by becoming
very "friendly" with the all-male faculty. These associations afforded her
many favors unavailable to the other students, including an all-expenses-
paid fellowship for her entire graduate course of study. The topic of titillating gossip in the intellectual community, she nevertheless continued to
"date" both the single and married professors responsible for granting her
degree.

The school's summer recess came and went. When everyone returned,
the other students learned that Brenda had miraculously received her
doctorate while they were in recess—and the library had been closed for
renovations. Everyone knew how Brenda managed to graduate in such a
short time; the art of sleeping one's way to the top was certainly nothing
new to the savvy student body. But many were enraged that someone so
close to them could "get away with" so much for doing so little, while
they researched and studied assiduously.

With her unrelenting Taskmaster drive, Brenda continued to sleep in to
move up. Enacting jaded Toastmaster behavior with men, she searched for
enhanced self-esteem and embellished credentials. But as she soared to
the top of her professional ranks, she still felt miserably alone. There are no
free rides.

Where does your power lie? Do you lean to the side of too much control? Do you offer too much abdication? Do you unwittingly vacillate between the two? Complete Self-Assessment #10 and find out.

SELF-ASSESSMENT #10

AM I MORE TASKMASTER OR TOASTMASTER?

Answer True or False to each of the following items that describes you:

_____ **1.** I complete my chores as soon as possible.

_____ **2.** When people don't fulfill their promises, I prod
them until they do.

_____ **3.** When plans don't go as expected, I become stressed.

_____ **4.** I often honk my car horn in traffic.

_____ **5.** The best way to handle anything is to do it myself.

_____ **6.** My critics upset me.

_____ **7.** I want to please people I'm with.

_____ **8.** I will alter my views when others object to them strongly.

_____ **9.** I put off my needs when others call on me.

_____**10.** I care about what people say about me behind my back.

SCORING KEY
ITEMS 1–5: TASKMASTER BEHAVIORS
If you have two or more Trues in this category,
study your Taskmaster traits.
Are they serving you or sapping you?

ITEMS 6–10: TOASTMASTER BEHAVIORS
If you have two or more Trues in this category,
study your Toastmaster traits.
Are they serving you or sapping you?

Neither Taskmaster nor Toastmaster behavior alone is harmful. Ask yourself two questions: (1) Is a behavior excessive? (2) Is a behavior serving me or sapping me?

Twenty-something single Tracy completed Self-Assessment #10. She evaluated her Trues in Items 3, 4, 7, 9, and 10. The first two items were in the Taskmaster category, and the last three were in the Toastmaster portion. First, she examined how she overreacted when plans went haywire. She noted how she sat on her horn in traffic. While she rationalized this behavior as part of living in a big city, constant horn blowing is a symptom of impatience. It is a childish outcry of someone who wants her own way _now_, someone who demands that everyone around her take note. _Honk!_

After completing this self-assessment, she realized that the Taskmastering sounds of impatience are both deafening and deadening. Tracy went on to examine Items 7, 9, and 10. She noted how important it was for her to appear as Miss Goody Two-shoes, an obvious call for approval. She wondered if it was her Toastmastering that pushed her to the brink when tasks were not accomplished to perfection and approval was not forthcoming as she had expected. She found herself too fatigued even to go to dinner after work with friends, much less to accept invitations for dates with men on weekends. Fulfilling our tasks should be joyful, yet so should our willingness to withdraw. Tracy knew that if she was going to be successful at life and love, she needed to change before she burned herself out. Self-Assessment #10 opened her awareness for the need to make some alterations.

She knew she had to strive for less perfection, patiently await life's outcomes, and not lose her composure when plans went awry.

Instead of the frantic jumping from one extreme to another, women need to learn *gentle style-flexing* between Task and Toast. For the sake of our physical and emotional health, the one most important requirement for this flexibility is to learn to trust our feelings about when to use which technique. That sort of trust requires that we learn to like ourselves.

When We Like Ourselves, We Trust Ourselves . . . When We Trust Ourselves, We Choose Appropriately

We have observed how many women vacillate between the extremes of Taskmastering and Toastmastering. This is because most women simply don't know what is appropriate behavior in this PC, judgment-prone world. As we've also seen, at the root of most women's actions is a need to be liked. The desperation of "Like me, want me, love me" propels us to remain in relationships we know are not healthy. There is just one way out of this dilemma:

👑 **Gilda-Gram** *Before we fantasize being liked, we need to like ourselves.*

When we *like ourselves*, we need not vacillate between the two extremes. Instead we can choose the one appropriate style that we ourselves judge as fit. But if liking ourselves involves empowering ourselves, and power is an unwieldy concept for a lot of women, how do we go from point A to point B without turning off the whole population, and especially our men? The answer is to avoid the extremes and choose the power source we need—Task or Toast—whenever the circumstances are ripe. To choose appropriately, we must not only like and trust ourselves, we must also be equally comfortable incorporating both behaviors.

Learning to Incorporate Taskmaster/Toastmaster Balance

By now you've seen that there are no absolute gender roles for Taskmasters and Toastmasters. Although we have outlined the stereotypical gender models, women can take on Task orientations as much as men can become the Toast of the town. The objective is to balance the two so that neither gets out of hand. Balancing the two is different from desperate vacillation in the name of not knowing which is appropriate and choosing on the basis of our wanting to be liked. Brenda never learned that the art of balance would make her whole. Neither did nurse Caroline or horn-honking Tracy.

Being in control is important, but so is giving up the crown to compromise. The positive traits of Taskmasters involve accomplishing quests quickly, competently, methodically. The positive traits of Toastmasters involve their consideration for others' feelings and needs. Neither alone is bad. But one without the other is impossible. Pressing task achievement burns a woman out as much as happy-making questions her own life's purpose. Healthy women exhibit balance between the two, with neither used in excess and each applied selectively at the prime time and occasion. The ability to assess circumstances for what they are and then style-flex the power base best suited to the situation is the true measure of a woman's power. Power draws from a woman's feeling that she is strong enough on her own to compromise with someone else. But it never means she should give so much away that she feels she is left with nothing.

Each personal compromise must be predicated on what a woman herself deems right for her, not something she does superficially for her man "just this one time." A truly balanced woman can style-flex from Task to Toast to Task again, without guilt, without regard for what others say, but always with the goal of achieving the greatest good for whatever her purpose at the time. By her own Toastmaster admission, Caroline aimed so much to please that she jumped frantically to satisfy others, however crazy or debilitating their demands. When Tracy recognized how much of herself she had given away, she tried to patch her losses with endless horn honking. Both women needed to understand that saying "No" without guilt would not lose them their Toastmaster status. They also needed to understand that not performing every task to Taskmaster perfection was all right. Caroline vowed to delegate tasks to others and to trust them to perform these tasks *as best they could*. Tracy vowed to accept life as less than perfect and to be satisfied when things didn't always go her way.

When women get off the merry-go-round of *nice*, when we believe in and trust ourselves to choose appropriately between Task and Toast, when we no longer feel the need to hold adamantly to one extreme or to vacillate from one to the other because of our insecurity about what's right, we will know that we have become balanced women. A balanced woman is adaptable, and she is free to choose. She is free to exercise her power. For she is in full control of her life. And if others don't like it, that's not her issue; it's theirs!

Who Runs My Life? Choosing Between Internal and External Control

Once we acknowledge our power, how do we project it unwaveringly? How do we put aside our fear of intimidating others with it? Simple. By understanding what this power is and what it isn't. Power is neither overbearing control like Arleen's nor exhausting abdication like Caroline's. Neither is it some finite force that we must trumpet loudly, dreading we'll never get the chance again. Power is our inner strength. We know we possess it, so we need not flaunt it. Once we establish it, it remains forever there, forever ours. During moments of weakness we may surrender it, but such yielding is temporary, and it is always within us to reclaim.

Power is never control *over* anyone. People who laud themselves over others to prove their potency only verify their insecurity. Real power is our deepest sense of inner peace, our comfort in knowing who we are and what we deserve. Knowing what we stand for, and being willing to state it, remains our greatest strength. Our power is also the pen with which we draw our boundaries. When someone crosses our sacred, private line, our power directs us to boldly hold to "No." When we honor this commitment and solidly stand firm, there can be no guilt.

In order not to bet on the prince, we must use our power to observe our innermost feelings and follow their lead. Our innermost feelings are based in Internal Control. Despite cries from the crowd, Internally Controlled people remain self-directed without swaying to the noise outside. Inner-oriented personalities pride themselves on their individuality. In more extreme instances, they may be named "wacky," "unusual," or "eccentric." But flouting society's rules and marching to the beat of their own drummer finds them happier and healthier by all medical accounts. Nor will these people oscillate between Taskmaster and Toastmaster to the tune of other people's standards. They know who they are, they pursue what they want, and they style-flex between the two power alternatives in accord with their own goals.

The opposite of Internally Controlled people are those driven by External Controls. People influenced by External incentives allow themselves to be directed by the arbitrary dictates of others. In kiss-the-right-ass confusion, Externally Controlled personalities want to impress, please, and seek acceptance by the in-crowd. Susceptible teens joining gangs, starving anorexics identifying with Hollywood starlets, upwardly mobile country-club wanna-be's, and brown-nosing workers all suggest the price inclusion costs. Unfortunately, women often fall into this category. One study from Brigham Young University points to other people's opinions of a woman's future mate as mattering twice as much as how well she believes the two of them communicate. I receive countless letters on this quandary, such as this one from an eighteen-year-old woman:

> *Dear Dr. Gilda:*
> *There is this guy in school who likes me. He's really nice and I like him, too. But when it comes to looks he's really not that good looking. I'm afraid of what people will think if I start going out with him. What should I do?*

Like this young woman, Externally Controlled people will undulate to the choreography of those who can't even dance, just for the sake of gaining approval. They are superb Toastmasters, happy-making ladies who honor others' impressions before considering their own. Why would this eighteen-year-old fear what others think about the looks of someone *she* cares about? I believe that the greatest killer of women today is not some physical ailment, but the overwhelming need for applause, especially from men. Admiration is an External need, independent of what we need inside.

External people may drive the task as hard as they must while the boss is looking, curse his mean spirit behind his back, but kiss his royal ass(ets) if it means a raise. Externally Controlled personalities can be bought by External rewards, but they can never be happy since they rely on reinforcement from people and circumstances outside their own sphere of control. Brenda is one example of a woman governed by External Controls. She slept with any number of men, craving their approval, but when the question of happiness arose, all she felt was alone.

As with the Taskmaster and the Toastmaster, every healthy person must balance her Internal and External Controls. While Internally Controlled people certainly exhibit more independence and self-awareness, living *totally* by Internal Controls could mean utter self-absorption. On the other hand, to be in a relationship with someone who is abusive or condescending, yet remain with him because "we were married for better or for worse," is an example of buying the External tradition at the expense of the self. As with everything, it is always the measure of degree and the question of excess that determines what we are to do next. Clearly, the optimal power balance consists of being *guided* by Internal Controls and *motivated* by External Controls.

To discover the power source that drives you—Internal or External Control—and where you fit on the spectrum, complete Self-Assessment #11.

SELF-ASSESSMENT #11

IS MY POWER INTERNAL OR EXTERNAL?

For each pair of statements below, circle the one [either (a) or (b)] you believe to be true:

1. (a) People usually don't realize all I do for them.

(b) I usually get the appreciation I deserve.

2. (a) I often have bad luck.

(b) My misfortunes are usually caused by my mistakes.

3. (a) Even when I try to win their favor, some people just don't like me.

(b) If someone doesn't like me, it's often because I haven't invested enough time in developing the relationship.

4. (a) It's tough to tell which people have my best interests at heart.

(b) My friendships require my time and energy.

5. (a) I usually have little influence over what happens to me.

(b) When I'm lonely, it's usually because I'm not reaching out enough.

SCORING KEY

Count the number of (a) responses you circled. If you circled only one, you are probably controlled Internally. If you circled two or more, you are probably motivated by External forces.

As an integral part of being balanced, our power may be Externally rewarded, but it must always be Internally motivated. Now that you've completed Self-Assessment #11, read each of the (a) statements aloud. Note their "poor me," victim language. Would you want to be friendly with someone so needy? Would you want to be the lover of someone so desperate? Would you want to marry someone so whiny? Men are not stupid. Such women need men too badly for their own good. Worthy men avoid the woeful, wanting woman who will suck their independence dry. Women must guard against projecting that kind of image or they'll be wiping the skid marks from their floors.

Read aloud all the (b) statements. Note the contrast between them and the (a) responses. Notice how each (b) statement sounds like an exciting person. If these were statements from a man you know, would this be someone with whom you'd like to converse, someone with whom you might want to make love, someone with whom you'd like to spend your life? Men want the same qualities in a person that women do.

If there is one common denominator in all the (b) statements, it is the Internal willingness to take responsibility for one's life. No one outside us knows our needs better than we. Unlike the dependent (a) statements that call on others to enhance us, the Internal Control mantra chants:

👑 **Gilda-Gram** *Take full responsibility for your own happiness.*

> *Dear Dr. Gilda:*
> *I have this boyfriend who keeps telling me he loves me. I never wanted him as a boyfriend; I just wanted to go out with him every once in a while. Now this has become an everyday thing. The day he said he loved me was the day I was going to break up with him. I don't love him. I don't even like him anymore. But I don't want to make him feel sad. What should I do?*

This twenty-year-old woman certainly does have a problem. She would willingly relinquish her own needs and be unhappy just so that she doesn't hurt some guy. I asked her a series of specific questions: "How did this relationship just 'become an everyday thing'?" "Weren't you part of it?" "Couldn't you say 'No' at any time?" "Whose needs are most important to you now?" "Is not hurting him more important to you than healing yourself?"

Remember Christine from chapter 2, married to abusive and controlling Howard? A bit older than the letter writer above, when she took this self-assessment she discovered that most of her energy was spent complaining about her bad luck, the dishonest people she met, how clients didn't like her, and how her husband was a brute. When clients avoided paying her, she said, "Do I have a sign that says 'Screw Me' written across my chest?" When Howard denigrated her, she whined, "How this man takes me for granted!" When her kids got into trouble in school, she complained, "The school doesn't appreciate their intelligence." When nannies left her, she screamed, "Nobody can be counted on to do a decent job anymore!" From this self-assessment, Christine noted that it was always *someone else* who caused her misfortune. Christine represents a culture that would rather lay blame than take responsibility. This is but another form of power passing, and in the end it destroys our ability to care for ourselves. Christine finally started to realize that it was she who had to take the reins of her life.

A fully responsible woman is inviting to a worthy man. (Notice I say *worthy*.) This is not to suggest that dependent, whiny women remain alone. But would you want their "princes"? Have you already had some of your own? Are you with one now? Remember, the purpose of this book is to guide you to partner with men of *substance*, men who appreciate your shining star, who support your wants, needs, and feelings, men who are not looking to control a malleable you. If you had been satisfied with the guys you had already met and/or married, you would never have picked up this book to begin with.

To become a person motivated by Internal Control, rewind your mind. Agree to alter some of the propositions with which you were raised. There are only three basic points you need in order to get started.

The Three Basics of Internal Control

Internal Control Basic #1: No matter what anyone says to you, be it positive or negative, understand that:

👑 **Gilda-Gram** *Praise and blame are both the same.*

People constantly offer unsolicited compliments and critiques—as though we asked! Of course, we welcome the positive feedback because we all love applause. But we're quick to balk at the negative barbs when they come our way. Protect yourself. Be careful not to become either devastated by your critics or dependent on your admirers, for none of their assessments really matter in the end. Ultimately it is only *you* whom you must satisfy. As long as your intentions are honest and you are performing at your best, why care what these External forces say? Welcome the positive and supportive people into your life, and bar those who are not. Don't return phone calls of people who cruelly dispense unwanted judgments. Avoid those energy vampires, as I do. If you are serious about betting on yourself, reserve your zest for important things. Review each of your actions yourself. Knowing that you are your toughest critic is plenty to have to withstand.

Internal Control Basic #2: Believe that you are fully responsible for your actions, mistakes, and future because:

👑 **Gilda-Gram** *We alone create our destiny.*

Life is not as tough as it's rated. Surely things happen that we have no control over. But we can control how we react to these things. We can either be negative or positive, lie dormant or take action, lay blame or take responsibility, withdraw or get help. We even have the choice of doing absolutely nothing. There are so many options, yet people often shrug and say, "I had *no choice*." Forget that statement. If we are guided by Internal Controls, we *do* have choice, and when we exercise it, we manufacture our fate.

The worst consequence of choice making is that it leaves us without anyone but ourselves to blame. And that's no picnic, either.

Caitlin, the middle-class teacher we met in chapter 2, divorced her mate after he slugged her one too many times. The moment she realized her marriage was over, she went to social functions, cookouts, parties—wherever there were men. Sure, she continued to mourn; sure, she continued to shed tears. But she said that she did not want to spend her life alone, and she was determined to find a healthy new relationship. After two years she met the man to whom she is now engaged. He was a respectful, refreshing contrast to her brutish ex. When a friend asked, "What would you have done if you hadn't met Leonard?" Caitlin replied, "I'd be with someone else." Since that is what she deemed, that is what she created, despite what her ex-husband said about it to their children (expletives deleted). Caitlin is living proof that we alone can create a much happier destiny if we set out to make it happen. As writer Somerset Maugham said, "If you refuse to accept anything but the best, you very often get it."

👑 **Gilda-Gram** *Expect your every need will be met.*
Expect that you will meet each one yourself.

Internal Control Basic #3: Consciously use the expression *"I choose to"* rather than *"I have to"* in all your language. Yes, we *have to* get up in the morning in order to get to work. But understand what those words *have to* do to your mind and body. That one expression tells you that your work is a chore, something you must somehow withstand against your will. Even if that's the way you really feel, how can you have a positive outlook if you're looking at the day ahead as drudgery? When you substitute the expression "I choose to" get up for work this morning, note the difference in your mind and body, in your overall attitude, and in the people you relate to. The same change occurs when a woman goes from saying "I *can't* put up with him anymore" to "I *won't* put up with him anymore." This translates to "I chose to put up with him once, but I don't choose to put up with him now." In this instance, a woman puts herself totally in charge of any decision she chooses to make, which, in turn, aligns her with her power. The way we program our thoughts makes a difference because:

👑 **Gilda-Gram** *Power is as power does.*
Power does as power feels.
Power feels as power thinks.
When we think power, we project power.

Remember corporate president Alice? After she came to grips with Mark's departure, her condo's manager rang her doorbell to inform her that the painter she hired could not park in the parking lot. There were no other cars there, and the painter was doing only a short-term job. She recalled recent instances when this manager rudely remarked about "all the money she was making." She knew he'd never pull that sort of behavior with a male unit owner. But she smiled about how intimidated he seemed to be over her success and his apparent need to upgrade his own lowly status. Without a hint of sarcasm, Alice called to the painter to move his car. She said, "Thank you," to the manager and gently shut the door in his face. Although she was displeased by his arrogance, she accepted the incident as his problem rather than hers. She was in control of whom she'd choose to be open to, and she *chose* to close the door on him. Her experience with Mark had taught her a lot—information that served her in all aspects of her life. It got her to start *thinking* power, and she was therefore able to take the first step in *projecting* power. Now she was ready to learn the specific and sequential steps to get a man to appreciate her for all she really was. A woman who is genuine in her power projection will attract a man of genuine worth.

How to Project a Power Image

You now realize that you alone own your power. You also know that it is Internal. It begins in our mind. When we know our power, we attract people who are comfortable with it, unafraid, unthreatened. We project a *Power Image*.

The concept of Power Image came to me while I was consulting for Fortune 500 companies with mostly men. I studied how the most successful among them strutted their power without acting imperious. Their posture, their pitch, their pronunciation, all subtly connoted that they were in charge. For these men, I saw their staffs willing to walk through walls. In contrast were the men who repeatedly needed to remind their employees that they were the boss. I noted how their staffs resented them and resisted their directives. Clearly their power was based purely on their legitimate authority as hired guns, not on their genuine likability and devotion to their troops. From my experiences, I summarized that a Power Image begins in our own home, our minds. It is then transacted through our body language, voice, and words. If we just think the thoughts we need to think, we will become transformed.

When I began to speak to women's groups worldwide, I took these insights into my workshops and applied them to women's lives. They achieved similar results, and my seminars drew standing-room-only crowds. Without knowing what I was doing, I had developed a solution for a problem all women knew existed but didn't know how to fix. Specifically, these insights into what creates a Power Image put an end to the major complaint women voiced throughout my seminars—that we are not heard, especially by men. Projecting a Power Image is potent because it doesn't scream, "I am woman, hear me roar!" like the words to Helen Reddy's song. The paradox is: *Real women don't have to roar.* Women don't have to choose between being Kick-Ass or Kiss-Ass. Women who project a Power Image know what they have, and their listeners sense it. A microphone will do where a megaphone was once needed.

Myriad studies by Albert Mehrabian have shown that our nonverbal communication accounts for 93 percent of the impact we make, while our words strike only a 7 percent chord. Women who are successful with men *know* their power and project it face-to-face through three channels: their body language 55 percent of the time; their voice 38 percent of the time (the two together are considered the 93 percent of our nonverbal communication); and their words a paltry 7 percent of the time. Yes, talk is not only cheap, it's almost worthless in getting your point across. Think back to Cinderella. We never heard any dialogue with the prince. We saw graceful, dancing bodies and imagined lilting, laughing voices. The power behind a Power Image, then, lies 55 percent in body language and 38 percent in vocal tones. It may be depressing, but 93 percent of what we communicate is nonverbal. No wonder harping on relationship issues with our men wins us the Nag Award. Maybe sign language and cooing would better motivate our guy to pick up his socks!

Power Image Part I: Body Language Spoken Here

Part I of projecting a Power Image consists of using our body language effectively. Sadly, many women are deeply misguided in their definitions of effective body language. I have appeared on loads of TV shows with women parading Victoria's Secret demi-clothes as *street wear* in hopes of being noticed. In a completely different setting, I have met women in my corporate seminars who don revealing sweaters and bustiers *to work*. Nationwide, women model the skinny TV sitcom beauties who sport skirts two inches below their designer suit jackets. As hard as they try, however, a woman's powerful body language does not emanate from resembling a pumped-up prostitute. It is pitiful to see how prone women are to alter their External packaging to be loved. In a "Make Me Over" contest conducted by a national newspaper, letters from women were strikingly sad:

I desperately need a makeover. I'm only 12 years old but age isn't the problem. I have not had a boyfriend all my life. With this makeover, I'll show that I have inner beauty. No matter what my weight.

Every day I go to school, my friends and their boyfriends are really happy together. Not having a boyfriend isn't going to get you far at school. Boys here don't go with girls unless they're pretty. I'm just plain. I really want a boyfriend. When I find Mr. Right, I will be happy. Please help.

I am not generally a bad-looking lady but I still have a lot to improve to knock men down. I may be in the pile of victims. I urgently need someone to marry not because I'm sexually insatiable, but because I want to stay in this country and I want it to be real. Please help!

Sit down. I'm here to tell you about myself. See me! I'm fat! I'm forty! You need me like you need fits! Sit down and get me a new life. You need a lawyer to put my husband away for the rest of his life, too.

Boy! Would I like a new me! I live in T-shirts and tennis shoes. I forget what a new dress looks like. I've never had a professional manicure in my life. I'm a retired, swinging 70-year-old senior. I'm divorced 20 years from an abusive relationship. Maybe I can still catch some worthwhile man's eye if I were all dolled up!

As these pathetic letters attest, if we were to buy into today's "perfect" woman, we would see that she has the legs and hips of an adolescent boy, yet the breasts of a mature woman. With the billion-dollar industry's Barbie sold every two seconds around the world, with the average girl owning at least eight of them, and with over a million of these dolls sold each week, is change in sight? It seems not. There's even a new rendition: "Barbie as My Fair Lady." (Now, in case we didn't have enough pressure, Henry Higgins does Barbie!) And if that won't depress women whose mirrors don't reflect a doll, toymaker Hasbro is giving Mattel a run for its money with its "Model Dolls," created in the likenesses of famous models wearing gowns by top designers.

No wonder so many grown-up women are unhappy with their natural endowments, most of them wondering how "fat" they appear in every mirror. Even with surgery, the largest bone in our body—our despised thigh bone—will never be thin enough, no matter what we do. Those without willpower use the scheme to "Pig out now, liposuck later," as liposuction becomes the current-day surgery for bulimia. What we won't control ourselves, another prince, our plastic surgeon, will control tomorrow.

When surgery isn't enough, the media airbrushes age away. In our culture a man is deformed if he loses a limb, but a woman is maimed purely by her increased years. With role models like the half-century-old Cher, with no two body parts the same age, the pressure mounts. But what will society do now that the fastest-growing segment of the U.S. population consists of women over eighty? People forget the successful late bloomers like Julia Child and Emily Post, whose finest hours came in their late fifties. "You can never be too rich or too thin" is still the theme, and it permeates the minds of our impressionable young girls. We need to teach them:

👑 **Gilda-Gram** *Nothing that you ever do can change the fact that you are you.*

Let's get real, ladies. The power we have is *Internal*, not the celluloid package we display. It's time for the "average" woman to wake up. Reconstruct someone else's view of "heavy" to yours as "voluptuous." Respond to the critical man with "I feel good about myself. It's *you* I don't feel good about. Good-bye." Envision a "Happy to be Homely" doll, to be loved for her inner goodness. This is especially significant since a new study from Yale University has found that men who marry ugly—er, "cosmetically challenged"—women live an average of twelve years longer than those who marry beauties! (Could less attractive females be less wearing on their mates?) We must constantly remind ourselves:

👑 **Gilda-Gram** *Only part of beauty is in the eye of the beholder; we carry the other part in our image of ourselves.*

Meanwhile, with all these alterations, no matter how enhanced we make our outside packaging, *women are still not heard* unless they have learned how to recognize, accept, and project their power. This requires a new definition of body language. To become an open and inviting communicator, begin your interactions with the use of the **S-O-F-A**. That doesn't mean lying in a seminude reclining position with the promise of sexual favors. S-O-F-A is an Internal technique that guarantees hooking your listener's attention without freezing from overexposure. Using the S-O-F-A, you enter a room as if you own it. You visualize yourself as being completely composed. The S-O-F-A consists of four distinct steps:

S—Smile.
O—Open your posture.
F—Forward lean.
A—Acknowledge your listener's uniqueness.

When you first meet someone, *smile*. Over fifty smiles have been documented, but the only genuine ones are—sorry about this—those that include the crow's-feet. Smiles that do not draw in the entire face are staged. Phony smiles may be asymmetrical, inappropriately timed, and last longer than a few seconds. Researchers have found that women smile more often than men. The problem is that when people smile, their voices rise, so with our higher pitches and smiling faces, women are often accused of being too emotional. Furthermore, smiling can become a problem for women because we tend to substitute it for needed discussions about our real feelings. Seems we can't win. Each woman, then, must devise her own genuine and authoritative smile that honestly reveals her wants without overbearing emotionality. Tall order, but not impossible. Rehearse in front of a mirror to get your personal insignia down pat.

Posture that suggests you can be pushed around will hold you back. Whenever you are meeting and greeting, *open your posture* from your body's center, your pelvis. This is your pivot point in all sports. The more open your posture, the more space you fill. The more space you fill, the more powerful you appear. People who stand with arms folded in front of them, or with their hands in their pockets, or their legs crossed, appear closed to people, ideas, and life in general. Who'd want to pursue them?

Observe your posture on a chair. Do you sprawl out or are you scrunched to one side? Men sit with their legs and sometimes arms spread apart. In fact, *Mirabella* magazine revealed that if male bus and train passengers would close their legs instead of spreading out "as if they owned the place," 15,765 more Americans would have seats. The female body is smaller than the male's. And to look more formidable we could spread out, too, but how can we spread our legs while wearing a skirt? What we can do, however, is make full use of the armrests or drape one arm over the back of our chair. This enlarges your form. When you stand, imagine a string running all the way up your spine and out the top of your head. Let the string hold you like a marionette. Tuck your pelvis under you. Align your upper and lower body as you lengthen your spine. Hold your head high with your chin slightly raised. This is the dancer's stance—and your power posture. Power posture focuses you. Powerful people are fully focused on their goals. Open posture allows you to be open to attracting the most wonderful men into your life.

Forward lean and touch someone you want to know better. Whether it's a simple handshake or an affectionate embrace, as the largest body organ, the skin is far more potent than ordinary verbal contact. It immediately sends the strength of your power to whomever you touch. That is the reason we reach out a hand to a friend in pain and stroke the brow of a crying child. When touch occurs, the hormone oxytocin is released into the bloodstream. This is the same molecule that causes uterine contractions during orgasm and childbirth, reduces stress, and functions as "relationship superglue" by triggering the desire to bond and even become addicted to a partner's face, fragrance, voice, and cologne. Oxytocin levels rise even at the *thought* of being touched by someone who cares. Not surprisingly, there is no sensation that men feel that is equivalent to a woman friend's offering a hand or hug of reassurance and connection.

A study from Northwestern University Medical School comprising twenty thousand people in twenty-five states found that 98 percent of Americans want to be touched and hugged more. Generally speaking, people need touch to survive, and most feel better after only a few hugs. It is often recommended that we get four hugs a day for sustenance, eight for maintenance, and twelve for growth. Do you give and get your ample share? To project a Power Image, reach forward and touch someone now.

Most men believe they are drowned by marathon monologues of women, preferring instead to participate in the Ping-Pong of dialogue, since they get a greater chance to speak themselves. But there's a stage before monologue and dialogue that primes your guy to attend to you and "hear" you *before you utter a word.* It is what I have coined "eye-alogue," prolonged eye contact that ropes in your listener through your enchanting eyes. *Acknowledge your listener's uniqueness* through warm eye contact. Everyone wants to feel special, and we can easily communicate that special feeling to someone through these "windows to our soul." Since the visual memory is reported to be two hundred times greater than our auditory memory, expert eye-alogue allows you to seduce the man you want to impress.

Eye-alogue can be quickly and easily devised and perfected. In our society, the general custom is for women to establish more eye-alogue than men, but to avert our gaze quickly so as not to suggest intimidation or its opposite, sexual innuendo. In our culture, eye-alogue for a period of about five seconds is considered appropriate. Women who are shyer often refrain from eye-alogue but wonder why they "never meet anyone" at social functions.

The eyes certainly are the windows to the soul. If you want to acknowledge your listener as particularly special, engage in a more commanding eye-alogue, the *power stare*. The power stare speaks volumes without uttering a sound. It has six parts:

1. Narrow your lids, but don't squint.
2. Move your eyes from point A to point B on your listener's face.
3. *After* repositioning your eyes, allow your head to follow.
4. For greater emphasis, tip your head and brow protectively over your eyes.
5. Hold your gaze for longer than five seconds. Don't just stare; have *ocular intrusion*.
6. Add a smile.

It intrigues me that after each of my workshops, so many women, still uncomfortable about speaking their mind, line up to review with me these six points of the power stare. Women know the power they have in their eyes. Now there's a means to use it without intimidation.

Power Image Part II: Your Voice of Choice

While your body language accounts for over half the impact you make, your voice accounts for over a third. The *power voice* includes your rate, pitch, rhythm, volume, and use of the pause. Since women's pitches are higher than men's, especially when smiling, and since we have greater and more frequent vocal range, we must guard against emitting sounds that only dogs can hear. The fact is that most women use a pitch that is higher than their natural one. Using the wrong pitch may project the impression of cute little girl, which gains them positive attention, but it can also damage their voice. I suggested that Christine lower her pitch, but she didn't understand my critique until she saw and heard herself on videotape at a party. Sometimes the little girl voices that women take on are so deeply ingrained, they don't even know they are using them.

Listen to your voice as you say, "Oh, how awful!" Most women would incorporate the four notes of that expression as one up-down sound followed by another. This is called the "high-low glide," but to a man it's interpreted as a "whiny woman." Although Fran Drescher's Nanny reflects the whiny woman stereotype as sexy and appealing, in real life most men find it a turnoff. Use a tape recorder. Practice repeating, "Oh, how awful!" with different vocal ranges. Do not be satisfied until you play it back as an unrecognizable sound. This vocal change is the start of expanding your voice and enhancing your power.

Next, find and use your proper pitch. Raise your arms over your head, or bend over while seated. Either of these postures will free your voice box and throat. Count, "Um, hum, *one*; um, hum, *two*; um, hum, *three* . . ." all the way to *ten*. Feel your lips and nose vibrate as you repeat each "um, hum." Using that same pitch, say, "Good morning." Announce your name. Return to your original posture, either by placing your hands down or by sitting up. Continue projecting the pitch you discovered when you were bent over or had your hands above your head. Do you hear how much deeper and rounder it now sounds? That is your correct pitch. It is powerful. Speak from that spot in your daily speech. Note how much more positive other people's reactions to you are.

Another requisite of the power voice is your willingness to speak slowly. For powerful people, time is plentiful and there is no need to fill the silence in a conversation with worthless chatter. Men forever accuse women of talking too much. The fact is, most studies show that men are the masters of schmooze, speaking far more than we do. But years of subordination have made women uncomfortable if a conversation lags. As the relationship police, we take on the role of maintaining the communication flow by filling the lull. Stop that habit immediately. Allow for silence. In fact, welcome it.

There is power in pausing. Dramatic pauses add to your presence and mystique. It minimizes saying things you'll be sorry for later. It prompts others to speak more than you, which sets you up to gather "free information" you can apply later. It offers others center stage, which everyone (especially men) enjoys. Finally, it directs your conversation by allowing you not to deal with certain topics. In short, patience is enduring; patience is power. Understand that the person who speaks first after silence is the less dominant of the two. Isn't it time you relinquished the subordinate role?

Power Image Part III: Words as Sounds of Silence

Unfortunately, words impact your listener least of all the elements because people in our society are such poor listeners. Just because you say something doesn't mean it's heard. And even if it is heard, is it heard as you meant it? While a speaker may be able to talk at 250 words per minute, a listener is capable of listening at double that amount. So what does the listener do? We know what *men* often do when a woman is speaking: they tune out. Actually, it's a physiological fact of life that the speaker's slower rate of divulging information motivates the listener's wandering mind. In the end, he processes only 25 percent of what he hears and remembers a mere 10 percent. Men probably fare worse as listeners because their mode of processing information is to listen for bottom-line deals rather than the familiar-to-females details. How depressing to most women, the bearers of the A-student mentality, the crossers of every "t," the dotters of every "i," the "perfecters" who over-rehearse their correct words, who remember every word of every fight they had with their men since the antediluvian days of their relationship. Men and women certainly do listen differently.

Yet women find great comfort in conversing. To make the most of the impact of your words, incorporate Yale University's twelve power words to help stimulate listener attentiveness: "money," "new," "proven," "results," "save," "discovery," "ease," "guarantee," "health," "love," "safety," and "you." Use these words along with active, rather than passive, terms. Passive terms are victim language that blames others' External Control for your present condition. Expressions such as *"You made me* cook dinner" or *"You get me* so angry" point the finger at someone other than yourself for the predicament you find yourself in. Such you-language guarantees a defensive response. But it also deenergizes you because while you are pointing one or two fingers at someone else, at least three more are pointing at you in negative ways. There is no worse enemy you can have than yourself.

A more appealing approach is to incorporate I-Language. Note that it speaks to you with a capital I rather than a wishy-washy lowercase one. I-Language puts the onus for your feelings on your own shoulders. Such expressions as "I *chose* to cook dinner" and "I *am angry* because you didn't call as you promised" are powerful because men prefer hearing your thoughts rather than being bombarded by your blame. In short, a responsible speaker is more often listened to. Are you adept in using I-Language? To find out, complete Self-Assessment #12: The Pride of I-Ship.

SELF-ASSESSMENT #12

THE PRIDE OF I-SHIP

Say each of the following sentences in Group I aloud, visualizing the small letter "i" at the beginning of each sentence. Since this is an unusual way to start any sentence, think carefully about each statement before you visualize and say it:

GROUP I
1. "i am going to work this morning."
2. "i am happy."
3. "i take good care of myself."
4. "i compliment myself."

Now in Group II, change each of these sentences to begin with a capital "I":

GROUP II
1. "I am going to work this morning."
2. "I am happy."
3. "I take good care of myself."
4. "I compliment myself."

- What was the difference between the way Groups I and II sounded?
- What was the difference between the way Groups I and II felt?
- How did your body language change between Groups I and II?
- How did your voice change between Groups I and II?

Most people experience a dramatic difference between the statements in Group I and Group II. Not only do they recognize the obvious change in pronoun, but they also lift their postures and deepen their voices. Participants also report feeling more powerful and better able to take on the world. At a New York Power Image breakfast I conducted, the instant changes in a group of three hundred women were so astonishing that I joked about letting them out to descend upon the city. "Heaven help the people you work with!" I said, laughing, as they swaggered confidently through the exit doors.

Now the big test. When you put together your confident body language, voice, and words, what is the overall image you project? Complete Self-Assessment #13 and find out.

SELF-ASSESSMENT #13

THE IMAGE PROJECTION TEST

Draw a picture of yourself as an animal. (This is not an exercise in zoological accuracy; the only element that counts is your perception of the animal's characteristics.)

Answer each of the following questions quickly:

1. Why did you choose this animal?
2. Is this animal a predator or prey for another animal?
3. Is this animal sociable or a loner?
4. How does this animal relate to other animals?
5. What gives this animal pleasure?
6. How do other animals perceive this animal's personality?

Think of a man you would like to attract. Draw him as another animal. Answer the same questions about him. How do you two animals relate?

Deb drew herself as a bear, hibernating in winter. Yet the picture she drew of the man she liked was of a dove. How could any hibernating animal actively attract anyone? From the Image Projection Test, this woman realized that she had to either alter her own image to one that could attract whom she wanted to attract or alter her fantasy of the man she desired. Polly drew herself as a purring kitten. The problem was that she wanted to attract a tiger because she enjoyed aggressive men, but the image she projected attracted abusers who used her as prey. She recognized that she needed to project a different image. Instead of the kitten, Polly reconfigured herself as a racehorse. Almost at once she attracted a new man who was aggressive but did not look to devour and exploit her. What a refreshing change! Then there was Sherry, a beautiful woman who drew a picture of herself as a tiger. She boasted that a tiger has strong traits, but that it is predatory. As she talked about her self-portrait, she recognized that predators invite fear, not trust. Sherry wanted desperately to meet a man to love for life. After creating her drawing, she concluded that she had to modify her predatory demeanor because no man would want to partner with a bloodthirsty carnivore that might devour him alive.

As we said, what we project, others reflect. Confident body language, voice, and words are the power tools that constitute a woman's Power Image. They help her style-flex between Taskmastering and Toastmastering more easily. They are derived from her acceptance of her Internal motives amid a world of External come-ons. They make a woman feel powerful, sound powerful, look powerful, act powerful. Projecting this power is invigorating. Women who are invigorated have spirit and style. They are a real turn-on to men who are enthused, rather than confused, by life. When your inner self is in charge of your outer surroundings, you attract men who are in charge themselves. These men have no need to control you or abuse you because:

👑 **Gilda-Gram** *People make contact with people they like, and people like people like themselves.*

I was being interviewed on a radio show about how to project a Power Image. As usual, this topic generated hundreds of calls throughout the program. The interviewer wanted to wrap up with a strong conclusion that listeners would recall. She said, "In other words, Dr. Gilda, what you're saying is like *The Little Engine That Could,* 'I think I can, I think I can.' " I smiled and said, "Well, not exactly. What I'm saying is, '**I know I will, I know I will.**' " There is a big difference between *thinking I can* and *being convinced that I will.* The first depicts a Wanna-Be Woman; the second shows a Will-Be Woman. A Will-Be Woman is someone who projects a Power Image. She knows that her power is a foregone conclusion. Because she knows it, so do the men she attracts.

The best thing about projecting a Power Image is that it sets the stage for a woman to both put forth her most honest self and share it freely with others. What she must learn, however, is to wisely apportion the amount of giving she offers so that her own needs do not go unnoticed and unmet. This is the issue at hand in the next chapter.

GILDA-GRAMS

FROM CHAPTER 4

Project a Power Image

▶ *If he doesn't want you on his team, form your own.*

▶ *The Taskmaster who feels her own life is out of control often tries to control others, but few people are willing to withstand such domination for long.*

▶ *The Toastmaster who feels without control often becomes depressed and/or angry that she has surrendered her voice.*

▶ *Before we fantasize being liked, we need to like ourselves.*

▶ *Take full responsibility for your own happiness.*

▶ *Praise and blame are both the same.*

▶ *We alone create our destiny.*

▶ *Expect your every need will be met. Expect that you will meet each one yourself.*

▶ *Power is as power does.*
   Power does as power feels.
   Power feels as power thinks.
   When we think power, we project power.

▶ *Nothing that you ever do can change the fact that you are you.*

▶ *Only part of beauty is in the eye of the beholder; we carry the other part in our image of ourselves.*

▶ *People make contact with people they like, and people like people like themselves.*

5

Give from the Overflow, Not from the Core

👑 **Gilda-Gram** *We will never be loved if we can't risk being disliked.*

W omen's lives revolve around relationships. Indeed, the success of our relationships is so vital to women that we gladly accept full blame when there are misunderstandings, or worse. As we've seen, caretaking is the only way many women know how to demonstrate their love, and unfortunately, our caretaking often involves taking better care of others than we do of ourselves. Abject devotion toward other people is called "overfunctioning," and it's usually accompanied by a cautionary equation:

👑 **Gilda-Gram** *When we overfunction for others, we underfunction for ourselves.*

Why are women such terrific Overfunctioners? For the same reason many are such superb Toastmasters and some are such reliable Taskmasters. We figure that if no one is listening or caring about what we have to offer, we will make ourselves essential, irreplaceable, indispensable. We will be constantly available and therefore likable, we think. We'll be noticed. The problem is, when women aren't discriminating about *how* we want to be noticed, we find ourselves out of energy to do the things we must for ourselves.

The Cost of Overfunctioning

Let's face it, each of us has only so much energy. If we expend it all on our men's problems (and/or our children's, our boss's, our friends'), either our own needs go unmet or we worry about his needs *and* ours, and we fizzle out from fatigue. Even the Bible advises, "Love thy neighbor *as* thyself," but never *instead of* thyself. But women belong to the *salvation* army. And while overfunctioning does not sound like the behavior of choice, it can be mighty inviting. Certainly it makes us feel important and wanted. The reasoning goes, "If you need me, you won't leave me." As we have seen, *needing* is not the same as *wanting*, and *wanting* is not the same as *loving*. A man might *need* us and *use* us for our kind offerings, but the question remains whether he'll stay around after he's used us *up*.

Occasionally, overfunctioning may give us a much welcomed breather from tackling our own life's problems. Although we can never escape from dealing with what we need to deal with, overfunctioning for someone else gives us a reason and a place to hide from ourselves. The trap is that at first our man not only enjoys our total attention, he encourages it. It reminds him of the mother who nursed him, groomed him, and was present when he got into scrapes. However, this same guy will eventually run from us because it was this same mother from whom he needed to separate once he realized he had to establish his own identity. So in running from our over-nurturing, our guy may be performing an overdue "motherectomy" at the same time.

Overall, the overfunctioning/underfunctioning imbalance is damaging to both partners in a relationship. The Overfunctioner is left feeling empty, while her partner, the Underfunctioner, remains with his emotional work still undone. For example, if we argue with neighbors because our mate doesn't get along with them or if we call our mate's boss with bogus absence excuses for him, then *we* are taking responsibility for his life, and *he is not*. When he does not take on his own issues, he absorbs a learned helplessness. At first we are flattered to be needed. But check out his needy ineptitude after a couple of years. For ever-ready relationship rescuers, in time the original lust transforms to disgust. "You're still asking where we keep the toilet paper? After living here with me for ten years?" Finally it's time to let him find the proverbial toilet paper himself—in whatever compromising posture he may be. 'Cause ya gotta start somewhere.

Teacher Caitlin from chapter 2 exemplified an ace Overfunctioner. For all those years, unhappy in her marriage, this woman put her emotional energy into her teaching job and her children. Her skill at overfunctioning elsewhere allowed her to hide from the hurt she felt in her marriage. No doubt her husband was an Overfunctioner as well. While it was he who did the money managing, household duties, and at first all the driving, neither of the two recognized the need to communicate about what really mattered. The angrier each became with the other, the more they overfunctioned in their chores. When their inevitable split finally occurred after a long twenty-five years, each was shocked into discovering how raw their emotions were and how neither had dealt with the real issues. Overfunctioning readily allows a person to escape from reality. Unfortunately, one can never run from reality forever.

Another teacher, Lisa, was employed by a parochial school while her fiancé, Jeffrey, had a salesman's job during the week. On weekends he paid his alimony by working as a waiter. It was okay for Lisa to spend weekends alone because when they met she had been working toward a master's degree, and she appreciated the time to study and write her final thesis. But as she got to know her future husband better, she found that his tumultuous temper got him fired from one sales position after another. Since Jeffrey needed to continue waiting tables to support the children from his previous marriage, Lisa took on the task of searching the Sunday newspapers for his job leads. She was also Jeffrey's official résumé writer, creating differently targeted résumés for each potential position. Then she became his private secretary, both submitting the résumés to the proper interviewers and responding afterward with thank-you notes. She was also his wardrobe manager, consoler, anger absorber, and punching bag when her fiancé couldn't take the long wait between jobs. In all, besides her regular teaching job, Lisa's whole life centered around Jeffrey, his temper, his job search, and his out-of-work depression. Even after he finally landed a new job, it had such a short tenure that the cycle soon began again.

Good-natured Lisa had no idea that this was Jeffrey's pattern. Overindulging his problems, Lisa took an extra year to complete her master's, which thereby held up her salary increase. Meanwhile she married Jeffrey—and extended her overfunctioning duties to his children, doing their homework and disciplining them when Jeffrey or his ex-wife could not. Lisa was so tired that the couple put off having children of their own, which Lisa had wanted desperately. They continued their marriage for ten years in the same vein, with Jeffrey getting fired a few times each year. Finally Lisa couldn't stand Jeffrey's down-time abuse any longer. She filed for divorce, not entirely recognizing her role in their lopsided dance.

....

♛ Gilda-Gram *There are givers and there are takers. Takers eat well, and givers sleep well . . . but not for long.*

....

Givers eventually become *used up*. They often lie awake at night trying to figure out what it is they did wrong. "Why doesn't he love me enough?" "What could I have done differently?" "What more could I have given?" On some level they recognize that the relationship they set up would never be reciprocal. They would never be their man's equal and would never derive the pleasure of being given *to*. But in exchange for their overgiving, they would forever be the one in charge because they would always be needed.

Are you a woman who is exhausted from expending too much energy giving to others and not enough giving to yourself? In Self-Assessment #14, determine how you would behave if it were *you* in each of the following three true scenarios:

S E L F - A S S E S S M E N T   # 1 4

DO I GIVE TOO MUCH?

SCENARIO A

Ted is arguing on the phone with his often nasty sister, Beth. For years he and Beth have had angry spats, some of which ended in their not talking for months. As usual, Ted hangs up in a rage and is visibly furious at what she just said to him. He vents to you, his wife, and at once feels better. Two days later, as though the incident never occurred, Beth calls your house again and asks to speak to Ted. You are still fuming over what Ted had told you about their argument. Suddenly appointing yourself constable over your sister-in-law's obnoxiousness, you treat Beth coldly over the phone. Ted, however, lifts up the receiver and is very pleasant to his sister, as though negative words between the two had never been exchanged. . . .

SCENARIO B

It is 5:30 P.M. on Friday afternoon. You are finally leaving work for a much needed weekend after having had a very rigorous week. Your good friend Linda passes you in the hall and groans about a problem she has been unable to solve regarding an important account. She asks you to stay for a few hours to help her resolve the issue. You are beyond exhaustion and have a splitting headache. You are anxious to switch gears and get home to prepare for a date with someone new and exciting. . . .

SCENARIO C

You and your spouse are both dashing out the door to catch the train to work. He has a job interview that he has been looking forward to for a long time. Together you have rehearsed how he will respond to some of the predictable questions he will be asked. Suddenly, in the rush, one of his shirt buttons pops. Although he knows how to use a needle and thread himself, he asks you to sew it on. If you performed this task for him, it would make you late for your scheduled morning meeting with your boss. You and your boss have not seen eye-to-eye lately on some issues. It is important for your spouse to look great this morning and be offered this job, but equally important is your relationship with your boss. . . .

• **How did you respond to *Scenario A*?**

Role playing this scene in one of my workshops, one woman was furious at Ted when he got off the phone. They ended up having a fight, even though the issue had nothing to do with either of them. How would you have behaved?

• **How did you respond to *Scenario B*?**

In another role play, a woman was angry at her friend Linda for asking her to stay. She was angrier at herself for giving in and canceling her long-awaited date. How would you have behaved?

• **How did you respond to *Scenario C*?**

In this last role play, a woman told her husband, "Darling, just because you have a penis, are you saying you can't sew your own button onto your shirt?" She wished him luck on his interview, kissed his cheek, and left for work. Her husband proceeded to do his own sewing—flabbergasted! How would you have behaved?

Of the three women's responses, with whom did you most identify? The first woman was someone who overfunctioned emotionally for her husband. Note how quickly Ted dumped his anger toward sister Beth in his wife's welcoming lap. For him, once Mount Vesuvius erupted the explosion was over. But the wife kept the angry embers burning. Little did she realize they were not her embers to burn. The second woman, too, was an Overfunctioner. Although she was physically wiped out and would have enjoyed a refreshing date with an interesting prospect, she did not take care of herself at all. No wonder she was angry. Truth is, it wasn't Linda's fault at all; just because someone asks does not mean that you must comply.

Finally there was woman number three. Although her flip-and-glib comment might have seemed acerbic, she was the only one of the three to recognize her needs, remember her priorities, and do what she felt was best for the *couple's* financial security. If her husband-in-a-hurry was momentarily miffed, too bad. All partners occasionally speak out of turn. The most important thing was that whether or not her husband landed his job, this woman had to take the proper action to protect hers.

Would you classify yourself as a world-class Overfunctioner? Complete Self-Assessment #15 and see if you display overfunctioning traits.

THE OVERFUNCTIONER'S CHECKLIST

Mark each of the following statements (X = My Partner) according to the numbers below:

> 0 = Seldom or Never
> 1 = Sometimes or Occasionally
> 2 = Often or Frequently

_____ **1.** I put my own recreation on hold for X.

_____ **2.** I am here to make X happy.

_____ **3.** I feel needed when I am available for X.

_____ **4.** The more time I devote to him, the less X will seek out someone else.

_____ **5.** When X doesn't do something right, I complete it for him.

_____ **6.** I postpone doing things I like if X doesn't enjoy them also.

_____ **7.** I often make plans for us without consulting X.

_____ **8.** I usually drop what I'm doing when X calls me.

_____ **9.** I offer X advice even when he doesn't ask me.

_____**10.** Sometimes I complete X's sentences.

SCORING KEY

Three or more points: You are *possibly* an Overfunctioner.
Five or more points: You are *probably* an Overfunctioner.

Like most women, Marta had learned to be a typical Overfunctioner when she was growing up. In her family she quickly developed the role of taking care of everything and everyone. But now she was married, and with that new role came a full-time job, part-time graduate work, and overtime mothering. To say the least, she was constantly exhausted. For this woman, completing The Overfunctioner's Checklist opened her eyes to the need to extricate herself from unnecessary burdens, including the role she had once played with her mother and father, the relationship from which she had originally learned Overfunctioning 101.

One day, Mom asked Marta the Overfunctioner to remind her father about her upcoming birthday but not to mention what she had repeatedly asked him to buy her. Mom wanted to see if Dad would forget. (Note how the mother wanted to "catch" Dad at *forgetting* rather than at *remembering*. The games women—yes, *women*—play!) For the first time in her life, Marta refused to be involved in this triangle. When the time came, her father did remember her mother's birthday, but instead of the necklace she longed for, he bought her an impersonal house alarm. Now, because Marta had dropped out of the overfunctioning role, her parents would have to negotiate their own skirmishes without her aid. Marta felt good that she had reclaimed her life with her parents. Now she was left to reclaim her life with her husband.

Marta was particularly struck by Item 2 on The Overfunctioner's Checklist, the one that said her role in life was to make her husband happy. She really did believe that that was her job. She agreed that she felt needed by her happy making (Item 3), and if she continued doing so much for him, he wouldn't seek out other women (Item 4) as so many of her friends' husbands had done. In short, she scored all ten points on this checklist, as her own needs and wants simply took a backseat to those of her husband. Obviously she could not continue. At once she knew that if she was to succeed at love, she would have to drop out of this role as she had with her parents. Otherwise she would remain only a shell of a woman—which might eventually cause her biggest fear to come true after all—having her husband lose interest in a vacuous wife and seek someone else.

Often, women like Marta feel that they *need* to overfunction to gain others' approval. This approval has the potential of making them feel better as they are needed and applauded for all they do for other people. Unfortunately, they often end up stressed and depressed as their own requirements for a happy life remain unmet.

Addicted to Approval

If you're still unsure whether to consider yourself an Overfunctioner, determine if you are addicted to other people's approval through the use of Like-Me Language. This is the indirect use of communication that avoids commitment to your real feelings as you look to satisfy the feelings of your man. Did I say *avoid commitment*? A *woman* avoiding commitment? Yes, while we lambaste our men for avoiding commitment in our relationships, we are certainly guilty of avoiding direct communication about our feelings—and committing to them. Okay, it may be because our feelings have been discounted for so long. It may be because we are trying to avoid being hurt. It may even be our only means of protection. But no more excuses. Truth in advertising must start somewhere. Anything short of honesty with your lover is manipulation. Is that how you want to start or continue your loving?

Like-Me Language is part of too many women's speech patterns. It includes five expressions that indirectly ask for approval, acceptance, kinship, or love.

THE FIVE EXPRESSIONS OF LIKE-ME LANGUAGE

a. Statements That Add a Question at the End:

"That movie was good, wasn't it?" "Our date is at eight?" These statements give the speaker an out in case the listener disagrees. They intimate how unsure of herself the speaker is.

b. Hesitation and Hedging:

"I think," "kind of," "maybe," "you know," "something like." Hesitations and hedges show that the speaker fears imposing her opinions on others.

c. Italics:

"It's so hot!" "I'm very upset," "He's really great!" Italics politely and indirectly tell the listener how the speaker wants him to respond, fearing her words alone won't carry enough weight.

d. Attention Getters:

"Guess what!" "Do you know what happened?" "You won't believe this!" Attention getters aim to stimulate advance interest for permission to continue to speak.

e. Disclaimers:

"No, I just wanted to say," "I know this is crazy, but . . ." *"I don't know anything about that, but . . ."* Disclaimers confuse and weaken communication between people. The listener doesn't know if he should respond to the disclaimer and soothe the speaker with "Of course I don't mind" or ignore the disclaimer and cut to his response.

Like-Me Language may use these five patterns, but it also consists of walking *around* an issue so as not to offend. In Self-Assessment #16, how would you respond to each of the three scenarios?

SELF-ASSESSMENT #16

DO I INCORPORATE LIKE-ME LANGUAGE?

1. Your friend has made a derogatory remark about a man you both know. She has no idea that the two of you are an item. You aren't ready to disclose this information yet, but you would like to defend his honor.
YOUR RESPONSE: _____

2. Your neighbor has just asked you a personal question about your sexuality, which is none of her business. You want to tell her that in some way, but you have to see her daily and you don't want a confrontation that will affect your mutual cordiality.
YOUR RESPONSE: _____

---

3. While being interviewed for a new job by a young interviewer, you are asked a question about your age. You know this is illegal. You want to be offered this job.

YOUR RESPONSE: _____

- Do you prefer to use the indirect Like-Me Language or a more direct approach?
- What do you gain from using your preferred style?

Christine, the unhappy housewife from chapter 2, had a real problem completing this self-assessment. She could come up with no "nice" answers where her listeners, she felt, would still like her. From this she recognized that she was unwilling specifically to address confrontational issues because her need to be liked was so great. Remember, Christine was the one who questioned if people perceived her wearing a sign that said "*Screw Me.*" This is precisely what happens when we are not direct: when we don't address things that affect us, we do wear such a sign. But:

....

👑 **Gilda-Gram** *When we state our preferences, we invite people to act as we want, not as they want.*

....

We began to practice how Christine could respond in a new way to each of the scenarios in Self-Assessment #16. For Item 1, she felt comfortable responding with "I haven't found that to be the case about John," shrug, and change the subject. For Item 2, she was able to tap into her good sense of humor: "My sex life keeps me so busy, I hardly have the time to eat or sleep," ended with a laugh. For Item 3, she practiced saying, "I've always believed I'm young enough to keep learning," with a smile.

We audiotaped Christine's responses. She was quickly able to determine that her Like-Me Language had been keeping her from direct and honest communication. She now understood that having confidence in her candor was the only path to gaining respect.

By now you probably recognize that it takes more work to conceal your feelings than it does to communicate them. Overfunctioners suffer undue exhaustion from trying to select the correct language and behavior. But that is not the only negative consequence of overfunctioning. An Overfunctioner's loss of self can be exacerbated when the recipient of her caretaking suddenly turns on her. It is very painful when the care-taker is ultimately accused of not having done a good enough job of caretaking after all. It may come from her adult child, from her spouse, from an employee, from a boss, or even her parent. Sometimes the accusation occurs years after she has played the role of wife, mother, company president, assembly worker, administrative assistant, or even "other woman." Having often sacrificed her entire life for the ungrateful recipient, the Overfunctioner feels spent and angry.

Joan gave up pursuing a career of her own to put her husband's interior design company on the map. His business soared. Sixteen years and two children later, he told her he no longer loved her and that he wanted a divorce. Divorcée Ellen often went without new business clothes because her three kids needed school uniforms, sneakers, music lessons, and camp. Now years later, two of her offspring resent her for not being home enough while they were growing up. The other doesn't talk to her at all.

Both these women were good, giving Overfunctioners, not unlike the women we met earlier—Christine, Caitlin, Lisa, and Marta. But what did any of them get in return? Joan denied herself her own career in favor of one for her husband, while Ellen may have been held back from career growth in unacceptable business clothes to accommodate the needs of her children. Overfunctioning hid both Christine and Caitlin from marital reality as they provided for the needs of their family at the expense of the need to be loved. It overdosed Lisa and Marta with exhaustion and stress from never feeling they were doing enough for their family. Meanwhile I smile at the license plate in front of me that reads, "Whatamom." I wonder if motherhood is this woman's only claim to fame. I'd like to get out of my car and warn her . . . but I'm a reformed Overfunctioner myself. I drive on.

In one of my graduate courses sat a very bright and competent woman. She was suffering from a serious knee condition and was about to undergo painful surgery. During one class session, her eyes appeared to be glazed over. Although her knee hurt horribly, it wasn't her pain or even the operation that worried her. Solely on her mind was her fear that her husband and twenty-seven-year-old daughter would fall apart while she was out of commission. She agonized, "How will they eat? Who will cook? With my new job, do I have enough time to prepare three weeks' worth of meals in advance?" This woman was clearly an Overfunctioner. Although her husband and daughter were adults, she had taught them to underfunction as dependent children. Her goodness was literally killing her. She was not only very tired, she was overweight by two hundred pounds.

A weight problem may demonstrate a person's disrespect for her body and her boundaries. Often, when people can't say "No" themselves, they create a body that will do it for them. It is no accident that the song title is "I'm Just a *Girl* Who Can't Say No," rather than "a *Guy* Who Can't Say No." Because of our bad feelings about hurting others, not saying "No" is clearly a greater problem for women than it is for men. Without the wherewithal to offer a firm negative response, good-natured overweight women typically protect themselves in a way others can't penetrate. Little do they know that their larger girth makes it more difficult for them to hide after all.

I videotaped this woman while she fretted over her fears of not succeeding well enough in her role as hausfrau. (Or did she fear that the operation would teach her family to fend for themselves and no longer *need* her?) She broke down. She watched the playback through her tears. Yet she learned that the lesson in getting this operation lay not so much in correcting her condition, but in agreeing to let go. This was one of the most valuable assignments of her life:

👑 **Gilda-Gram** *Give from the overflow, not from the core.*

Don't get me wrong. Our ability to give someone something they can get nowhere else is a special gift, and one of the beautiful attributes of women is our capacity to care and nurture and support in ways men usually don't. But relationships must have balance. And the giver must exchange roles with the receiver from time to time to eliminate resentment of static role typecasting. If too much giving places our needs on the back burner, we must watch that we don't fall off the stove along with them. Overindulging may increase our short-term likability, but it will never gain us long-term respect. And who will care for *us* when we're burnt to a crisp?

How Relationships Exhaust Us: It's All in the Numbers

If the possibilities of burning out, being unappreciated, getting disrespected and dismissed, and preventing others from doing their own healing are not compelling enough to avoid overfunctioning, consider the numbers. Every relationship's interactions enter into the following basic Relationship Formula:

$$\frac{n \times (n-1)}{2}$$

n = *the number of people in the relationship*

Couple A has two people in the relationship, so their formula is:

$$\frac{2 \times (2-1)}{2} = 1 \text{ interaction}$$

For example, Jim and Donna alone constitute Couple A. They have only their own communications with which to deal, or one interaction to nourish. That seems simple enough. But notice what happens when Jim and Donna have a child. The n, number 2, now becomes number 3, or:

$$\underline{3 \times (3 - 1)}{2} = 3 \text{ interactions}$$

By adding just another (little) person, the relationship amasses to three interactions, rather than the former one. They consist of Donna + Baby (Interaction #1), Jim + Baby (Interaction #2), and Donna + Jim (Interaction #3). Not only are there three basic interactions, the nature of the interactions becomes more stressful because the tiny new infant legitimately requires his parents' constant attention.

Now, let's say Jim and Donna expand their family to two children, or four people in all. The Relationship Formula would grow like this:

$$\underline{4 \times (4 - 1)}{2} = 6 \text{ interactions}$$

There would be Jim + Donna (Interaction #1), Jim + Child 1 (Interaction #2), Donna + Child 1 (Interaction #3), Jim + Child 2 (Interaction #4), Donna + Child 2 (Interaction #5), Child 1 + Child 2 (Interaction #6). Again, the younger the children, the closer the need for more parental supervision. With six interactions in all, it is easy to understand how stressful family life can become as each interaction develops a life and personality of its own.

Many families have three or four children, an elderly parent, and a pet or two. Let's say Jim and Donna, now married ten years, have expanded their family to four children, Jim's elderly aunt, and their dog, Rusty, all residing under the same roof. That would be eight people if we counted Rusty. The Relationship Formula for this group would then be:

$$\underline{8 \times (8 - 1)}{2} = 28 \text{ interactions}$$

Okay, you think we ought to omit Rusty from the formula? Then there would be only twenty-four interactions! Staggering as these numbers seem, *the Relationship Formula as it stands does not tell the whole story.* While you have just observed the myriad interactions everyone has with each other, the formula omits one thing:

👑 Gilda-Gram *The most basic relationship we have is the one we have with ourselves.*

What about the special, private time we devote to ourselves? What about spending time alone? What about taking a "time-out" from our busy day just to watch TV, or go to an afternoon movie, or go shopping, or make love to our partner, or do whatever it is we passionately love? Usually, because women are such fine nurturers, we save time for ourselves as the last thing of the day or we put it on hold indefinitely, where it usually remains.

Imagine if Donna were an Overfunctioner. The more complex her family connections, the more she would try to control the flow of everyone's interactions. In reality we cannot control other people's behaviors, even when they are our children, but this is especially true with our grown-up, adult mate, who has a mind of his own. So the Overfunctioner's two choices are to continue her control, seeking to organize everyone's disarray, or give up overfunctioning entirely and *take charge of her own life*. The first choice inevitably leads to such stress that the Overfunctioner spins out of control all together. This is not only anxiety producing for her, but it is extremely agitating and unpleasant for others to be a part of. Her mate, for instance, may start yelling at her for tending to everyone else while not spending a quiet moment with him. He's now angry—and so is she. How can her good intentions not be appreciated? And the cycle continues. Clearly, there is only one healthy choice, and it is the second.

Letting Go

If I were to name the most difficult challenge for me in my adult life, it would be learning to keep quiet and *let go* of other people's issues. It still takes much restraint for me to keep my mouth shut when I observe someone I love sabotaging his or her life. Like the majority of women I know, I always considered fixing someone's ills an act of love. But I have learned the hard way that my overfunctioning for other people is not love at all, but an attempt to control according to *my* way of thinking and behaving. It took me some time to let my ex argue with his former wife without my interference, to free him to discipline his kids without my counsel, to tell friends it was their choice to decide what to do with their mates, to allow the family I love to naturally process their mistakes and grow from them. Nationally known relationship expert that I am, I vowed never again to receive such feedback as "What do you know?" or "How can you advise me about X when you don't Y?" But they *asked me*, I rationalized. Then, after their attack, I'd be hurt. Well, no more. I learned that in order to live in peace, I need to allow others to follow their own path. Besides, it was time for me to grow up and tackle my own life's issues. Finally, when I did, I became successful. It wasn't until then that I shined in my own light instead of in my ability to repair someone else's.

Letting go is not to stop caring about someone, however. It's recognizing that people must traverse through their own dark tunnel alone, where they learn to process the ebbs and flows of their life. Letting go is not for us to care *for* another person, but to care *about* that person. That means that we are now being called upon not to *fix* another person's pains, but to *support* the road she or he needs to travel. In essence, it requires our ability to love more than we've loved in the past, because now our love is based on trusting this person to do for him- or herself. When we do for ourselves we take the most responsible step toward our own self-growth.

From seeing herself on videotape, my graduate student learned that it was finally time for her to substitute her travails for her family's. I explained to her that taking responsibility for her family's issues had sidetracked her from taking a responsible position for her own. Great shopper that this woman boasted to be, she understood when I said that that was just too expensive. Unfortunately, while most women may know the price of many things, they often don't understand the value of the soul. In addition, I was preparing my student to face the world in the raw without the safeguards from her added weight. Being out of commission while she recuperated from knee surgery was probably the best thing that could happen to her. She realized that when things happen *to* you, they really happen *for* you. Nevertheless, while this woman found her need to let go refreshing, she was also terrified. Now she would have to star in her own commercial, rather than direct the actions of her husband and daughter.

It has been a year since the class ended. I recently bumped into her on campus. This woman has dropped about one hundred pounds already, and I've never seen her smile so broadly. She thanked me for pushing her off the fence. But in reality it was she who was ready to drop the artificial barriers and take an active role in her life. She said she has little time now to engineer the actions of the other grown-ups with whom she lives. As a result, they, too, are happier. Her daughter just found an apartment of her own—finally—and my student and her husband have more disposable income now to take lengthy vacations together and rekindle their love. Ahhh, how far-reaching are the benefits of letting go.

Without Boundaries We'll Fall Off Life's Stage

We need to set boundaries primarily for ourselves, so that we are clear as to where we stand. But boundary setting also lets others know where they may be crossing *the line* into territory that we regard as off-limits. When we paint our perimeter from the outset, we both learn and teach the rules of our loving. But when a relationship becomes our sole sustenance, we alter our boundaries in wishy-washy form just to keep the prince around. For each woman, individual and respectful boundaries must be drawn at the *start* of every relationship. They subtly set the standards for the kind of treatment we will ultimately permit.

Denise was a physical knockout, a drop-dead beauty who had been living with Roy for four years. Any woman would have wanted to have a body and face like hers, and no woman could imagine any man not desiring her in all her splendor. A fast-moving entrepreneur, Roy suddenly decided that he wanted to move to New York from California to start some new business ventures. But Denise had a small business of her own in California, and she was in the midst of completing an MBA there. However, she loved this man, so she agreed to continue their monogamous relationship on a commuting basis, which is not easy for short distances, let alone cross-continental travel. While the couple had been apart, she learned that he had taken the baby-sitter of her best friend on a business trip. (Huh?) Then, on another occasion, when they were together for a long weekend, she observed how rudely he spoke to his doorman. Finally she actually caught him in bed with another woman after she arrived home "too early." That was the proverbial last straw. Denise cashed in her chips. After such a devastating breakup, many women blame their luck on "If only I were prettier . . ." "If only I were smarter . . ." "If only I had been better in bed . . ." But by stating her boundaries and announcing what she would not accept, Denise at once recognized that the problem was not hers, but Roy's. She decided it was time to pack in the poor treatment and put her efforts into herself.

👑 **Gilda-Gram** *Boundaries don't close people out; they contain you so you don't disperse your energies where they are unappreciated.*

By knowing her boundaries, a woman also knows the allowances she'll make for a man's transgressions. She understands that she can always leave. When boundaries are solid, it doesn't take twelve whole steps to determine our next move.

👑 **Gilda-Gram** *Forget the 12-Step programs. Women in pain need only two steps: Get up. Get out.*

Women who forever seek acceptance find that delineating boundaries they can stick to is not easy. A lovely young woman worked with me for two years, seeking me out primarily to learn more assertive managerial skills. When we got into her story, she realized that she had to start first with becoming a more assertive *woman* and that her concern over her management style was just a smoke screen for issues that lay deeper. She needed to draw up boundaries around the way her husband treated her at home before she could demonstrate her boundaries in the great beyond. At one point in our therapy, her challenge was so great that she joked whether there was a store where she could simply *buy* some boundaries. It would have been far easier to purchase what she needed than to painfully stretch herself into new terrain. But after her mission was completed, she not only commanded better treatment at home, but she went on to gain thousands of dollars in raises for her superb managerial abilities. It all begins with the self.

It's been said, "Good fences make good neighbors." Intimate intrusions are shaky business, and it's not just physical space we long to protect, but emotional space as well. If we transfer ownership of our fence, the holder has the power to knock it down at any time. If and when he does, unless we have reserve power, oh do we suffer. But love merges us, and boundaries are the last thing we have on our minds when we begin to care.

When they coupled, Caitlin had given her entire life over to Lou. This is what happens when a woman is male-centered instead of self-centered. Being self-centered means that a woman is centered on her own growth, talents, ambitions, and passions. As a woman who put her man on a pedestal, Caitlin began the marriage with ceasing to see her friends and family and simply living to wake up with and come home to her man. "Pedestalizing" a man can be very dangerous. When they finally split, she was totally alone. Except for the children she neurotically overfunctioned for, Caitlin lacked one person by her side. After a year of nonstop crying, she finally decided she could no longer continue as she was. She needed to reclaim herself. It took her two long years and a lot of therapy, but even though she is now engaged, she still sees her friends and family regularly, adjusts her boundaries when necessary, and retains her private time. From that devastating experience of overlove, she learned to maintain her *self* in the equation of life. Her new flame not only loves her for her independence, but he respects her—which is a whole lot more substantive. When her invisible billboard flashes "No trespassing!" everyone respects it.

Priscilla had a different kind of boundary issue. When she came to me, she described her marriage as falling apart. She was a college graduate once with a well-paying job. She gave it all up after their baby was born, and now Priscilla admitted that she looked to her husband for everything. Another game of pin-the-tail-on-the-alleged-prince. But now this woman suddenly came to realize "I hate my life!" She felt stagnant, she was overweight, she had no self-confidence, and she was totally dependent on her husband for affection and adoration, which he was often too tired to shell out. Together we outlined what she could do to repossess the life that was once enjoyable to her. But as we listed activities she could engage in, she broke down. She said, "If I become more independent, I don't think my husband will love me." Ahhh. Second-guessing the prince. We had to return to the boundaries she had once set when her husband had first fallen for her. "Did he love you then?" I asked. "Oh, yes," she said. Then what makes you think things would be different now? As we spoke, it became obvious that the boundary restrictions were in Priscilla's mind, not in her man's. Priscilla has returned to work. As she has grown to feel better about her self-worth, the couple is now doing fine.

Many women erroneously assume that boundary busting allows us to be liked at all costs to prevent abandonment. But other people's opinions of us fluctuate, often without warning, and usually have nothing to do with us per se. This happens to female best friends at every age, from elementary school to adult women. Suddenly one turns on the other for no apparent reason, and the recipient is shocked and devastated. Learning to cope with an abrupt dumping early on is good training for women later in life. Down the road, a man could see in us the same hair color as the boss he hates, or we may unknowingly mirror mannerisms of the mother he never got along with. Without warning, he leaves. Everlasting popularity might be nice, but it's unrealistic. We can never please all the people all the time. I certainly needed to be rid of the need to be liked before I could appear daily before millions of people on worldwide television. Now I know that whether people praise me or blame me, I always return home with the power with which I left.

Gilda-Gram *When we quit trying to please others, we please more people than we know.*

That's a lesson we all must learn.

What about the woman who wants to marry the "I'm not ready to marry" man? Giving a guy an ultimatum is another form of boundary building. Everybody must lay down laws and stick by them. If a man wears a sign that says, "I'm not ready," take him at his word and recognize that he's not ready. You might want to wait around a bit to see if he changes his mind. But no woman can make a man want her. Nobody comes around unless he wants to, until he's ready. You must determine in your own heart what is right for *you*. Give yourself—and him—a time-line. If he meets it, fine. If not, move on. Sometimes, as soon as a woman wakes up, throws in the relationship towel, and reclaims her life, her rudderless ex calls and proposes. The relationship that ensues afterward is far more respectful then because this guy has learned that his woman keeps to her agreed-upon boundaries. But remember, issuing an ultimatum should be a last resort, because once you say it, there is no room for negotiation. And if you don't keep your word about walking out as you said you would do, you'll never be believed again.

Boundary maintenance gains respect. Being respected draws from our inner control so we're free to achieve the tasks we love without the need for outside applause. Sure, it's terrific to get it, but we need never count on someone else's willingness to dole it out. In contrast with being liked, respect upholds and honors our promises to ourselves. People who respect us first may come to like us later. But even if they don't, our power directs us to proceed with our goals. We have ourselves on our side—and that's what really matters.

Each woman must draw up a Bill of Boundaries. These non-negotiable statements protect a woman from allowing others too much leeway over her freedom and personal territory:

- We have the right to say "No."
- We have the right to offer an opinion.
- We have the right to remain silent.
- We have the right to enjoy pleasure.
- We have the right to pursue passion.
- We have the right to prefer solitude

👑 **Gilda-Gram** *When you know it's your right to say "No," you can freely choose the times you say "Yes."*

Practice adhering to your boundaries. Do you have problems with any of these? Does your partner currently, or did he ever, violate these boundaries? Sometimes people test us, and we find ourselves having to defend our boundaries. If we remember that this is how others determine how far they can go with us, we'll understand the necessity to stand our ground. We must honor our needs before we honor anyone else's. At times we may even be called that dirty word "selfish." Keep in mind, that word is preferable to its opposite, the doormat we may have traditionally been.

Proudly Becoming Selfish

Yes, some people will call us names when they don't get their way with us. We may not win a popularity contest when we defend ourselves, but the more we reiterate our unacceptance of poor treatment, the more we gain respect. Respect is the nourishment of Will-Be Women. While it is nice to be liked, and there's not a person on the face of the earth who doesn't want to be liked by those around her, it is respect that ultimately wins the greater rewards in terms of jobs, pay, and men.

It's Better to Be Respected Than Liked

So why don't women seek respect before liking? In large part, we are uncomfortable and unsure about telling someone "No." Listeners sense our waffling and wavering and take advantage of our vacuous words:

> If a lady says "No," she means "Maybe."
> If she says "Maybe," she means "Yes."
> If she says "Yes," she's really no lady.
> —Anonymous

From childhood, the word "no" was associated with pain, danger, punishment, and withdrawal of love. As grown-ups, "No" relates to hurting someone, getting into unwanted negotiations, angering someone, turning someone off sexually, coming clean with our true feelings—and most of all for us, feeling guilty, as we've discussed. Women often tell their friends they have broken up with a man before they cough up the courage to tell him themselves. *New Woman* offered advice on how to break up with your hairstylist, while *Cosmo* advised how to say sayonara to your shrink. We know, nobody loves the umpire, the person passing judgment, the sayer of nay. So, to keep our relationships intact, we became the "nice girl." Nice girls don't upset people. Nice girls have that one last drink with their colleague though they want to get home. They take that one last call from their boss though they're rushing to pick up their spouse. They do that one last favor for their lover though they are bone tired. They are the picture of the preferred low-maintenance employee, spouse, lover. Quick to say "Yes," they disown their wants, needs, feelings—and any approximation of substance.

> *I ended our relationship because of what her kindness symbolized. She had no emotional boundaries. Her fences were down. I could, and did, walk in and take over. My boundaries became hers.*
>
> *Fences make a relationship interesting. We do not really want to fall in love with ourselves; we want to match wits with some other person who has her own definition.*
> —Jake: A Man's Opinion
> *Glamour* magazine

Indeed, it seems that women have traditionally put the wrong concept in the wrong sequence. The inescapable truth that we've never been taught is:

....

👑 **Gilda-Gram** *We will never be loved if we can't risk being disliked.*

....

For most of us, likability in a woman depends on her success in being a Toastmaster, or its overfunctioning alternative, a Taskmaster. But likability is arbitrarily *given* and alters with the changing tastes of people. Sadly, our desire to be coupled sometimes prompts us to transform our own tastes to those of the man we hold dear. One woman met someone she definitely considered "husband material." While he was attracted to her, he disliked her "Laura Ashley" taste in clothes. Putting pressure on his new girlfriend, this man got her to transform her entire wardrobe to resemble Frederick's of Hollywood. Pleasing your mate is one thing, but this woman's new garb made her feel like Lady Astor's pet horse. Fortunately, before it was too late (and she was into a predictably miserable marriage), she recognized that she had been Eliza Doolittled into someone she was not. She broke off the relationship, not a moment too soon for her to refurbish her former self and go on her way to find a more appreciative partner. Quickly enough, she recognized that she would not sway her Internal Control for the alleged rewards of an External prince. To protect ourselves from doubting our own judgment, it is best to know our boundaries before we bond. Then, at the very least, we can prevent the unnecessary outlay of money on garments that are not our style!

In contrast with likability, *respect* is achieved through noteworthy tasks. Respectability is solidly *earned* and is clearly non-negotiable. Unfortunately, our society generally doesn't count marriage and motherhood as earned achievements. So while providing the necessary love to our impressionable babies, many women question the meaning of their lives. With the projection of questionable worth comes the reflection of questionable respect.

The problem arises when the need to succeed at nurturing is so great that it supersedes the desire to achieve personal goals. Lots of women may enjoy running the household and carpooling the kids, but these roles must never become all-encompassing to the exclusion of other passions. Journalist Anna Quindlen calls wifehood and mothering "an iffy line of work, with nothing else to fall back on" should the prince outgrow the castle and leave you stranded. To protect themselves from who knows what, these women must also establish a separate identity. Whether "identity" means selling cosmetics door-to-door, doing volunteer work for a local charity, or having a full-time job, every woman must set personal goals that are not dependent on the return love of someone else—man, job, children, or any friends. This doesn't seem to be a popular thought with a lot of men today, and, in fact, a woman pursuing any passions aside from wife and motherhood might receive that nasty label—"selfish." Only a short time back, a large store chain yanked a T-shirt off its shelves because it had Margaret, the Dennis the Menace character, beneath the legend "Someday a woman will be PRESIDENT!" The store claimed it was offensive to "family values." After much public outcry, the company retreated from its position. The shirts are reportedly flying out of the stores now. A second T-shirt was created with Margaret in traditional male roles, including astronaut and firefighter. One of the store's buyers refused to carry that line unless it also featured Margaret as housewife. Seems there's a lot of resistance to women realizing their dreams. Be in the position of being able to take care of yourself. Reap your own rewards. If you want a man to join you, you'll attract someone worthy of who you've become. Instead of what we've been taught,

👑 **Gilda-Gram** *Seek respect first, then liking.*

Let's decide what we really want in our lives. Do we have goals? Do we have ambitions? Do we have dreams? In order to achieve these things, our objective must be *not* to be liked, but to be heard and understood (remember the S-O-F-A technique from chapter 4). People attend to us and listen when they feel we have something important to say. This is their measure of respect. Again, respect is something we work for, something we draw from the content of our character and the excellence of our achievements. It isn't something that's arbitrarily given. It can *only* be earned. Are you respected? Do Self-Assessment #17 and determine if you project the notion that you deserve respect from the people who listen to you.

SELF-ASSESSMENT #17

PROJECT RESPECT, REFLECT RESPECT

1. Repeat this statement aloud ten times—"I am respected"— as you visualize capital "I."

2. List three words you associate with respect.
   a.
   b.
   c.
   Are these words positive or negative?

3. Imagine yourself with a man you respect.

   • Visualize how he respectfully treats you.

   • Smell the respectful surroundings.

   • Touch this person with respect.

   • Hear his respectful words.

   • Alter your body language to elicit his respect.

   • Envision slipping into a silk robe with the word "respect" written on the back.

Did your responses to this self-assessment surprise you? One of the most effective ways a person gains respect is by not saying "Yes" to everyone for everything. Yeses must derive from what remains after we have provided for ourselves. Saying "No" protects our basic core of emotions, those we must deliberately keep intact at all times. Besides, when we say "No," we are only negating the speaker's *request*, not negating him as a person. If he thinks otherwise, that is clearly his problem, not ours. Knowing this, we cannot *feel bad* about turning down someone's request.

If your sister has borrowed countless pieces of your jewelry and never returned them, it's not only your right, it's your obligation to safeguard your possessions. If your boyfriend circulated a personal secret of yours that you asked him to keep under wraps, it's your right to confront him about it, then to protect your other private information in the future. It's better that other people rather than you are disappointed. Can they take it? Wrong question. *Do you care?* If so, examine your need to be liked.

This chapter has made it clear that overfunctioning women place being liked on a higher priority rung than being respected. Of course, their ability to be respected is questioned by their obvious lack of respect for themselves. People who respect themselves don't work so hard for love that they become others' sacrificial lambs. Clearly, as an overfunctioner such a woman's objective is to be loved, but at the price of devaluing her needs—which she all-too-willingly agrees to in order to get love. In reality, then, she often gives not out of a genuine desire to serve, but in order to get something back. That would make her a master manipulator. If she's forever present because she's forever needed, she gets to have a say in others' lives. In the driver's seat, she feels good about the power she wields. So while overfunctioning may actually be viewed as selfish, it is also self*less* because the penalty for damages is to leave this woman without a sense of who she is.

Of course, no woman deliberately sets out to barter her soul for a chunk of control. These behaviors are unconscious, and until the Overfunctioner understands what she's doing, she usually has no clue that she suffers from the disease to please. One would wonder if, with all this manipulation, it wouldn't be easier for such a woman to go about her business and satisfy herself. Regrettably, an Overfunctioner with years of experience at this gig usually no longer knows what her business is. If this is your case, ask, "Am I a bellboy? If not, why do I carry other people's baggage?"

Taking Good Care of Yourself

Are you reluctant to cease your endless giving? Do you use excuses like "But he's my son," "I'd never disappoint a friend," "I have to be there for my lover," or "I owe her"? Sometimes your virtue can become your vice.

Nobody says that a woman has to be a bitch, nor must she give up being polite and pleasant to express her needs. What I am saying is that she must take care of her own needs without being addicted to someone else's approval. Are you subject to other people's opinions of you? Find out by rating each of these women's statements in Self-Assessment #18:

SELF-ASSESSMENT #18

AM I SELFISH?

How would you rate each of the following statements according to the following definitions:

    S = Selfish: Self-seeking and self-loving

    SL = Selfless: Self-denying and later feeling used

    C = Compromising: Willingness to give in exchange for something

Imagine having these conflicts with a partner:

_____ **1.** I don't want to see that movie because I hate action flicks.

_____ **2.** Your brother is so nasty to me, I'd rather not attend your family gatherings in the future.

_____ **3.** I've been supporting this family for three years while you looked for work. Now I want to return to school, so it's your turn to support us.

_____ **4.** I find your friends loud and embarrassing, and I don't want to go out with them again.

SCORING KEY

(1) S if you truly refuse to see this movie.

    SL if you don't want to go but go anyway and later feel cheated.

    C if you willingly go in exchange for a favor from your partner.

(2) S if you decide not to go.

    SL if you go against your will just to please your partner but are miserable afterward.

    C if you agree to go in exchange for your partner's defending you when attacked.

(3) S if you enroll in school.

    SL if you put off school enrollment until your partner fully gives his permission.

    C if you agree to begin slowly to see how the family's new scheduling arrangements work.

(4) S if you happily do something else when your partner sees his friends.

> SL if you go with your partner and his loud friends, then complain later.
> C if you negotiate accompanying your partner in exchange for his doing something you want.
>
> ---
>
> Count the number of S's you checked. If you had fewer than four, your willingness to be self-caring is questionable.

We are using the term "selfishness" here to mean self-caring. Scoring some SL's may mean that you have problems giving generously without strings. At times, however, being selfless may be appropriate. For example, at work you may be coerced to contribute to a charity because the unwritten rule is that people who don't contribute don't get promoted. In this case, although you complain about it, your giving is a career decision and a compromise with which you are comfortable. The real test is your ability to understand the motive behind each act of giving and then decide what is appropriate for you. You must be able to balance putting off your needs, as well as protect yourself by saying "No." You must know when it is appropriate to compromise your own values for the sake of someone or something else. I had a client who was so incensed that her company coerced their employees to contribute to a particular charity that she went to the extreme of quitting her job to preserve her sense of freedom. Most of the other employees at this organization were dismayed about this contribution policy because it meant less money in their take-home salaries. But they chose to go along to get ahead. Who is to say what is appropriate for someone to sustain self-respect?

Every relationship requires a balance between selfishness and selflessness, depending on the people and the circumstances. Each of us must decide what is right for us. Your taking a stand against a popular view might be termed "selfish" by onlookers but might be considered "self-nurturing" by you. A woman who operates from her own power point knows what she must do. Eating and thinking and breathing are selfish, but would anyone consider ceasing them?

Proving Our Power Through Selfing

Life requires compromise. The compromise we choose is what I call *Selfing*. Selfing encourages a woman to give, but it also warns her to protect herself from giving too much. It therefore balances the art of being selfish with the act of being selfless.

Selfing has three components:
1. F.E.A.R.
2. The Feel-Good "No"
3. The "3 + 1 + 1 Rule"

The Avoidance of F.E.A.R.

Until now, what has held you back? If you're like most people, the answer is probably F.E.A.R. On some level, many people fear that if they let others know exactly how they feel, they will be abandoned, dissed, disliked, dismissed. That's fairly serious for someone who values being liked.

There are four truths that will counteract your irrational fears of hurting and/or disappointing others and be disliked in return. They are easy to remember in the form of a **F.E.A.R.** acronym:

F— Fear will never go away as long as we continue to grow.
E— Everyone experiences some fear when they are in unfamiliar situations.
A— Adopt the philosophy "Feel the fear . . . and do it anyway."
R— Ridding yourself of the fear is more powerful than the helplessness of inaction.

F—As long as you are growing and experiencing new adventures, it is absolutely normal to feel some fear. Rational fear can be a protective device that warns you to be more cautious before taking risks. The consequence of not fearing is not risking, not stepping beyond the limitations, never discovering what lies beyond, and therefore staying where you've always been. There are plenty of people who stay stuck in their comfort zone. You may have magnetized some of these types of men into your life. If so, have they been interesting, exciting? At first they may seem stable. But later you probably became bored. Do you always want to eat in the same restaurant? Shop at the same stores? Hang with the same friends? If we want adventure, we also have to put up with the fear of breathing air that is new and different. Take a risk and see how in control you really are.

E—Everyone experiences fear occasionally, whether in the supermarket or in Hollywood. The "impostor syndrome" documents how doctors, judges, lawyers, professors, and others at the top fear that people will discover they are not as great as others think. Know that feeling fearful is a natural occurrence for everyone from time to time. This is one case where misery not only loves company, it *depends* on company—especially of such a high caliber—to make us remember that we're still okay.

A—Adopt the philosophy that you will feel the fear—and do it anyway. Admit to yourself that you are frightened when you are. Ask yourself, What exactly is frightening me? What's the worst thing that can happen? Take your scariest steps in small doses. After each, reward yourself for getting through it. Just keep knocking down those pins. You're in control now.

R—Rid yourself of the fear by pushing ahead and gaining leverage. If we do nothing with our fear, it hangs over us like a dark cloud. Instead, take action and flush it out, once and for all. With each tiny step forward, we project greater power. When we project our power, others reflect our power. Before we know it, we are treated with respect. And it wasn't so hard after all.

As my graduate student discovered, making changes in your life means leaving the protection of passivity. This is frightening because if you remain passive, you already know what to expect from your life, even if it's misery. But by enacting something different, you're faced with the unknown, and that can be scary even for the most courageous and adventuresome. Are you in touch with your feelings and your fears? Complete Self-Assessment #19 and find out.

SELF-ASSESSMENT #19

AM I IN TOUCH WITH MY FEELINGS AND FEARS?

1. The most difficult feelings for me to show are: _____

2. Discover which fears conceal your feelings. Complete the following statements:

   a. "I don't show people I'm _____ because I'm frightened that _____.

   b. "I don't show people I'm _____ because I'm frightened that _____.

   c. "I don't show people I'm _____ because I'm frightened that _____.

Did your responses surprise you? Why?

After completing Self-Assessment #19, one woman recognized that she would not tell her nineteen-year-old daughter "No" when she asked for money because she was fearful that her daughter would withdraw her love. Another woman admitted that she would not say "No" to sex with her abusive husband because she didn't want to get him more angry. In both cases these women's unwillingness to deliver a firm and final "No" kept them jailed by the people they refused to confront or to erect proper boundaries toward.

As we've seen time and again, saying "No" is a difficult chore for most women. Of course, there are alternative ways to suggest your disinterest. I have heard some people say sarcastically, "I don't think so." I have heard still others drop the heavy artillery with "No way, nohow, not now." Each of these alternatives to "No" will gain you more enemies than friends, and that's what most women try to avoid. Instead, a simple "No" might seem more comforting. It is possible to say it and actually feel good.

The Feel-Good "No"

Let's change the old myth that saying "No" will make you feel awful. Actually you can feel *good* about saying "No" because you know that you're standing up for yourself, maintaining your boundaries, and protecting your right to express your feelings. When you use the Feel-Good "No," your listener will thank you for sharing your honest feelings. Follow the steps from 1 to 7 and experience how much stronger you feel.

1. Remind yourself that you have a right to turn someone down.
2. Hold steady eye-alogue to instill strength.
3. Incorporate the three B's: *Be* friendly. *Be* brief. *Be* firm.
4. Give a simple explanation for why you can't or won't.
5. Refuse to be drawn into negotiations that your listener may try to counter with logic.
6. Offer an alternative if you have one.
7. Use your time-buying options:
   "I'd like to think about your request for a while."
   "I can't deal with this now. I'll have time at one this afternoon."
   "For me to lend you the car, I'll have to see if I can make other arrangements. I'll get back to you."

Once you've set the stage, the third step involves your actual delivery. Follow the *3 + 1 + 1 Rule* and know that you will feel protected.

The 3 + 1 + 1 Rule

This rule for personal caretaking sandwiches your "No" between three positive statements and one strong exit. It is so easy to use that you will find you don't even have to actually utter the "No" word. When you follow this formula, you will feel good about delivering your "No" statement, you'll set up an environment where you will not be assaulted to change your mind, and your listener will get your point immediately.

The 3 + 1 + 1 Rule
EXHIBIT A

Your lover wants you to spend the weekend with him and his two bratty teenagers. Ordinarily you would agree to join them. But this weekend you feel exhausted from your job stress. You even fear that you might say the wrong thing while your nerves are stretched to their limit. You are sure you want to say "No" to this trip, but you don't want to hurt your lover's feelings or damage your relationship. You say:

> **Positive #1**: *"Dick, I'm pleased you included me in your family weekend."* (Always use his name to get his full attention and personalize your intimacy.)
> **Positive #2**: *"I know that spending time with your children means a lot to you."*
> **Positive #3**: *"Including me with your family is a beautiful way to tell me how much I mean to you, and I love you for that."*
> **"No" Statement**: *"I am emotionally spent from work this week and I need to spend some quiet time by myself."* (Never begin your "No" with "But" because once he hears that word, he'll negate all the positives you already offered.)
> **Strong Exit**: *"Please invite me again the next time the kids join you."* (During the strong exit, touch Dick if you are comfortable doing that. Touch maintains a stronger connection between the two of you and makes it easier for him to hear you.) After delivering your strong exit, disengage eye-alogue. Change the topic. He'll understand you are unwavering in your decision.

The 3 + 1 + 1 Rule
EXHIBIT B

Your boss's boss keeps asking you out, always under the pretext of discussing your business future at the company. You love working where you do, and you're interested in moving up as quickly as possible. He's married. He's also someone you find downright unattractive. But you understand that if you continue to refuse his advances, it could possibly damage your income and promotions.

> **Positive #1**: *"Tom, I'm flattered that you'd like to spend time with me outside the office to discuss business."*
> **Positive #2**: *"I know that you're a busy man and that you value how you spend your time after you leave work."*
> **Positive #3**: *"I think that what you've done as senior vice president has been positive for our company, and I'd enjoy discussing my future with you on a professional basis . . ."*

"No" Statement: *"And I have a policy of not mixing business with pleasure."* (Smile pleasantly; you're there not to teach him a lesson in business ethics, but to state your position.)

Strong Exit: *"Let's sit together and have coffee or do a business lunch next week. I'd like very much to pursue some of the ideas our department has been working on. When's the best day for you?"* (You certainly don't want to touch this lech to underscore your point. After you have delivered your strong exit, disengage eye-alogue. Change the topic. If you're seated, rise from your chair. Leave. He'll understand you mean *business, not pleasure.*)

To give from the overflow and not from the core, a woman must demonstrate the art of Selfing, occasionally giving yet occasionally holding back. Saying "No" in whichever way she is most comfortable is a woman's ultimate self-care. The opposite of self-care consists of holding back. When a woman withholds her real feelings, she is being dishonest with herself. Such dishonesty could incur others' disappointment, anger, or hostility when they discover they have been misled. Offering an honest "No" requires the ability to balance the three potent forces of:

- Taskmaster vs. Toastmaster
- Internal Control vs. External Control
- Selfishness vs. Selflessness

After completing the self-assessments in these chapters, Christine felt that she was slowly progressing in her success at love. In particular, she felt that she was making headway in enhancing her love for *herself*, which she now understood was primary before she could be successful at love with her husband. She conceded that she had never asked for what she needed because she never believed she deserved much. In her need to be liked, she had exhibited more Toastmaster kindness than Taskmaster determination. She acknowledged that she was motivated primarily by the External Control of others, and especially that of her husband, rather than an Internal drive to satisfy herself. She became aware that each time Howard threatened to withdraw his love, in order to make him happy, she erased any boundaries she might have set and accepted his tantrums. Since she accepted the idea that *what we accept, we teach,* she now recognized that by supporting Howard's tirades, she was guaranteeing their continuation.

Finally, she observed how her self*less*ness was based on her fear of displaying her feelings, frightened of the possibility of being left, as Howard often threatened. In short, Christine was so desperate for love, she did not project a Power Image, and consequently was rarely treated with respect. She noted how her negative self-image projected its way into all her relationships and was reflected back in the way others treated her. Her parents favored her older brother, her children ran wild over her, her clients withheld fees they owed. In the end, she agreed that she ought to have had a monopoly on the "Screw Me" signs she indeed wore across her chest.

Christine's new awareness was astounding. She understood that betting on herself simply required developing and honing these needed skills. Just because she had mislearned the lessons of self-love while growing up did not mean she would have to remain stuck for the rest of her life. Each "No" she delivered encouraged her advancement. Each time she told her husband to take his tantrums elsewhere, her body language grew stronger. Most outbursts by her children were met with newfound discipline. Each client from whom she demanded her fee further strengthened her boundaries. These may have appeared like small steps, but every one of them proved to Christine that she was on her way. She had already begun to feel better.

Balancing these three forces should be no great strain for any woman today. We have been doing a balancing act in a male world since the beginning of time. Our ability to give is nothing new, but our capacity to take care of ourselves is an art we must develop and practice. After we perfect it, we are on our way to developing the other side of giving, the ability to receive.

GILDA-GRAMS

FROM CHAPTER 5

Give from the Overflow, Not from the Core

▶ *When we overfunction for others, we underfunction for ourselves.*

▶ *There are givers and there are takers. Takers eat well, and givers sleep well . . . but not for long.*

▶ *When we state our preferences, we invite people to act as we want, not as they want.*

▶ *Give from the overflow, not from the core.*

▶ *The most basic relationship we have is the one we have with ourselves.*

▶ *Boundaries don't close people out; they contain you so you don't disperse your energies where they are unappreciated.*

▶ *Forget the 12-Step programs. Women in pain need only two steps: Get up. Get out.*

▶ *When we quit trying to please others, we please more people than we know.*

▶ *When you know it's your right to say "No," you can freely choose the times you say "Yes."*

▶ *We will never be loved if we can't risk being disliked.*

▶ *Seek Respect first, then liking.*

6
Know How to Receive

One wintry Sunday, Krista sauntered into a large, crowded shoe store, hoping to get warm. Instead she found some astounding sales on quality boots. She picked up a pair from the display rack and found that a tall, dark, handsome stranger was admiring her choice. She remarked that it would be difficult to try on the knee-high boots over her jeans. He offered to help. Afterward they exchanged business cards. He was from California, she from New York. She wondered about the purpose of the card exchange since the two were so geographically distant.

But two weeks later the good-looking stranger trumped up some business appointments as an excuse to return to the East Coast and Krista. They revisited the scene of the crime, the shoe store. This time he generously purchased four fabulous pairs of boots with stiletto heels for the woman to whom he was so attracted. Trading in the proverbial glass slippers, Krista was now a veritable "Puss in Boots." She had no problem receiving the stranger's gifts.

This is a heartwarmingly true tale of a man intrigued by a woman and his desire to demonstrate his feelings through his ability to give. A man's generosity toward a woman he adores is nothing new. Shāh Jāhan built the Taj Mahal for the wife he loved. But the most interesting part of Krista's story was the reaction she got from her friends. Unlike her, they were meeting and/or married to men who were often cheap and withholding. More often than not, they found themselves invited to dinner with guys who asked *them* to pay. They were amazed by this stranger's kindness. In Krista's mind, a woman paying for a man was like a cow buying feed for a farmer. Krista somehow mystically knew how to turn Kismet into Camelot, as her friends looked on in amazement. In fact, after having dinner with a man who had taken one of her friends to lunch some years earlier, the two women compared notes. Krista's friend called the man "very cheap" while Krista, only halfway through her salad, had gotten an invitation from him to take her to Europe! Was her boot man acting out a foot fetish? Maybe so. But it was also something more.

What was Krista's secret? A high-earning professional, she could certainly have afforded to buy all four pairs of boots herself, as well as take herself on any fabulous vacation she desired. But she knew that a woman's giving to and nurturing of a man is only one side of the seesaw. Although most women enjoy being able to give, we must also show our openness and vulnerability by knowing how to receive. It begins with our ability to receive our own goodness. In other words, receiving builds on the ability to be kind to ourselves, to count ourselves as number one, and to consider our needs first and foremost.

Be Willing to Receive Your Own Goodness

Before a woman can receive a man's generosity, she must be able to receive her own. When she takes care of herself, she signals to men the way she wants them to treat her. So the first question to ask is "How do I bestow kindness on myself?"

Carol had enrolled in one of my "Don't Bet on the Prince!" workshops. She was a single, middle-aged guidance counselor who lived with her frail and crippled father. For years her life had been lonely without a partner and totally devoted to caring for her dad. The woman not only received little emotional support in return, when she got to the workshop, she discovered that she did not believe she was entitled to any. I asked Carol, "What do you do to make your life happy?" Sadly, she replied, "Nothing." Clearly she had not even thought that her life was her own. Being an only daughter, she felt she could not leave her father alone.

The workshop lasted ten weeks. At our very last class, Carol surprised the group. She had had a sudden epiphany, and slowly she began to describe it. It was Christmas, and the snow was falling every day. Traditionally this can be a time of sadness for someone without a loving partner. But Carol announced to the class that she would not spend another holiday feeling blue. She told the group that she had gone out and bought something she wanted very badly, but which she had always believed ought only to be given to a woman by a man. There was no man in her life, and she *chose* to wait no longer. From our class discussions, she said that she had recognized it was time for her to give to *herself*. At last she was willing to receive.

That Christmas, Carol placed a big box under her tree. On the card she inscribed, "To Carol. From Carol. Love, Carol." Under the fine wrapping, silky tissue paper, and variegated ribbon sat the mink coat Carol had longed for. The group gasped when she related this. Then they applauded . . . but some of the women also cried. They cried for those who never took time for themselves, for those who worked long hours for their families without appreciation, for those who never rewarded themselves for jobs well done, for those who never knew they deserved more. Too many of these women had been in the same situation, and some of them still had not learned that to have a loving relationship with a soulmate, they would first have to have a loving relationship with themselves.

In only ten weeks Carol had stepped up to happiness she had not even known she lacked. She had learned that:

👑 **Gilda-Gram** *The art of receiving begins by giving to yourself.*

Once Carol had broken the ice and decided to buy herself something she had wanted for a long time, she was able to be open to a man's love. Carol is now happily married to someone wonderful and generous, whose kindness she freely accepts. He has invited Carol's father to live with them, and she recently helped her dad move in. This art of giving to yourself works toward your ability to receive because:

👑 **Gilda-Gram** *When you give to yourself, others learn how you want to be treated.*

Unfortunately, not every story ends as beautifully as Carol's. There were women in that very workshop who returned to their lives and continued their habitual self-denial. There are other women who become compulsive shoppers, misconstruing buying frenzies as emotional fulfillment. Still others sho*plift* in an effort to *steal* the emotions they've been denied. Obviously, material objects can never assuage the pain resulting from emotional holes. However, when the desire for affection is filled, the acceptance of material things is simply an extension of the notion of "I deserve."

Be Willing to Receive Gracefully

After she has learned to be a recipient of her own caretaking, a woman can receive both a man's emotional kindness and his material generosity. A woman's eagerness to be accepting and receptive in both arenas is important for a relationship to thrive. Women who won't receive deprive and cheat their partners of sharing, and in the long run, the entire union suffers from one-sided caring.

While some women are, indeed, "gold-diggers," trying to get from men whatever they can, it is surprising how many women distrust a kind man's attempts at courting them with occasional material offerings. As much as we can certainly fault Caitlin's ex-husband for his womanizing, gambling, and physical abuse, Caitlin herself was a woman unable to receive. Occasionally, at the start of their marriage, Lou would come home from work with a surprise present for his wife. But she continued to blame him for spending too much money on frivolous things for her that she would never use. Eventually he stopped bringing them. He sought others more open to receiving—and to him.

Some women hesitate to ask for what they want, while others want more than what they ask for. None of these women feel they *deserve* what is rightfully theirs. Caitlin began to explore her receiving patterns from the beginning of her first marriage. Because giving and receiving are two sides of the same coin, not surprisingly she discovered that she was also parsimonious in her material giving. Raising two little daughters, she had refused to traditionally celebrate their birthdays with parties. She had reasoned, "If we have a party, children will bring you gifts, then we'll owe them a gift in return. I never want to be in a position of owing anyone anything." As a result of their mother's miserly attitude, the two girls grew up not knowing that birthdays are celebrations of their own special day. Neither did they celebrate the parties of their little friends. Worse, they grew to believe that receiving always came with a price tag. As they moved through life, they perceived most people as users, usually wanting to profit from them. As a result, in all their relationships, they had difficulty in the area of trust.

Just as little ducks in the water follow their mother's lead, human mothers condition their daughters for what is to come in their lives. More than the words they tell their children to live by, mothers' behaviors clearly delineate *the way*. Sometimes daughters observe mom's lead step-by-step; other times they overcompensate for what they missed. Now thirty, Caitlin's older daughter was invited to her best friend's home for a sumptuous dinner. Divorced twice and suspicious of any generosity offered her, she could not fathom that anyone would slave so long and hard in preparing such a loving meal for her. As she was leaving her friend's home that evening, she revealed through teary eyes, "This was the first time in my life anyone cooked me dinner without expecting me to sleep with him."

Meanwhile the younger daughter compensated for her stingy mother's behavior through the opposite extreme, by holding expensive birthday banquets for each of her two children. Whether her children were celebrating their first birthday or their Sweet Sixteen, this daughter often got herself into debt proving to her kids that they were special and that this was how a family traditionally valued their special day. Of course, the unnecessary party expenses the younger daughter incurred were wasted on kids happy to play video games with their pals and eat any kind of junk food. How our traditions are passed on! Witnessing her children's reenactment of her own faulty reasoning had helped Caitlin recognize that her weakness in this marriage had been her inability to receive. She vowed not to repeat these mistakes in her next marriage.

These stories are all tales of material receptivity, beginning, of course, with the willingness to receive what you give to yourself. In order to get and keep the man you want, you must also set standards of *emotional* receptivity. In other words, when people around you offer love through simple kindness or personal assistance or glowing compliments, note if—and how—you accept their offerings. Some women have so much difficulty with emotional receptivity, they would rather inconvenience themselves or relinquish positive feelings than reap the benefits of emotional kindness.

Megan's mother suffered a sudden stroke. When a good friend offered to visit Megan's mom in the hospital, although it would have been wonderful to share the emotional burden with her, Megan did not know how to accept this kindness. Instead of welcoming her friend's offer and letting her know when she could drop by, Megan conjured up every excuse possible to keep her away. Later, after her mother was fully recovered, Megan bemoaned her lonely fate as the sole caregiver to her elderly parent. Whose fault was that? She was a woman who was emotionally closed.

Holly was a plain-looking woman with a smile that could light a room. This was, by far, her most outstanding feature, offsetting every other on her face and body. But whenever someone complimented her beautiful grin, she dismissed it with "Oh, you really like it?" or "Well, I'm not crazy about my crooked front tooth" or, worse, "I hope it compensates for my big nose." Never once did she say, simply, "Thank you." As a result of her rejecting responses, after a while people stopped offering their praise. Eventually Holly began to wonder if her smile had lost its appeal. This was another woman who was emotionally closed.

The interesting part about emotionally unreceptive women is that not only are they unwilling to receive, but the other side of the coin, their ability to give, is also lacking. Since emotional receiving seems to be more difficult to achieve than the material kind, I recommend to these women that they begin by buying something wonderful for themselves, something they've always wanted but always denied themselves. Since material offerings are obvious, it is for this reason we began this chapter by explaining material receptivity. If emotionally unreceptive women begin by accepting some *thing* they value, they will eventually be able to move their willingness to receive into the emotional arena.

To be openly receptive to her man, there is one small price a woman must pay. That price is forgiveness. It may cost her her pride, but that is a mere pittance in comparison with the amount of love she will ultimately derive. Forgiveness is a woman's willingness to let go of the reason she has been closed down. Anger blocks us. But for many women, the act of forgiveness is a hefty request. In essence:

👑 **Gilda-Gram** *You cannot receive if you cannot forgive.*

Graceful Receiving Means Generous Forgiving

Mark Twain called forgiveness "the fragrance that the violet sheds on the heel that has crushed it." The truth is, often without reason, human beings cause each other to suffer. More bizarre, it is not our enemies, but the people we love most, whom we injure. Our ability to forgive someone who has hurt us is usually a problem for most of us sometime in our lives. But it does not have to continue to be that way. Are you willing to overlook being hurt by your ex? Are you ready to stop steaming over that salesman's rudeness? Are you free to get over the guy who didn't call? Your neighbor and her noisy parties? Your husband's late cavorting with his buddies? Pretending that things are fine when they really aren't will not heal you or your relationship. But getting your feelings out and getting on with your life will loosen the hold your negative emotions have over you. In short, forgiveness of others releases *you*, and as such it is healthy—and selfish in the best sense.

Forgiveness is an act of elimination. It is a ridding process of the things that do not serve you. We can't force new good into our lives when we haven't made room to receive it. Being upset with others serves no other purpose than to make us ill. Is it worth it? Since you will never change these people anyway, and they probably won't ever see things your way, let them be. Kick your memories of them to the curb.

While this is the best antidote for a woman's pain, after a romance ends, some women want their share of revenge. For them, the affair may be finished, but it's not *completed* until they have gotten their last licks. Before running off to flatten his tires or cut his power suits in half (I met a very angry woman who had done both to her ex), consider the universal law of giving out and getting back in kind. Okay, he lied to you, cheated on you, or dumped you for your "best" friend. First, remember that problem people are in our lives to teach us something. If we resent them, fight them, criticize them, or resist them, we *retain* them. The objective is to learn the lesson you were destined for and clear these people from your consciousness as soon as you can. Then:

👑 **Gilda-Gram** *Spend your time willing your happiness rather than willing your man's misery.*

What time and energy you'll save—which you will be able to invest in *you*.

Marsha had borrowed $8,000 from her boyfriend of three years to put into her foundering business. They agreed that she would repay a few hundred dollars a month. But she found that he was cheating on her, and after many confrontations about the "other woman," Marsha decided that she could not tolerate the pain. After she broke it off, throughout the following year, she still carried a torch and hoped that he would "see the light" and return. Instead she learned that he had actually married the woman with whom he had been involved. Marsha was livid. During one of their arguments, he had even told her that he couldn't stand this woman. Marsha decided not to repay him the remaining money she owed.

When she told me the story and asked my advice, I suggested she rethink her decision, because *what goes around comes around*. However, like most people who request free advice, Marsha chose to ignore my input and stand her ground.

Two months later we accidentally met on the street. When I asked how she was doing, she told me she was suddenly having continuous "losses" around her—in her business life and in her personal life. A light bulb went off in my head. I asked if the sum total of these losses was worth $8,000. She replied, "No, it's been more than that." She looked at me, startled.

Yes, revenge may be sweet—but is it worth the price of your precious time and energy? Okay, you still feel pissed *off* for being pissed *on*? You still want an instant pain reliever? Then do get revenge, but invent it in your mind, with a *creative fantasy*. Fantasize your partner stepping in doggie-do while he's trying to impress his most important client. Imagine him losing his hair or his job or his erection. Laugh heartily and have your catharsis. But at least with this revenge fantasy you won't have to wonder if the coronary you might have wished on him will instead plague you. Know, too, that time not only heals all wounds, it wounds all heels, and he will suffer his own indignities when the time is right. Just don't have a hand in them. With good care and a lot of prayer, you'll be somewhere nearby to gloat about the news when it does occur. In the meantime, instead of waiting for New Year's to write a new set of Resolutions, create a List of Elimination now with your ex's name on it.

👑 **Gilda-Gram** *Your will to love must be stronger than your wish to hate.*

You will at once be unfettered and unbound by contaminants that block your growth.

When you have cleared out the old negative feelings, allow their absence to make way for those who matter, people who support you and everything you stand for. Welcome those who can give to you, people from whom you can receive. Forgiveness has to begin somewhere. What about here? What about now? Complete Self-Assessment #20 and begin the forgiveness process at once.

SELF-ASSESSMENT #20

FORGIVING AT LAST

- Think of a man who has hurt you.
- Name one good thing about him. (Come on, everyone has at least one good quality.)
- Name the things he had done *to* you.
- Name the things he has actually done *for* you.
- Complete the following statements:

> I forgive myself for _____.
> I forgive my ex for _____.
> I forgive my partner for _____.
> I forgive my friend for _____.
> I forgive my boss for _____.
> I forgive my client for _____.
> I forgive my company for _____.

REPEAT THE FOLLOWING STATEMENTS ALOUD:

"I not only *forgive* _____, I *thank* _____, because I have grown by _____ from having known him."

"I not only *forgive* _____, I *thank* _____, because he's the reason I left this _____."

"I not only *forgive* _____, I *thank* _____, because I learned _____ about _____ from him.

Add more reasons you are grateful to the person you are now willing to forgive.

While she had made great strides in completing the other self-assessments, Christine, like many women, was still uncertain about offering forgiveness for her past grievances. After completing this self-assessment, Christine understood how *not forgiving* was holding her back. She knew what she had to do next. Still somewhat reluctant, she agreed to forgive her husband for humiliating her, her children for haranguing her, her clients for not paying her, and most of all, herself for not believing she *deserved* better. At once she recognized that her continuous whining was doing nothing to improve any of these situations. If anything, it kept her victimized and exhausted, as one form of "Screw Me" enveloped another. But it was the last mantra in particular that stunned her into the reality that all these negatives might have occurred for a positive purpose after all—if she chose to learn from them. She realized that had she not had these troubles, she would never have developed her strength. Instead she would have continued to mirror her mom's life of a woman controlled and forlorn. At least now she mouthed the words of thanks to all her troublemakers for kicking her off the remaining-and-complaining fence, motivating her to take stock of her sorry existence and finally make changes. From the assessments in the previous chapters, Christine knew what she needed, wanted, and *deserved*. She would build on these requirements by opening the way to getting them. She knew the answer began with her vow to forgive. She was ready to open the way now.

When the subject of *thanking* a person who has been hurtful arises, a common female question is "Why must women do all the work?" The answer is simple:

> ♕ **Gilda-Gram** *Whoever is hurting must initiate the healing.*

And the reality of our gender differences is:

> ♕ **Gilda-Gram** *Life dents us. Women work to fix the dents. Men just work.*

Yes, men would rather sublimate their personal problems into their careers, while women are forever looking toward self-improvement. So if your initial reaction on this self-assessment was "I should thank *him*? No, he should thank *me*," well, maybe so, but you may wait a long time to hear him utter the words you want. In the meantime, your negative energy is holding *you* back. Isn't it time to put *your* chaos to bed?

Twenty-something Danielle wrote:

Dear Dr. Gilda:
I've been going out with my boyfriend for 2 years now and it
has become a very boring relationship. He never wants to do
anything but stay home and watch TV. I can't stand this! I'm
not saying that he needs to take me out every night, but this is
ridiculous! Also, he has gotten very rude with me in his words
and actions. I am no longer happy with him. But I don't know
how to break it off because I'm scared I might be doing the
wrong thing. Please help me.

One reason we remain in unhealthy relationships is that we are afraid of the possibility of having no one to love us. Instead of worrying about how we will be *without*, consider how much *richer* our life could be with someone who supports us. Thank the negative person in your life for having brought you this far. Then leave. You have gained the strength to finally determine what you *don't* want. Now you are ready to accept what you not only *do* want, but what you realize you *deserve* to get.

How does the transition from hurt to harmony come about? Think of the people in your life who have given you the hardest time. Didn't they motivate you to change? Didn't you eventually find that the change was always for the better? If not for an incompetent school administrator I worked with, I would still be a miserable civil servant, teaching in the classrooms of the South Bronx rather than influencing millions of people today on TV. Now, not only do I forgive this man, I actually *thank* him for doing me such a favor. Unfortunately, or perhaps fortunately, where there's no pain, there can be no gain. Understanding this makes us better aware of the reasons for our down time. It makes it easier for us to shorten the hurt and lengthen the love.

Nonetheless, forgiveness is a difficult human undertaking because of its enormous emotional impact. An injury to our soul can bring about shock, confusion, anger, and self-blame. We may be entitled to our resentment. But it is important to recognize that forgiving can serve to release us—not just the person we forgive—from the burden of continuing these feelings. Forgive . . . and one day it won't hurt so much to remember. Remembering without anger is key. We must remember to protect ourselves from similar incidents in the future. Remember to say "No." Remember not to wait a full 12 Steps, but to get up and get out after you've tried everything and the relationship is still not good. Ahhh . . . freedom. It is the freedom not only of now being able to *find* a better partner, it is the freedom to *be* a better partner.

But what if you are one of those women who absolutely doesn't want to let her perpetrator off the hook? Although you don't want to see him get away with how much he hurt you, you may be unconsciously feeling the need to maintain your connection because:

👑 **Gilda-Gram** *Not forgiving someone is just another way of remaining together.*

Contrary to popular belief, anger does not keep us separated; it keeps us together. Caitlin took many angry years to get divorced even though she knew the marriage was not good. Originally she said she remained because of the children. Then she blamed it on their inability to reach a property settlement. Most people prefer to hang on to the devil they know rather than connect with some unfamiliar new version they are yet to meet. Nora, another divorcée, finally signed the legal papers, but she immediately went through withdrawal and depression. For all those years, the turmoil that she and her husband experienced had kept the two of them adjoined. Now, at last, she's actually divorced from the guy, but she's still wedded to the memory . . . and although physically apart, she may never leave him emotionally. Evelyn took five years to leave a six-year marriage. The issues they debated included the usual money and property settlements, but it also extended to custody of the dog. They tangoed from mediation to litigation, but their negative emotions cemented their strong connection through the ordeal. Now they both live in apartments in the same building. Some disconnection!

Finally—and the only viable reason for not forgiving is this last one—we fear we will be hurt again, and our continued emotional turmoil is our protection even from ourselves. While this is a valid fear, and a good excuse to remain upset with someone, it is also too draining. Ask yourself if you want to feel spent for the rest of your life. Putting someone totally to rest is far healthier than having him continue to contaminate your thoughts because:

👑 **Gilda-Gram** *What we think about, we bring about.*

Test this "think about, bring about" Gilda-Gram by doing The Thought Test Arm Extension:

The Thought Test Arm Extension

- Extend your dominant arm to the side and make a fist.
- Have someone face you. With as much force as possible, have that person attempt to push your arm down with his/her outstretched hand. *(Note that he will not be able to budge your arm.)*

- Leave your arm outstretched. Close your eyes and repeat ten times, **"I am weak and I am worthless."**
- Open your eyes.
- Have the other person attempt to push your arm down again. Resist as hard as you can. *(Note all your strength leave your body.)*
- Try the exercise again. This time change the words you say to **"I am strong and I am worthy."** *(Notice how you regain your strength.)*

Our positive thoughts make us physically strong. They empower us and make us rich. Our negative thoughts make us physically weak. They limit us and make us poor. There is no judgment a woman can pass that is more significant than the one she passes on herself. So unless you're convinced that you really want him out of your life, your continued consideration of him will loom in your mind until you dismantle it. Is he worth your time and energy? What great activities could you be involved in instead?

When we choose to let go, it is not another person's *action* we forgive; it's the *judgment* we've made about that action. We can either forgive and forget it or forever hold a grudge. We have a choice about this and can decide ourselves how we perceive our hurt.

👑 Gilda-Gram *There are no victims, only volunteers.*

We can choose to be a fault finder or a love finder. Or we can be apathetic about the entire matter. Choose whether you want your negative emotions to own you or to get on with your life. As soon as you release the victim mentality of being owned by someone else's thoughts, you release yourself from bondage. Volunteer to let go. When you do, you freely allow your hurt to float toward the sunset. Then, in your next love, you can respond out of strength rather than weakness.

Forgiveness completes the past for us by gently untying the knot around our heart. We live life forward, and we analyze it backward. It would be easier if it could be the other way around, but we have to experience the ups and downs before we can understand them. Each person who enters our life is our teacher in some way. There are no accidents, only opportunities. Let's not muddy them with mere inconsequentials.

Healing a relationship is a unilateral choice: yours alone. And you can be downright *selfish* in your determination to heal because:

👑 Gilda-Gram *When you heal your relationship with someone else, you heal your relationship with yourself.*

All that you must remember, and keep remembering, is that you *deserve* top-notch treatment, but it has to begin with your receiving such treatment from yourself.

In chapter 5 we questioned your use of Like-Me Language. We noted the importance of projecting respect and thereby reflecting respect. The question of how a woman respects herself is reflected by the man she chooses. When you have forgiven one who has hurt you, your floodgates open to receive one who is as respectful of you as you are of yourself. Begin your process by receiving answers to questions you are finally willing to ask *yourself*.

Ask Better Questions of Yourself— and Receive Better Answers

Many times women ask themselves the wrong questions. Wrong questions bring the wrong answers, and the wrong answers lead to needless anger and frustration. From the women I meet and the letters I receive, these are the top ten Bad Questions women ask about their relationships with men. Which of these questions do you find familiar?

Ten Bad Questions Women Ask— and the Ten Better Questions We Should Ask Instead

1. **Bad Question:** "Why didn't he call when he said he would?"
   Better Question: "Did he promise to call? I was so busy with my life, I don't even remember."
A woman who is living a passionate life will not live from moment to moment awaiting a phone call. Males and females suffer from a time differential, where a guy may say, "I'll call you," and mean "when I've straightened out my life." A woman takes "I'll call you" literally and often waits impatiently. If she is dependent on this promise for her sustenance, she denies herself her own life adventures. If your heart has stopped beating by the phone, get a life! We become so much more attractive when our availability is scarce.

Robert met Eleanor at a popular New York restaurant. After a fabulous first date, he promised he'd call during the next week. The call never came, but Eleanor, while mildly disappointed about it, was so wrapped up in her work, she proceeded to live her life with her usual humor and passion. When Robert did call during the second week, he began the call with "Is this the beautiful and vivacious Eleanor?" Recognizing her caller's voice, she responded playfully, "It depends on who's asking." Robert said, "Why? Does Eleanor have so many interested male callers?" She joked, "Oh! So many men, so little time. *Who is this?*" Robert identified himself. She offered a friendly "Hi!" He immediately launched an apology for not having called the prior week but said he was "so busy." Eleanor chided with her **Better Question**: "Did you promise to call? I forgot. I've been very busy myself." She immediately shared the woes of her workload, not even asking about his. He saw she was indifferent about his broken promise. But when he said that he was traveling to the Far East in the next week, and he'd call her from there, she joked, "If you couldn't call me from the same city, why call from Japan?" Robert teased back, "Ah, that's a low blow. . . ." But the nonchalant wit with which she dealt with this casual caller got his attention. She knew she'd hear from him from Japan—and she *did*!

Meanwhile, a recent letter asks:

> *Dear Dr. Gilda:*
> *How long does a guy normally take to call you after you give*
> *him your number? I met this guy and we had a great time. He*
> *said he'd like to get together, but then he never called. It's been*
> *3 days. Maybe I acted stupidly when we were out.*

The thing that worries me most about this letter writer is her last two sentences. "It's been 3 days." To that I respond, "Is that all?" and "Don't you have anything else to do with your time than be hung up on one guy's phone call?" The last sentence, "Maybe I acted stupidly when we were out," is also disconcerting, as she blames herself for his inattentiveness. I respond, "Why would you ever consider that he hasn't called because you acted stupidly?" Finally, I leave her with these words: "If he hasn't called, then he hasn't called. Maybe, simply, *he* is stupid for not recognizing what a fine woman you are. Or maybe he's just busy for now. In any case, get on with your life. You might also begin to concentrate on someone who appreciates you enough *not to be able to wait* to speak to you on the phone." *Click!*

2. Bad Question: "Why is he afraid to commit?"

Better Question: "Do I somehow threaten his independence?"

Women so often pressure a guy to commit when he's not ready that he becomes frightened and runs in the opposite direction. If you're in a relationship now that seems to be going nowhere, ask yourself where you want it to go: to cohabitation? to the altar? to the baby-making factory? Give yourself a make-it-or-break-it deadline. In fairness to the relationship, and without putting pressure on your man, choose a date that is realistic and fair. Wait it out while you continue to enjoy your partnership. At your agreed-upon time, let him know what you want. You have discarded being a "nice" woman for being an "honest" woman, and you have set your boundaries. If he offers a compromise when you want a commitment, that's an answer for you to determine your next step. But if he tells you he, too, wants a commitment, arrive at a mutually-agreed-upon date. Keep to that date. If your partner doesn't meet it, move on. You have a life, so honor it according to your preferences. You've given the timeline your best shot, you've offered him leeway, and his behavior has shown you what he will do. While talk may be cheap, behavior tells all.

Cathy and Jay were seeing each other for two years. It was time, Cathy reasoned, for this guy to own up to sharing a future together. Jay often told Cathy how much he loved her, but his first wife had left him after twenty years of what he thought was a happy marriage, telling him that he now "bored" her. He was terrified of being abandoned again. So although he adored his new woman, he was reluctant to enter into another painful liaison. Meanwhile Cathy was becoming impatient. She told her friends that she was quickly coming to the end of her rope. This guy, she said, had better commit. Her friends reasoned that he *had* indeed committed. He upheld their monogamous relationship, he took her three children on camping trips, and he included Cathy at all his workplace parties. To the world, they were an item. To Cathy they were a couple with a questionable future.

Whenever Cathy pressed him for more, Jay often ran home to his own apartment for defense. He was, without a doubt, terrified, and he needed to take comfort in his cave. When she asked her **Better Question**, she realized that she was exacerbating his fears with her pressure. In her mind, she gave *herself* a deadline and stuck to that as the time she'd deliver an ultimatum with another deadline to Jay. When that date arrived, she calmly and strategically told him what she wanted. Since she had been planning her speech for several months, she was direct and to the point, avoiding the usual emotion that sent him flying. Jay smoothly accepted Cathy's message. She was now willing to let the entire matter go. Jay would have to work out the issue himself. When the time actually did come, Jay moved in, and now they are planning their wedding. By letting go, Cathy allowed Jay to realize *in his own time* and *at his own pace* how much he loved this woman. But if the story had not turned out this well, Cathy was determined to pack in the romance and take her suitcase elsewhere.

3. Bad Question: "How do all these losers find me?"
   Better Question: "What payoffs do I derive from magnetizing jerks?"
Whenever we attract someone into our life, there are mutual payoffs. If a woman continues to magnetize men to her who are out of work, whom she must support, she must examine if her caretaking of them gives her a sense

of feeling superior and in control. Is she mirroring what she saw growing up in her house, giving her a false sense of comfort with the familiar? Or maybe she learned somewhere that a man's acting out translates to his being strong. The most salient thing to remember is that whoever we are attracting is providing us with some payoffs; otherwise, we would not be there. It is for us to discover what these payoffs are and whether the payoffs are really payouts, with a price that is too steep. When we understand the cost, we can lose the loser without feeling a loss.

Remember, for years Christine whined how everyone took advantage of her. She bemoaned the imaginary "Screw Me" sign emblazoned on her chest. Yet never did she imagine that she complained—but remained—*because of the benefits she derived from each painful, yet profitable, entanglement.* Sure, she was overweight, her kids were out of control, her husband was a bully, and her clients did not pay. But one by one, she finally examined the *payoffs* she reaped from each predicament. Her **Better Question** asked what they were. To her dismay, she discovered that her weight protected her from getting intimate with her horrible husband. Her out-of-control kids prevented her from keeping reliable nannies so that she could save the day in Supermom style and thereby feel important. Her husband's bullying mirrored the false comfort she derived from the familiar parental relationship she observed. Her clients avoiding payment demonstrated her deserve level at an all-time low. These were not easy answers, especially since they pointed to her overall desperation to be *liked*. But once she was open to receive the information she gleaned, she could at last reclaim her life.

4. Bad Question: "Why does he upset me?"
   Better Question: "Why do I not only allow him to push my buttons, but hand him a direction manual?"
As soon as we become upset about someone's behavior, we hand him the remote control to our heartstrings. With it, he is free to pull and pluck them as he wishes, we the marionettes at his hand. We are no longer the proud owners of our emotions. When we instead walk away and let him resolve his own issues, we can use our energy to satisfy our goals. Meeting our goals is the reason we are on this earth and the only pathway to our growth. After our goals are met, we can combine our resources to problem-solve together.

Marisa went out with Frank as often as he called. She saw him perhaps twice a month, and she enjoyed his company more each time they were together. They had probably become intimate too soon, she reasoned, and now she found that she missed him when he wasn't around. He traveled extensively and often griped about his unruly life.

Marisa was invited to the wedding of a special person in her life. Appreciating Frank's busy schedule, she asked him a month in advance to escort her. From nowhere he responded, "With any luck I'll be out of town that weekend." She was shocked by his cruel and caustic reply. Without thinking she shot back, "Fuck you!" Now he was shocked. He laughed uncomfortably. Then he offered sheepishly, "I have other plans on that date." She was silent. Uncomfortably, he filled the space with another excuse: "Maybe I'll visit my son on the other side of the country." Angry over his dispassion, she quickly ended the conversation and hung up.

At first, Marisa's question was why this man upset her. Her **Better Question** became why she *allowed* him the power to penetrate her emotions. Her response was surprising even to her. Her intimacy with Frank had obviously accelerated her level of oxytocin, and the "relationship glue" adhered her to this man more than she believed could be possible. She knew this was more a woman's issue than a man's. But she also recognized that she *needed* to take care of herself to avoid such diminished emotional control in the future. She vowed to refrain from sex with Frank unless their relationship took a turn toward deeper meaning. That remained to be seen.

5. Bad Question: "Why can't he see how wrong he is?"
   Better Question: "Why must I be his teacher and preacher?"
Life has few black and white answers, which leaves us with a lot of gray to sift through. When you are part of a team, you must let go of your need to be right. We process our decisions through our own experiences, socioeconomics, education, upbringing, religion, political bent, gender, and momentary mood. To solve a problem, each person must do the necessary research that is right for him or her. For example, you might insist your man give up a bad habit, but if he is determined to continue, you can't save him. Although your insight might be helpful, he would probably consider it more if you offered it as a measly suggestion, not a directive. Overall, your job is to concentrate on your own life, where your efforts will place you on the next step of your growth.

Many years ago I was involved with a heavy smoker. When we met, I was struck by the filthy, unemptied ashtrays throughout his apartment. His clothes stank from the odor, the apartment reeked, and his kisses were punctuated with breath mints, mouthwash, and toothpaste. Besides these environmental perils, smoking, we all know, is bad for our health. I loved this man to pieces, and I wanted him to survive. Besides, with my psychological insight, a sometimes offputting occupational hazard, I reasoned that he would be incapable of fully loving me unless he could initiate his own caretaking. So I began my Mother Teresa salvation. I kicked my man out of the house when he needed a butt, I enrolled him in stop smoking classes, I set up appointments for him with acupuncturists, I hung color photographs of dirty lungs on the mirror where he shaved, I cried when I caught him "falling off the wagon." Notice, it was I, I, I. *I* did everything in *my* power to save this man from himself. When I finally came upon the **Better Question**, the information I received made me aware that I needed to save *him* because I was too scared to invest time in saving myself. Okay, amid some resistance, I got it. I let go. Freedom from his concerns induced my independence. I enrolled in graduate school for my mind and joined a health club for my body. I began to caretake *me* rather than someone else. Years later, when *my man* was ready, he decided to quit, cold turkey. Sometimes in our life we get a wake-up call. We choose either to answer the phone or not. This time it was not I on the other end of the receiver. It took only a ten-session course for *my beloved himself* to cease his lifelong habit. He had finally saved himself.

This issue of being the savior continues to plague many women and often smacks of overfunctioning as well. From a radio show I did titled *How NOT to Date Jerks* came this question:

> *Woman: My boyfriend is an alcoholic and smokes dope. Sometimes I feel that he likes his addictions more than he likes me. What should I do?*

> *Dr. Gilda: Now that's a jerk. This guy is dependent. Why do you want to be with such a jerk? Don't you think you deserve more? Substance abuse is a tough habit to kick. If you continue with him, you're the jerk. Make a better life for yourself by attracting someone who treats you better than he does his drugs and alcohol.*

But this woman wouldn't give up. Later in the show she responded:

> *Woman: You told me to lose this guy. But since I care a lot about him, shouldn't I try to save him? Why should I just give up?*

> *Dr. Gilda: Oh, pleeeeeease! For all us women out there who have tried to save our men, here's the big question, "Who's gonna save us?" I've been there and done that myself. Nobody can save anyone else. This is a drug-dependent guy, and you already feel that your needs are going unmet. Do you wanna be Nurse Nancy forever? Helloooo! Yes, I recommend you lose him—and instead find you.*

Now that I am single again, when a man says he needs to do this or wants to do that, I tell him simply, "So do it." I am responsive to his needs, but I don't feel responsible for them. I will not do my partner's emotional work for him. I have at last abdicated my role as savior.

6. Bad Question: "How can I get him to love me?"
   Better Question: "Why must I *manipulate* anyone to get love?"
No one can get anyone to do anything. Even if this were possible, why should we have to get someone to love us? Our best shot is to enhance who we are and let the chips fall as they may. If he's going to come around, he will. If you're into your own life, you won't be waiting till he does. Explore all your options, date as many people as you like, and go to as many varied functions as possible. Sometimes while we're waiting for the person we think is "the one," we meet someone better suited for us after all. Had we sat home and pined away for the first one to love us, we would never have known.

I recently received a note from "High School Dropout, Jacqueline." Remember her from chapter 2? She admits to pining away for that "asshole," Mike, for eleven long and dismal months. She said that she continued to wait for him to come around, rearranging her schedule to be where she knew he would be, hanging out in places she thought he'd find her, and barraging him with phone calls, freely offering him sex. As miserable as she was, in the meantime she decided to recondition her body. She lost weight and began attending a health spa. She also got her GED and enrolled in college. She confesses that with each step toward personal growth, she still kept Mike's image ingrained in her mind: what would he think of her new look, would he be pleased she was attending college, would he be proud to walk down the street with her?
   One day, during her desperate yearning, she bumped into a guy she had briefly known when they were both in high school. Jacqueline was amazed at how he had matured. He at once was taken with the new and improved Jacqueline. They began to date. And Jacqueline began to open her eyes. Her **Better Question** was now "Why waste my time over someone not interested in me?" It had been eight months. When I asked about her prior obsession over Mike, this once crazed woman asked, "Mike *who*?" Clearly she learned the futility of love through manipulation. If love is not mutual, it's obsession. Obsession is built on *need* rather than on *want*. *Need* projects desperation; *want* projects power. Our power propels us to invest in our assets. When we do, a worthy man is willing to invest in *us*.

7. Bad Question: "Why won't he leave her?"
   Better Question: "What do I find attractive about an unavailable man?"
When a woman pursues a man who belongs to someone else, she may fear

intimacy herself. Or she may want to create a fantasy triangle where she will come out the winner, replaying the childhood roles of mommy, daddy, and baby-makes-three. Being the winner would make her feel mighty. Neither of these possibilities is healthy, because in the first case, most "other" women must constantly play to their married man's schedule, as their own lives are insignificant. In the second case, if a woman does win a married man away from his wife, the winner ends up with a booby prize she can't trust. Trust is the ability to count on your partner as you count on yourself. If he's a guy who's cheated before, what's to say he won't repeat his disloyalty? How can this woman ever be sure? Women who pursue unavailable men must discover the reason they avoid someone of their own. It usually centers around what a woman believes she deserves.

Paula decided that she did not want to fall into the traditional wifely category like her mother. She noted how her father had left the family after the overwhelming responsibility of two kids and a whopping mortgage. As she watched her mom cry for years, she vowed never to put herself in the similar position of feeling abandoned. So she chose to devote her "career" to her married lover. The never-knowing-the-schedule suspense was "oh so exciting" that Paula was sure it was love. She anxiously awaited the day he would leave his wife. Meanwhile she just kept giving to and doing for this man she adored. Although she herself did not have an advanced degree, she wrote each term paper he needed to get his master's degree and admitted that she would even take his exams were that possible. When her concerned friends asked about his wife, she said that she never wanted to know. She was happy with things as they were.

Eighteen years (that's right; you've read this correctly) down the road, her dreamboat sank and the life she planned with her man went out to sea. He told her he had tired of her, it was great, but he was staying at home where he belonged. *He could not leave his devoted wife after all.* Paula wanted to die. Instead, she developed breast cancer and at least toyed with the idea. Had she asked the **Better Question** early on, she would have seen that her submission to an unavailable man was simply her desire to avoid pain similar to her mother's. However, in this case it is questionable whether Paula would have accepted the information she received. Sometimes it takes a shock to our system to get us to realize the truth.

8. Bad Question: "Why won't he change?"
   Better Question: "Why can't I accept him as he was when we met?"
Women are forever seeking a guy for his potential, whether it's his earning capacity, his ability to be more sensitive, or his willingness to someday be committed. In all my years of working with women, I'm convinced we have

a special gene called "change-'em." Well, here's a flash, ladies. You know those dresses on the rack marked "As Is"? The way you find the guy hanging on the rack is the way he is. Nothing more, nothing less. Nobody changes because someone else wants him to. Change and growth are motivated and initiated by the person himself, if and when he finds the need. So look clearly at the rack and get off his back. Your need to change him is arrogant. Save your energies for bringing yourself up to par. Could be you'll attract someone worthier than the one who arrived with all these flaws and foibles.

Unlike Question #5, in which a woman may seek to become her man's *savior*, this is an issue of alteration for alteration's sake. In chapter 2 we met eight perfectly rational women, young and old, rich and poor, who believed that frogs do *change* into princes. Princess Di believed her real-life prince would leave Camilla; clerical worker Selena believed the guy who didn't care would cough up renewed interest; teacher Caitlin longed for Lou to grow up; secretary Karla hoped her Casanova con man would reform; a baby with a baby Shimeika believed her street-smart boyfriend would accept the responsibility of fatherhood; high school dropout Jacqueline convinced herself that user Mike would come around; corporate president Alice thought her lover would change his womanizing ways. Then there's Christine, who continues to hold out hope that Howard will get kinder and gentler, even in the face of her realizations about the changes she needs to make in herself. Eight women, different lives, all with the same dream—that someday their prince would come . . . *around*. In every case, the handwriting on the wall was inscribed in indelible ink. In every case, the woman thought she could *change him* to be better.

The desire of women to change their men has become a national epidemic. It falsely promises our gender, traditionally of lesser status, alleged control. Not over *our* lives, where it should be, but over *our man's*. When we ask the **Better Question**, we may discover that if we really wanted *this man*, we would not want to change him into something—or someone—else. For many women, finding *a man* represents the mistaken notion of having *any man* to show the world we're loved. It is about time that women exchange this evil influence of the External Control mechanism for a hefty dose of our own Internal standards. Otherwise the nineties divorce rate will reach its predicted high of 67 percent, with a couple splitting every twenty-six seconds!

Complete Self-Assessment #21 and discover what motivates you to have a man.

SELF-ASSESSMENT #21

WHAT MOTIVATES MY DESIRE FOR A MAN?

Which of these most represents what you desire? Repeat each of the following statements, accentuating the emphasized word as it is written:

1. I *want* a man.
2. I want *a* man.
3. I want a *man*.

ANALYSIS

Statement #1 stresses that you want a man in your life more than most other things.

Statement #2 suggests that any man will do.

Statement #3 asserts that you want someone with male attributes—for whatever your purpose.

There are no right answers. This is just an indication of where you stand.

Each of these statements emphasizes a different reason you would like a man in your life. No matter what your reason, however, a man must represent an enrichment to the already strong you, not someone you lean on to make you stronger. If you are dating someone, ask, "Is it okay to just date this person casually, or do I want a full-fledged relationship?" It's your choice. If you are already in a relationship, ask, "Does this man *enrich* my life, or is he just someone I want to be seen with?" Conclude this self-assessment by answering, "Is it love I want, or is it my fear of being alone that attracts me to my partner?"

For once and for all, our men may be dense when it comes to dealing with us, but they certainly aren't stupid. No man wants to feel that he is being used to prove a woman is lovable. Women must choose the man they want on the basis of who he is. But to do that, they must first accept themselves for who *they* are. When women are satisfied with their own power and how to project it, they will be able to receive the goodness of worthwhile men. No alterations needed. End of story.

9. Bad Question: "Why does he take me for granted?"
   Better Question: "How can I assert my boundaries so I give myself what I need?"

Do you find yourself adjusting your life to meet his demands? Do you hurriedly drop your plans to be available for his? How can he even know what your goals are if your goals have become his goals? At the beginning, tell him what you need and want. Plan your goals in pencil, but be sure to use the eraser only when you need to meet your own desires. Once he respects you and your boundaries, he will stop taking you for granted. By doing what turns you on, you'll be sending the message that you count. It's tough to take anyone for granted when their presence is pronounced.

One of Christine's marital issues has been her husband's demand that she adjust her life according to his. From forbidding her to have friends to instructing her when to cook meals, the problem is less that he *commands*, but more that she *complies*. Part of Christine's "Screw Me" communication is that she accepts, and thereby teaches people, that it's okay to take her for granted. A responsible Overfunctioner, she has always been there, has always been prompt, has always been giving. Remember, before completing the self-assessments, she thought that *selfish* was a swear word used against women who didn't obey. Until now, she really didn't know any better.

As much as Eleanor in Question 1 molded Robert's calling behavior, and Cathy in Question 2 pressed Jay to commit, and Marisa in Question 4 closed the bedroom door on revisits by the old Frank, Christine had to learn that people took her for granted simply because she *let them*. Her **Better Question** showed her that if things were to change, it was she who had to design and delineate boundaries in bold hues, unwashable by her first predictable tears. She recognized that at first her noncompliance would be met with anger. But she now knew that others' external motives mattered less than her own internal drives. Although Christine naturally feared making these daring changes, she also acknowledged her deep unhappiness and exhaustion. It was time. She was ready to state and stand by her boundaries. She prayed she had the strength to overcome her years of subservience.

10. Bad Question: "Why doesn't he share his feelings?"
   Better Question: "Do I make it safe for him to be vulnerable?"
When men have a problem, unlike women, they don't want to discuss it. Instead they retreat to where they can be left alone to resolve it themselves. The way the male brain works is to block out emotional interference and unscramble issues logically, step-by-step. When your man is visibly upset, although it might require much resistance on your part, let him be. Allow him his privacy, however long it takes. Without pressure, invite him to share what's on his mind when he is ready. Once you pave the way according to his timing and comfort level, he will open up. When he does, it will be because he feels safe.

Cliff's entire department had already been downsized, and at any moment, he feared, he would be the next to be pink-slipped. He had been married to Georgia for six years, and he had proudly formed the union believing it was his obligation, just as it had been his father's, to support his wife and family. Georgia did not work but stayed at home with their three-year-old son. She left the household finances to her husband.

The day of workplace reckoning finally did arrive. But Cliff could not get himself to tell Georgia the truth. He hoped that by the time she found out, he would have secured an even better position at another organization. So, committed to living the lie for as long as he could get away with it, he dressed for work each morning and left the house at his usual time. He spent his days reading want ads at the park, secretly going on interviews, or simply sitting in the library, researching job leads. He didn't know what he was going to do, but he surely wanted to protect his wife from the fear of financial ruin. He also recognized that eventually he would have to tell the truth.

As checks began to bounce, Georgia tried to confront Cliff, but he shut down. Georgia was unwilling to give up. As ignored women often do, Georgia began to follow her husband around their apartment and nail him with more probing questions. But she noticed that this technique caused her man to close down even more. Finally unable to get his attention, Georgia replaced her Bad Question about her husband's distancing with a **Better Question**. In desperation, she now decided to wait it out. She said affectionately, "Cliff, I love you. I know there's something going on. Please let me know what it is as soon as you feel comfortable discussing it." While women need to feel safe before they have sex, men need security before sharing their feelings. So if a woman wants to get to the heart of her tin man, her job is to warm him up before she wears him out. Georgia downplayed her own fears and reiterated their team effort in working out whatever it was. This allowed Cliff to get off his macho stance and open up. It wasn't immediate, but within the next two weeks he revealed the disappointing news. When she immediately offered to get a part-time job until he reconnected with another employer, he was sorry he had not leveled with her sooner. Women have to learn that when a man closes down, it has nothing to do with us. It is their process, and they must be left to explore it on their own. Just another reason for a woman to have her own life in which she's involved and passionate.

All ten Better Questions have one thing in common: they place the woman as keeper of her own castle. To ensure that the castle remains yours, become comfortable with the differences between the Bad and Better Questions. Feel self-centered as you receive the information that you need. Your power is your insurance policy against weak and worthless men.

Ask these Ten Better Questions of yourself without involving your lover. Practice reading each one aloud. Really receive your responses. The Chinese characters of the verb "to listen" include your ears, eyes, heart, undivided attention, and *you*. After you include all five of these elements in listening to yourself, you can ask artful questions and listen to your man. Listening is the nicest thing you can do for someone.

Ask Artful Questions of Your Man— and Receive His Honesty

If the first step to receiving is giving to yourself, the second is forgiving in order to make way for your man's generosity, and the third is to ask solid questions of yourself, then the fourth is to ask artful questions to get the lowdown on your man. Artful questions center around his family relationships, love history, reasons for breakups, morals, values, and attitudes about love, commitment, and personal goals.

The trouble is that most women's questions to men are based on our insecurity in the relationship. But when our man tells us something we don't like, we feel hurt, we get angry, we scream, we cry, we defend ourselves. We fear abandonment so much that we think anything he says that is less than loving must be cause for splitting. After our reaction, our man doesn't want to risk the aggravation of leveling with us again and ending up in the doghouse.

If this guy ever does trust us with his info again, he may decide to brighten the truth just to keep us quiet. For instance, since part of the Toastmaster's smiley-face syndrome is to want to hear good, happy things, a man unquestionably will feel pressure to say something nice, even if he doesn't mean it. How irritating! Unfortunately, that's what happens when women desperately press to know and men vehemently refrain from telling.

Women often cannot balance their need for information with the need to let a man divulge his truths at *his* pace. When we ask too much too soon, we are accused of being Curious Georgette, trying to penetrate the guy's protective facade. His "Danger!" sign flashes and he clams up. But instead of backing off, we become Attila the Hun and ravage the guy's privacy more forcefully. With the threat of our permeating and puncturing, he runs for the hills. There may be another, seemingly more placid woman waiting there. But if she doesn't ask probing questions *at first*, don't worry, that will change in time because no woman will tolerate a distancing man for long. As she begins to fuse toward him, he is astounded by the way she resembles the one he left behind. In fact, he might even find himself longing for the one he left behind. This "should I go, should I stay" dilemma is the porcupine's dance of push and pull.

The porcupine is an animal whose back is covered by fifteen thousand to thirty thousand barbed quills that can be driven a half inch or more into flesh. As one porcupine tries to survive a cold winter, he huddles with another for warmth. However, each animal's sharp quills prick the other, so they quickly pull away. But then they become cold again, so they return to their huddle. Porcupines keep adjusting their distance to keep from freezing but also to save themselves from getting pricked. Men and women relate the same way.

Like porcupines' quills, male/female communication is both comforting and painful. Both women and men push to get close as they start their relationship, but often the man feels engulfed as he senses that the woman has encroached on his comfort zone. He pulls away to maintain his territory. But missing the warmth he once knew, he returns for sustenance. The couple continues the dance, continually adjusting the temperature of their love.

While a man self-protects by closing in, a woman protects herself by opening up. She longs to discover more about her man. That requires asking questions. Receiving his answers about family background, morals, values, love history, reasons for breakups, and his attitudes about love, commitment, and goals gives her the feeling of becoming closer to him, more intimate, and more secure.

Those women unwilling to receive honest answers to questions at the beginning of a relationship perpetuate the dance as the relationship unfolds. Openness, then, becomes the forbidden fruit instead of a means of protecting a woman's investment in a relationship and stopping her from committing too much too quickly. Infidelity is often in the wings. Why risk a man's straying when everything we need to know is right before our eyes? The answer is probably that we are not in touch with either our feelings or our fears, the ones we discovered in Self-Assessment #18. Yes, before we are ready to receive honest information, we must come face-to-face with the fears of knowing, for it is these fears that conceal our feelings. Overcoming the smiley-face syndrome is a thorny problem for most women. It certainly has been one for me. If it is still a problem for you, return to that self-assessment and again complete the sentence that reads: "I don't show people I'm_____ because I'm frightened that_____." When you become less frightened of discovering the truth, you will be more inclined to ask questions that will tell you the worth of a man.

Whether or not her man likes it, a woman must protect herself by asking solid questions. This is not only her *right*, it's her *reward* for self-respect. It exemplifies her Pride of I-Ship, the language she applies with capital "I." It underscores her Internal Control, the drive that motivates her self-respect. It projects her Power Image, the way she communicates that she *deserves* a man of substance.

When women feel secure in asking the *right* questions, we can receive information as to whether a guy is interested in buying or just in browsing.

If a guy is defensive about responding, there is a reason. If his stories don't jibe, we must discover why. The *way* he answers gives us cues about whether something is missing, if he's sending mixed messages by saying and behaving in different ways, and even if he's willing to be open.

When Claudette first met Harold, a Frenchman, she found herself overwhelmed by his great looks and international charm. Because she was so happy that anyone so fabulous would want her, she was careful to avoid conversation that could be controversial. Claudette must have sensed, on some level, that certain topics were taboo, so she simply steered clear. Her objective was to *hook* Harold because he was a terrific *catch*. (Did you ever wonder if women were *fisherpeople* in another life?) Claudette was so determined that she would prevent anything from standing in her way. Harold had courted Claudette for less than a year when he proposed marriage. She was ecstatic. But only three years into the marriage, Claudette "accidentally" learned that Harold had been cavorting with a young *man* while he was away on his "business" trips. How could this be? As she began to review their courtship, she noticed some early signs that she had chosen to ignore, like Harold's chummy way with young males, his urgent "business meetings" that cropped up suddenly in faraway places, his altogether passive interest in sex with her. Because she wanted to see this relationship end in matrimony, she had been unwilling to ask questions that might jeopardize her future. As any woman in a long-term marriage will support, matrimony is only the beginning. For it to be a good beginning, it must be founded on solid ground. Remember, just having "the relationship" should never be your goal. Growth is.

Firm questions make informed women. As the saying goes, "Knowledge is power." To receive this knowledge, we must structure open-ended questions that involve responses of more than just one word. Open-ended questions include "How?" "Why?" "In what way?" and "What?" As a man responds, listen between the lines to get the real scoop. Silently assess the accuracy and importance of the information you are hearing.

Open-ended questions are the only way to go. To be sure you're on track, avoid other, less effective questioning devices, such as:

1. *Closed-Ended Questions:* "Who," "When," "Where," "Which," "Are," and "Do" invite abbreviated answers that could quickly cut short your research. "Who did you see when you went to the store?" or "Are your folks having their usual anniversary celebration?" or "Do you want to rent a video tonight?" are questions that many women later blame their guy for answering with monosyllabic responses. What we can control we ought not find fault with.

2. *Questions That Place a Man on the Defensive:* Be sure your style is not as probing as a job interview and as serious as a morgue. Lighten up with

humor. When his girlfriend asked a probing question, one man replied nastily, "Are you writing a book?" His lady humorously retrieved her power by responding, "Only if your story is good enough." Had she reacted angrily or hurtfully, their communication would have halted.

3. *Too Many "Why?" Questions:* These are often used not so much to derive information, but to assert power over a partner, put him down, express hidden anger, or punish. Questions like "Why can't you act more loving?" "Why don't you call when you promise to?" "Why don't you ever ask how my day went?" "Why don't you express your feelings?" "Why do you always defend your children?" "Why can't you pick up after yourself?" really don't require an answer. They are meant merely to be critical barbs at a man's behavior. Usually a man who feels so assaulted bolts.

4. *Questions with No Options:* Some questions expect a "Yes" answer without giving the other person the right to say "No." For example, "Honey, I've invited my folks over for dinner tonight. Do you mind?" will probably cause a revolt in your home as well as a withdrawn invitation.

Receiving answers to well-formulated questions is a female's prophylactic. You will have the information you need—albeit not necessarily the information you like—but enough to go on to cease forfeiting the goods as soon as you meet an attractive prince. Question asking takes time. It will slow the rush of potential partners to christen the bed. It will delay the three-date rule, where by the third date he's pressured to orchestrate a performance and you're under the gun to comply. Hormones aside, three dates is hardly long enough to know if intimacy is even an advisable option, especially in light of our three-letter fears of getting an STD and the four-letter fear of contracting AIDS.

Therefore, to get responses to valid questions, *make your bed*! Engage in nonsexual activities outside the home, and discover if your association can get a G-rating before it progresses to R. Later, if you decide to interplay to the next step, you won't be wondering if he's there for the peaks and gone for the valleys. You'll feel you are waking in a bed in which you both belong. It all comes with asking the right questions and your willingness to receive the truth.

When you are willing, the question remains as to whether he's able. How do we get our man to feel safe about the information we request? The answer is to be receptive without badgering, pouting, sulking, or punishing him if you don't like his response. If you end up violating his trust in being truthful, he will return to square one, withdrawn and protected, and you will return to the point of frustration.

Enhance Your Listening Reception— and Receive His Openness

Improving your listening reception to your man is easy if you offer him gentle feedback through the Four Steps to Prompting Male Openness. To his relief, this technique does not tell him what is wrong with him or how he should change. Rather, it offers your perceptions and describes your nonjudgmental feelings. This spurs your man to drill a hole through his airtight armor. Before you offer these steps, you should:

1. Examine your motives to be sure your intention is helpfulness, not superiority.
2. Consider your partner's readiness to hear what you are about to offer.
3. Avoid overload by focusing on only one item at a time.
4. Observe your partner's behavior to adjust your message while you are talking.
5. Invite feedback yourself.

When you are fully ready to begin, follow the four steps in sequence:

1. *Hearing.* Repeat what he said, word for word.
2. *Interpreting.* Interpret his words by what they mean to him, not to you.
3. *Evaluating.* Value his information.
4. *Responding.* Respond with ease. Because you now have the total picture, you will not react emotionally.

These four steps take no longer than a few seconds. They eliminate the "wild" emotions women are accused of demonstrating. By receiving information according to these steps, you mirror the way a man processes information himself, in a step-by-step logical progression. Remember, people appreciate people like themselves. It makes sense that if a man speaks in English, you will want to respond to him in the same tongue. By being logical yourself, you can encourage his willingness to share. A man who feels accepted chisels away at his stone wall. Isn't this what you've been complaining he hasn't done all along? Follow these four steps, but be sure to listen twice as much as you talk, using two ears to receive and one mouth to offer. And don't interrupt him, especially while he's on a roll.

This is how it works. Nathan tiredly dragged home from work. He walked in and became his usual mum self as soon as he hit the couch. When his wife, Ellen, asked about his day, he responded in a melancholy moan. He remained silent for some time. Finally, he embarrassedly began to tell her how his boss blasted him for being rude to a customer over the phone. Ellen repeated without judgment, "Your boss blasted you." (Step 1, hearing.) Nathan felt heard. He continued, "I was going to ask my boss for a raise this week. Now I don't dare." Ellen silently thought, He's worried how his rudeness will translate to our finances. (Step 2, interpreting.) Nathan went on, "I am so pissed!" Ellen thought, We all have our days, and today was one of his. He's often said his boss forgets things like this quickly. (Step 3, evaluating.) Ellen offered her thoughts out loud. She was not critical, but understanding. (Step 4, responding.) Nathan apparently felt relieved. They began dinner and dropped the subject.

Notice how, although Nathan was openly describing his day, he still spoke with few details. Most women want details and feel that if they're absent, the relationship lacks depth. After you have followed these four steps, you may want to jolt your partner's expansiveness further. If so, expand Step 4 by responding more specifically. Select any one of the following three responses to stimulate your man to tell more:

1. *The Clarifying Response.* Ask a "What," "How," or "When" question: "What does this mean?" "How are they going to . . . ?" "When will this happen?"
2. *The Accuracy Response.* Restate his facts: "So you mean that . . ."
3. *The Feelings Response.* Show you understand how your man feels about the information he is sharing. "It sounds as though you feel that you . . ." "I can understand that you are annoyed about this."

Whichever one of the three you choose, be sure your body language openly displays your receptivity by using the S-O-F-A technique.

After Step 4 of Ellen's response, before launching directly into dinner, Ellen offered, "I understand how you feel about asking for a raise now. Maybe the timing was not right. We don't need the money that badly now, and we can wait a little longer. . . ." (The feelings response.) Then she remained silent, to allow her husband to fill the space with his own feelings. He began, "The garage door needs to be replaced, and . . . I wanted to surprise you with a weekend vacation," he confided sheepishly. "We do need the money for those things." Ellen offered sympathetically, "That vacation idea is so sweet! I love your thoughtfulness, and we will take a long weekend together soon. And look, the garage door has been broken for a while, so there's no rush to fix it now. Don't worry. They like you at work. You'll get that raise—just be patient." Now Nathan felt comforted. He said, "And when I do get the raise, I want to buy you a new outfit for being so terrific." One simple feelings response instantly opened more discussion and brought the couple closer. As women do, men just want to feel their women hear them. Demonstrating our receptivity makes a world of difference in how we relate.

Trash the Male Bashing—
and Receive His Trust

We have discussed that a woman's knack for giving is not enough for her to succeed at love. She must also know how to receive, from the goodness she bestows on herself to others' generosity toward her. She must also be able to forgive. By asking for better answers, she will receive early information to prevent future heartache. Asking artful questions of her man allows him to offer her his honesty. Enhancing her listening reception allows him to offer her his openness. Now there is one final step a woman must follow, one that will open the door to receive a man's trust. This step requires that a woman stop the naming, blaming, and shaming of him that our gender has perfected to a tee. In today's parlance it's called "male bashing," and today's men are paranoid in guarding against it.

People in every relationship enter into the usual power struggles of who's in charge at different times. But it's become chic for women to point a manicured finger at someone other than themselves and name, blame, and shame him for their lackluster love and for not being man enough to make it right. We are still convinced that pushing harder will force our partner to conform and reform. But since force and fear do not entice, our partner avoids our wrath instead. He stonewalls. How interesting that men stonewall to keep their distance, and we too, stonewall by silencing our voices in an effort to get close. Either way, stone walls do not make relationships stronger. Such noncommunication serves no purpose except to erect greater barriers.

As much as we pat ourselves on the back for our deep conversations with our female friends, when it comes to men, we're not really such great communicators. Instead of announcing what we really want, we offer a litany of his faults. Maybe we don't know what the real problem is, or we aren't aware of what we are really feeling, or we aren't sure how to express ourselves without wounding him, or we're just afraid to open up for fear he'll leave. Whatever the reason, our man never learns what he can do to make us happier. By naming, blaming, and shaming, we try desperately to change him, but our attempts usually backfire, because these are nothing more than put-downs, and a man simply has to defend himself against our tongues.

Male bashing is an evil enemy that gets us the exact opposite of what we want. It focuses a magnifying glass on our man while discarding the looking glass that reflects the power that is ours. It deenergizes us, and without stamina, how can we be successful lovers? Or is it not our guy at all, but *we* who really fear intimacy?

As the earth is round, so is love, and it goes full circle. When we love our man, he in turn loves us back and chooses to be honest, open, and trusting. It depends upon how he feels we accept him into our life.

👑 **Gilda-Gram** *Receive your man:*
Lovingly with your eyes,
Thoughtfully with your mind,
Understandingly with your heart.

Like us, men want to be heard and embraced without judgment. When they feel they are safe, they will surprise even themselves by offering more. "Puss-in-Boots" Krista knew just how to do that.

Love is a two-way street. Not only does it involve giving but it also requires being able to receive gracefully. A woman must know the rules of reception, from receiving her own goodness to accepting kindness from a man. Smart women prepare themselves for the giving/receiving cycle by enunciating their strength when they are solo. In this way, they are ready to be either in or out of a relationship, and they are able to feel fine no matter what their status. That is why the next chapter deals with the enjoyment of being alone.

GILDA-GRAMS
FROM CHAPTER 6
Know How to Receive

▶ *The art of receiving begins by giving to yourself.*

▶ *When you give to yourself, others learn how you want to be treated.*

▶ *You cannot receive if you cannot forgive.*

▶ *Spend your time willing your happiness rather than willing your man's misery.*

▶ *Your will to love must be stronger than your wish to hate.*

▶ *Whoever is hurting must initiate the healing.*

▶ *Life dents us. Women work to fix the dents. Men just work.*

▶ *Not forgiving someone is just another way of remaining together.*

▶ *What we think about, we bring about.*

▶ *There are no victims, only volunteers.*

▶ *When you heal your relationship with someone else, you heal your relationship with yourself.*

▶ *Receive your man:
Lovingly with your eyes,
Thoughtfully with your mind,
Understandingly with your heart.*

7
Enjoy Being Home Alone

👑 **Gilda-Gram** *We attract not who we want but who we are.*

As disappointing as this may seem, we are not on this earth to remain as we are. Although most of us would prefer to remain stalled in our comfort zone, life is about learning. Learning is about change, and we change a lot, especially when we're in love. Love changes are particularly challenging because of the necessity for two lives that were once separate and distinct to suddenly become *inter*dependent. Now each person's individuality is called upon to meld into a new and integrated form we call "us."

It is for this reason a woman must put such effort into herself *before* she falls in love. She must be skilled in the areas we mentioned in the preceding chapters to be able to offer a solid contribution in her new union for her end of the bargain. She should be armed to ask for what she needs as she believes she deserves to get it. She should be geared to project a Power Image, combining her strong shell and naturally soft sell. She should be dedicated to preserve her emotional core while she generously gives from the overflow.

"Us" takes on new proportions that look nothing like either of the two original lovers. Just as your new bicycle may have a sturdy body, its speed depends on the support of its tires. Similarly, the success of a relationship depends on the individual strength of its two people, because even though two people are sleeping in one bed, and their hearts appear to beat as a single loving soul, in actuality there are not one or even two people any longer who need nurturing. Now the number swells to three. It consists of *you*, *me*, and *us*. And it is the adding of the "us" that makes love tricky.

While it's important to nurture all three elements of a union, it's just as vital that none of the three crosses the boundaries of the others. Brains may be sparking with opposing demands. Needs and wants may be screaming to be met. Preferences for solo, peaceful pasts might be beckoning. This is what happens when two separate lives entwine. It is a time of testing and discovery. To be sure that one person doesn't go into a swoon while the other packs a weapon, couples must recognize their differences yet somehow maintain their individuality.

During this loving time, men, traditionally fearing their loss of power, posture to hold on to it all the more. And it is during this phase that women somehow construe that their power has all along had a shelf life, and now they must submit it to their man before its expiration date. As we observed in chapter 2, no matter how beautiful, educated, wealthy, and successful a woman is in other parts of her life, most women abandon their individuality early on in the face of love.

Yes, the bond is new; yes, many men fear the loss of the freedom they once had; and yes, each partner questions what the other expects. Yet while each may prefer to downplay his or her differences, this is the time for both to honor their contrasts and get off the comfort fence. For women, especially, it is vital not to lose the "me" that attracted their man to begin with. When "me" maintains its essence and distinctness, it becomes a far more competent contributor to "us." And it is the unique and healthy "us" that makes the relationship work. For each person, it includes the balance of self-centeredness with relationship-centeredness. And for each individual, the mix is matchless to any other.

Scheduling Time Alone

When some pollsters asked 1,104 women to choose one thing they wanted more of, 15 percent selected *time alone* over extra cash or steamy sex. *Only* 15 percent? It seems that women deny themselves what they need most—to be away from their relationships and sift through the things that matter to *them*. Even when they are happy and devoted to each other, people must find time to enjoy their own company, to be totally alone.

Whether married, single, or in between, being alone teaches a woman to come to grips with the power of one. She recognizes that she can leave a relationship at any time, which thereby affords her the freedom to stay in one. After she's broken a relationship, spending time alone gives her a breather until she is ready to try again. As she observes her lonesome toothbrush and lowered toilet seat, she examines where she was when she gave her heart away. But even if she is married, alone time pushes her to collect her thoughts and concentrate on the hobbies and activities that make her happy. Since a woman's happiness is vital to attracting and becoming a worthy partner, time alone is necessary at every stage of relationship.

Time Alone at the Beginning of a Relationship

To be sure that "me" remains intact, it is essential that each woman schedule time alone at the very beginning of her relationship. Planning time alone is another test of love, because it is at this time that a woman would rather spend every waking hour with her new partner. But by maintaining her "me" from the start, she ensures that her growth milestones will not become sorrowful millstones should the relationship dissolve in the future.

Like other forms of protection discussed earlier, a woman's ability to maintain her "me" at the beginning of a love affair is an emotional condom. At first love can, indeed, conquer all, even amid distinct signs that a person may be bad for us. Because our budding hormones have us rushing in with our hearts instead of with our heads, we often choose to ignore the truth. Not giving themselves the necessary time to gain clarity, many women stay when they ought to leave. Deep down they fear that if they see too clearly— or, as we discussed, ask the right questions—their only chance at love will escape.

Sitting beside me on a TV talk show panel one afternoon was the gorgeous Janice Pennington, former hostess on *The Price is Right*. As twelve million people watched this beauty daily, no one could know the hidden nightmare her life had become. She unraveled her romantic story of meeting a handsome ski instructor in Aspen, being wooed and wowed, falling madly in *lust*, and marrying him. Suddenly, a few years into the marriage, he disappeared. After seventeen arduous years of searching—from the Kremlin to Mozambique, to Pakistan, and to Afghanistan—she finally discovered the unthinkable truth: her husband had been a spy. What feelings of betrayal! She agreed with me that the warning signs of her despicable and deceitful spouse had always been right before her, but she was so in love, she'd simply blocked them out. On the stage sat a bevy of less beautiful but similarly duped damsels in distress from all walks of life. All of them now, after the fact, admitted that the caution bells had rung while they were with their stud-turned-dud, but they allowed their ears to be permanently clogged. How sorry they were today for not having taken time out during the affair to assess the romance.

What most women eventually discover is that:

....

👑 **Gilda-Gram** *You are the only person who will never abandon you.*

....

So treat yourself well. In indelible ink, place your needs high on your list of necessities. As men find protection in escaping to their caves, protection for women comes with ridding themselves of their desperation.

Dear Dr. Gilda:
Life is miserable. I just found my unemployed-but-gorgeous
lover rifling through my wallet. He swears he wasn't doing it,
but he was standing next to my wallet, which was opened
mysteriously. I could have sworn my wallet was closed before.
Now there's money missing. Should I believe him?

Yes, as the foregoing letter confides, life *can* be miserable when you're living it with a man you can't trust. Women must learn to recognize the signs for what they are while they are occurring. The best way to do that is to take time alone to clarify the signals. When you finally realize you can live your life without a man, you will know that you can negotiate your differences with one. The most important thing to remember is that while men in your life may come and go, it is *you* who are constantly there and *you* on whom you must focus.

👑 Gilda-Gram *If you plan to love someone, recognize he could someday be gone.*

With this attitude, when you ask "What if he leaves?" you respond with "I'd go on." Relationships don't have to last forever to be profitable. From each we learn another lesson and grow another step. We carry our own currency of authenticity. We must spend it on ourselves. Accept a man as an External factor, someone whose whims you cannot control and whose ebbs and flows may influence you but won't affect you in life-shattering ways. No one else can match the magnitude of your own self-love, and you need to be alone and quiet to discover how vital it is for your sustenance.

Maureen had sensed specific signs of danger while she was being seduced by Stephen in his Chicago penthouse apartment. On the night they met, he showed her around the place he had just moved into. He explained that every bachelor who had moved into this apartment ended up getting married. *Just what every single woman longs to hear from a gorgeous guy!* The view of Lake Michigan was breathtaking, with the illuminated glass buildings and slow-moving boats reflected in the water. Stephen led Maureen in and out of each and every room, and when he reached the clothing closet, his voice crescendoed: "Isn't this a large space? This is where you would put your clothes." Silence. Although he had invited her to stay the night (on this, their first meeting), she said, "I don't think so," and left. Stephen didn't call Maureen for two weeks, claiming to have "lost her business card," although he was a highly detail-oriented Taskmaster. Unlikely, Maureen thought. More like a control gesture, since he didn't get to sleep with me last time, she figured. When he did call, he asked her to walk with him in the park during the afternoon, but it was Sunday and she had already made plans, so she declined gracefully, telling him to give her more advance notice next time.

In his "busy schedule," he somehow found time to call her during the week. She agreed to have dinner with him, which was terrific. In her car, before she drove home, they spoke for about an hour and kissed lovingly. When sparks began flying, she said, "Look, before I give my body away, I want to know what you're all about, what you like to do, what you can't stand, the things that piss you off, your plans, your goals, your needs."

His response told the whole story: "I know women want to know those things, but I don't feel the same about having to get to know a woman that well before intimacy. What are we going to do?"

"I guess each of us will have to give a little if we want to go to the next step," said Maureen. Somewhere in her impassioned mind, she either didn't believe Stephen or she felt that she could get him to change his mind. The old "change-'em" gene at work again! But in so many words, Stephen had told Maureen that all he was interested in was a short-term roll in the hay. She chose instead to concentrate on his "marriage" and "closet" comments. A schmoozer, a user, and an all-time loser. If only Maureen had taken some time alone to listen to the truth.

👑 **Gilda-Gram** *Love at first sight is lust with potential. But we need time alone to sort it through.*

No woman need suffer from lust blindness. Every woman must open her awareness to the signposts that already loom large and visualize what life would be like some years down the road if she stays—and fill each pothole as she finds it. But she cannot be objective when she is constantly with her lover. This is work she must complete alone.

Whether you are just starting, or in the midst of a relationship, complete Self-Assessment #22 to open your awareness about the man you love when you met him. See if you glean additional insight into the person he now is.

SELF-ASSESSMENT #22

TEN-POINT CHECK-YOUR-MATE

Mark Yes or No beside each of the following statements:

_____ **1.** Is he still angry with his ex? with anyone in his family?

_____ **2.** Does he hide behind a mask of humor?

_____ **3.** Does he talk only about himself without asking about you?

_____ **4.** Does he never talk about himself and ask only about you?

_____ **5.** Do you find his friends irritating?

_____ **6.** Do you find his values upsetting?

_____ **7.** Does he criticize you? Does this put you on the defensive?

_____ **8.** Does he confide in others instead of confiding in you?

_____ **9.** Does he refuse to apologize?

_____**10.** Is he rude to service people and other strangers he doesn't have to impress?

SCORING KEY

Count your Yes responses: 1–2 = Proceed, but with caution; 3+ = Get out while you can.

If you are already involved with this guy, use this self-assessment to follow the path you are now on together. Decide what is truly important to you now.

When corporate president Alice did this self-assessment, although it was after she and Mark had split, she discovered some truths that she said would have been helpful before she wasted so many years of her life waiting for him. She recognized that he was still angry with his ex (Item 1), he rarely asked about her (Item 3), she found his friends irritating and his political values upsetting (Items 5 and 6), she noted how he often criticized her baggy clothes and light makeup in his effort to transform her into the airbrushed type of woman he preferred (Item 7), and he was consistently rude to waiters and doormen, whom he looked upon as "lowlifes" (Item 10). Alice counted six specific items about Mark that were wrong for her. She pledged to be more aware of these issues the next time she loved.

Know Your Heartfelt Passions

These ten assessment items work fine if you're sadly single and ready to change the channel. But maybe you're not beginning a new romance. Maybe you've been dismally dumped. Or maybe you want to boot the bozo out of your life. Maybe you're in a relationship with a wuss who won't commit. Perhaps you're boringly wedded to couch-potato complacency. Or you've already stitched the scarlet letter _A_ on your chest with crimson guilt. Or you simply want to send your beau off with a sandwich for no particular reason. Whatever your situation, _stop_! Finding and keeping someone to love has eclipsed the fact that you already have someone. _Look in the mirror._ Have you forgotten her? Accept her, love her, want her, reward her, warts and all. She, and not a man, must be your _primary passion_. You've already written a commercial for her. Now it's time to *buy* what she's selling. In short, *make that woman in the mirror your passion*. And let your passion about yourself dictate the activities you are passionate about performing.

No matter where you are on the relationship roller coaster, decide which activities propel you into personal distraction. If these included "a man," or anything else External, now you will have another chance to re-vamp your Internal Control mechanism. You can no longer afford to be influenced by his achievements, to be unsure of how to feel until you've gauged his mood, to place a man center stage while you live in his shadow. Yes, what are *your* passions? We're talking here about the heat that hurls you to follow your heart. Everyone needs new ways to dream, and now is the time to discover yours. Shake, stir, presto, chango. Your internal light may have inadvertently gone out, but it will be easy to re-trieve after you complete Self-Assessment #23. Do this exercise and look at yourself in a way you've probably long forgotten exists.

SELF-ASSESSMENT #23

PROBING YOUR PASSIONS

Quickly list five examples of passions you feel in each of the following categories:

1. HEALTH
2. SOCIAL
3. SELF-IMPROVEMENT
4. SPIRITUAL
5. FINANCIAL
6. FAMILY

There are no right or wrong answers. Your objective is to recognize your heart's desires and to see whether you are honoring them. If you are not, why not?

Leaving any of these categories blank suggests that there is a void of some kind in your life. *Health* passions include enthusiasm for eating and exercising well, taking care of our inner and outer housing. *Social* passions include recreational and play activities, time when we vacation or "vacate" our usual routines to explore new adventures. *Self-improvement* passions include things we do for ourselves, rewards we give ourselves, and time we spend alone in peace and harmony. *Spiritual* passions include how we honor our beliefs and others', and offerings we give and receive, both of which are equally important. *Financial* passions include short- and long-term money and investment plans, managing the nuts and bolts that maintain our security, and assessing our abundance. *Family* passions include the time and activities we devote to people who matter to us most, people who may not necessarily be our blood relatives but who are the folks we include nearest our heart. Expand these six categories to include any additional passions you find important. Pursuing your passions differs from pursuing your goals. Goals are "gotta do" items often legislated by others. Passions are "love to do" items motivated and directed by ourselves. When you "choose to" rather than "have to" enjoy yourself, your success ratio soars.

For each passion category, paint a picture in your mind of what you *want*. For example, in the Social realm, you may have a passion for elegant parties, for walks on moonlit beaches, for drinks with friends on a seaside veranda. These are the passions you must pursue. When you follow your fervent desires, you will establish friendships with people who share them. So while you enjoy the things you love, you meet and mingle with folks who love them, too. Picture the end result and how it *feels* to achieve it. Will you be a happier and more complete person after you accomplish this passion? You already know the answer.

There are no unrealistic passions, only unrealistic timelines for fulfilling them. If you plot your passions in the beginning, the process plots itself as you go on. Hopefully these are new experiences for you, distinct from anything you have done in the past.

To achieve each passion successfully, be sure it consists of the following six **S.M.A.R.T.S.**:

S— Specific in language
M—Measurable
A—Attainable
R—Results oriented
T—Time rationed
S—Seen in your mind's eye

Choose one passion from each of the six categories. For example, in the Social area you recognize that you love to play tennis. But because your latest honey prefers golf, which you don't play, you have allowed your passion for tennis to wane. Is this not typical of what we females tend to do as soon as an alleged prince enters our life? Now, change your habits.

This is how it works. Once you've pictured what you want and how it feels, you are ready to commit the S.M.A.R.T.S. technique to paper. Vow to rekindle the passion you once enjoyed. A statement like "Someday I'd like to return to playing tennis" is wishy-washy. A more *specific* statement announces, "I have scheduled a return to my tennis passion on Saturday mornings." Since it is now on your calendar, its accomplishment is *measurable*. To be sure it is *attainable*, plan your schedule so that it accommodates your baby-sitting needs, your weekend chores, and your willingness to rise early on your day off. To assure your plan is *results oriented*, be certain you set up enough players in case of last-minute dropouts. Your plan will be *time rationed* by your prepared schedule—for example, 10:00 A.M. to 12:00 noon. Finally, when you *see in your mind's eye* the actual enjoyment you will derive, you have a greater chance of accomplishing it.

Committing your S.M.A.R.T.S. to paper guards against your being swayed to substitute your honey's preference for golf for your own love of tennis. Just be sure to perceive this plan as a rubber band: elastic, flexible, and able to be altered at any time. And alterations will be necessary; as the joke goes: "Do you wanna hear God laugh? Tell Him your future plans."

Acknowledging their elasticity, you can change and reprogram your passions at will. This ability protects you from the possible fear of a failed commitment. Continued growth, not perfection, is what you're after. The key is to be alone while you are doing this exercise so that you will not be influenced to rush your ardent desires.

Bridget had just gone through an ugly and emotionally devastating divorce. In deep agony, she began to bury her pain by doing volunteer work with crack babies. Volunteerism has been found to offer physiological healing, including a lowering of blood pressure and increased circulation. But Bridget was running out of money, and it was time for her to find a paying job. From Self-Assessment #23, I asked her to fill in one passion from any of the six categories. Writing our passions on paper pays off. When we *write* that we will succeed, we *see* that we will succeed; when we *see* that we will succeed, we *know* that we will succeed. When we *know* that we will succeed—*we succeed*.

Bridget went to the Financial realm at once, since this was her most pressing need. She wrote, "I need to find a job. And I'm also worried about these babies." I looked at the paper in disbelief. "These babies?" I asked. "What do they have to do with your taking care of your Financial passions?" Bridget's fear of more emotional upheaval in her life had fogged her personal agenda. I said, "You need to garner your core energies to survive now. Give to the crack babies later from the overflow of emotions you have left." She rewrote her passion statement: "I deserve to find a marketing job by June." She changed her "need to find" a job to "deserve to find" a specific job in a *measurable* amount of time. Marketing was what she had *loved* before her divorce, and now she probed her passions to remember her feelings of joy in this area. Once she committed her passion to paper, she devised the logical steps to get her to her destination. "I will research companies I am interested in pursuing," "I will make three appointments a week," "I will attend two networking functions this month." Bridget was on her way to taking care of herself. As she pursued the passions that turned her on, her fears vanished.

Being alone induces clarity of mind to acknowledge what it is *we* long for. Women who wait for their External Controls to direct them relinquish their power to take initiative on their own.

Faye tried to get into a graduate program in genetic counseling, but she was not accepted at any of the universities in the Midwest, which was her preference. Since she had been a little girl, she had loved the sciences and excelled in them throughout school. In the East there was one program in this field that did accept her, but she said that she couldn't stand the thought of living there. She said she really wanted to pursue her passion, but her unwillingness to sacrifice to achieve it said more. Remember, words are cheap, but actions say all. A passion is a burning desire to do something, be someone, get something. Olympic champions discuss the sacrifices they make to get the gold. Students bemoan sacrifices they make in their social lives. People on diets lament their sacrifices to lose a few pounds. Faye clearly was *not* passionate *enough* about what she wanted. She was more interested in being comfortable, having things her own way, and not making waves. Amid her own self-deception, her impatient father directed her to "go where the money is" instead of pursuing the lower-paying sciences. Ah, how easy it is for a woman, especially a young one, to fall prey to the offers of External Control. Following his advice, she enrolled in an MBA program in finance. At twenty-five she is now out of school and working for a bank. She asks, "When will I be happy?"

Faye is typical of women who pursue other people's goals rather than their own personal passions. We must be willing to forgo the minor and momentary inconveniences to get what we want. This, ultimately, is the test of how badly we want it. When we get what we are passionate about, we are happy.

Once you have discovered what your passions are, the next step is to further enforce how you will accomplish them. That's simply a matter of making a pact with yourself and programming your promises. Since you are the only one who will see the results, if you renege on your promises, it is yourself you will disappoint.

Complete Self-Assessment #24 and program your passions now.

SELF-ASSESSMENT #24

PROGRAMMING YOUR PASSIONS

- On six different index cards, write one passion from each of the six previous passion categories.

- On each card, enumerate the steps that will get you to where you want to be, followed by completion dates.

- Place each card in a different envelope, seal it, address it to yourself, and on the outside, mark the date to open your envelope.

- When you receive the mail, mark your calendar to remind yourself to open each envelope on the date marked on its outside.

This self-assessment demonstrates how you kept your promise with yourself.

Self-Assessment #24 is so powerful that a woman said she had accomplished exactly what she had written on her index card after having forgotten ever completing the card. When she found the envelope and opened it, she was astonished. In the Financial arena, she was earning within $2,000 of the annual salary she had listed as what she deserved. In the Spiritual realm, she had begun a collection of New Age CDs by which she had begun meditating. In the Family dimension, she had restructured her wobbly relationship with her father, which was affecting the way she behaved with men. The will to achieve these passions had been buried in her unconscious. After her commitment to them on paper, they became ingrained and habitual. She conceived, she believed, she requested, she achieved. Finally, good-bye suffering. She had met a fascinating new friend—herself. She was in charge of her life.

There are 1,440 minutes in a day. Do you spend some of those minutes each day exploring your passions? If not, when was the last time you totally immersed yourself in your own fun? Was it long ago? Too long ago? If you don't like your response, it's time to change.

Time Alone at the End of a Relationship

How often we fill others' needs before our own so that they will simply pay attention to us. The need to be noticed, to be valued, to be liked, with the bottom-line objective of them all: to be loved. That desperate need for External support from others who may themselves also have trouble living in the world alone. Eventually those of us who evolve recognize that *no one* can make us whole. We are the ones who emotionally separate from those we foolishly bet on in the beginning who didn't fulfill us after all. If there is emptiness in our lives, it is there to provide a specific purpose. We must not run from being on our own because:

👑 **Gilda-Gram** *At times, it's necessary to be a single bookend.*

A single bookend is always preferable to being part of an unmatched pair. Use your time wisely during your single introspection. Discover who you are, what you want, where you are going. To fill the hole of loneliness, conduct an archaeological dig and shovel your own earth into the hollow. Encourage others who feel empty to do the same for themselves, but your mission is to serve yourself first.

Ultimately there is only one way to really count, and that is by counting yourself. We cannot alter our behaviors according to whether or not others approve because not everyone will love us, no matter what we do. We must accept who we are with the freedom to be ourselves. Otherwise we are living a lie.

As men have bet on the "prince" and lost, so have women. Although we're talking about different princes, the lesson is the same. We must all become entrepreneurial, enterprising, and self-protective so we don't suffocate when one option leaves, disappears, or dies. Our men are learning to enhance their equipment and parlay their skills into other possibilities. Give yourself the goodwill you were hoping to get from others. When you give yourself your own goodwill, you are getting your own castle in order, rather than waiting to be swept off into some prince's.

Scheduling personal and private time is a gift you give to yourself. Time for yourself is the pause that refreshes. But it's especially important after a relationship ends. Why is this private time so special for women? Because while men have learned to move up, climb over, and move on, it is we who hold on for dear life through the muck and mire, the zaps and zings. It is we who somewhere learned that love and pain are synonymous.

> *When I was first asked to write an article about how women*
> *get over a broken heart, I figured it would be the easiest money*
> *I ever made. Are you ready? We don't.*
> —*Comedienne Stephanie Miller*

Women simply hang on for too long. We rationalize, "I have so much already invested in him"; "If I try harder, things will improve"; "I know I can fix things." In contrast, many of these women's exes are more capable of camouflaging their grief in their work or in the arms of someone else.

During time alone, a woman is able to clearly process exactly what went wrong and why. Since most bad partnerships involve a woman's loss of part of herself, this is her time to discover her role in the duet and to reclaim her value. It is vital that she do this work. Otherwise:

👑 **Gilda-Gram** *To ignore our past is to repeat our past.*

Who wants to repeat the same painful events, even if they are repeated with someone we now deem magnificently new and "different"? Many women are held at bay by men who they hope will commit but who suddenly up and leave. Relationships that keep us guessing, keep us hurting.

> *Dear Dr. Gilda:*
> *I am in my 20's. I have trouble with relationships. I have no*
> *self-esteem, and can't be in a relationship longer than 2 months*
> *without the guy breaking up with me. Then I become suicidal*
> *and I feel terrible for months at a time. What should I do?*

Is any man—or person—worth such pain? It's time to take the rocks out of our backpack. Who said love's gotta hurt? We may be bummed out and burned out, but it is only we who hold the salve to anoint our wounds. And only by being alone will we take the time to apply it.

It is time to move on, the needed mourning is over, and the brilliant sunlight is shining through. As she scouts the signals of risky Romeos, being alone makes a woman look before she loves again. As she reflects on the past, she now questions her actions with greater insight. It is no longer "Did I love him?" but "Do I love *me*?" Being home alone gets a woman to recognize that:

👑 **Gilda-Gram** *Even if you're a couple, you're always a person away from being single.*

Remember young Shimeika from chapter 2, the baby having a baby? For two years now she has spent much time without a man raising her child, completing high school, and beginning college. She feels she is much wiser now. As she studies to become a nurse, she looks forward to graduating and moving away from the ghetto apartment she shares with her mother. She is so happily busy with her activities that she will only date men she feels can enhance her life, not pull her down, as Lloyd would have done had she remained with him. Time alone taught Shimeika the value of her self-worth. Another young woman from chapter 2, Jacqueline, the letter writer who wanted to get back with Mike to make him suffer for the pain he inflicted on her, was at first disappointed that her lover never returned. But in this lonely space of time, Jacqueline learned to provide for her own needs, feel better about herself, and recognize that she need not exchange sex to gain love. As she slimmed down, she began to think more highly of herself and project an image to new men that she was special. She recently admitted that as much as she kicked and screamed about it, spending time alone was what readied her to meet the real love of her life. Finally, she discovered who she was. Even fifty-something Karla learned necessary lessons about being alone once her Casanova con man was put behind bars. Having to now fend for herself, alone and without love, she began to draw from strength she never knew she had.

All three of these cases involved women who ended up without a man despite their initial plans. In all three cases, however, the women benefited from their newly found freedom. Most of us live our lives backward, looking for love to be happy, not realizing that it works in reverse. To achieve intimacy, we must love ourselves and be ourselves before we meld ourselves with someone else. We must choose our own self-esteem over mere accompaniment by a man. The number one rule for partnership success is:

....

👑 **Gilda-Gram** *To be a good* we, *first become a good* me.

....

Once a woman understands that she is fine *as is*, she can get on with her life—with or without a man. And the paradox is that when she's least expecting it, another relationship possibility will appear. Hasn't it ever happened to you that way?

Becoming a Good Me

How does a woman become a good me? After she's left a relationship, she must sit with remorse and examine her circumstances for all they are. Eventually she will arrive at the magic of "Ah-ha, I see . . ." This is called having an *epiphany*, and it is cleansing.

Are you ready to have an epiphany yourself? You will be after you complete Self-Assessment #25.

THE MAGIC EPIPHANY

The magic epiphany is the moment of Ah-ha! You suddenly realize that your signs—water and earth—could only make mud. Clearly he's two tacos short of a combination platter. It was pure infatuation. Were you crazy? You can look back and finally see the signals you missed at first—and laugh! This epiphany will make you wiser in choosing better your next time out.

- Describe your first impressions of this man.
- When did your feelings wane?
- How do you feel about him now?
- What did this experience teach you?

Women know more about themselves than they think they do. By assessing your misguided loves, you are guarding against repeating bad relationships. As you luxuriously take the time to binge on things your former lover was not crazy about, you get to find new things that turn you on. One door closes and a bigger door opens. Sure, it may be hell in the hallway for a while, but perform the necessary appraisal alone and be better equipped to make smarter choices tomorrow. Vow that:

Gilda-Gram *My next mistakes will be new mistakes.*

Planting the Seeds of Patience

You are now ready for new beginnings. Where do you start? Back at the farm. Are you a miner or a farmer? Miners take from the soil. Farmers, too, take from the soil, but they also put back. Have you been mining for too long, taking too much out of your own rich earth, or allowing others that right, without the necessary replenishing of your nutrients? Spending time alone mandates that you put back into your soul the vitality you once had. It begins by planting the seeds for your future.

The old adage "All good things come to those who wait" is wrong. It should instead read:

Gilda-Gram *All good things come to those who plant.*

Women have waited for centuries. *Someday* my prince will come, *someday* he'll tell me he loves me, *someday* he'll commit, *someday* we'll have kids, *someday* they'll leave home, *someday* he'll stop pestering me for sex, *someday* he'll die (now I *can't* wait!). Planting has a waiting cycle all its own. Farmers can't go out and pull the roots to hasten growth; roots sprout when they're ready.

It's the same in relationships. After falling into the depths of the dump zone, people must wait before they play the next round of rebound roulette. While each person requires a different amount of time before jumping to another love, one thing is for sure: one must remain alone, if for no other reason than to catch one's breath and discover what really went wrong. However long that takes depends on the person and her pain. Some people mourn for a week or two, others grieve for years. No good friend can get you over the hump until you're ready. But you won't be ready to try again until you cultivate your soil with the **Five Steps to Healing**:

1. *Let Go:* Let go of trying to control people and conditions. Get out of the "If only . . ." mentality. Life has dished you these circumstances, okay. Now you control the emotions you use to respond.
2. *Plant New Seeds:* Identify your passions. Decide how you will pursue them. Begin pursuing now.
3. *Have Patience:* By pursuing your passions, you are not sitting and waiting idly. While your seeds are being sown beneath the earth, above the soil you are tap-dancing till ready.
4. *Let Grow:* When the shoots appear, don't tug at them to grow quicker. Let them emerge gradually, in their own time. Why worry? You're enjoying your life as is.
5. *Let In:* Welcome the refreshing changes into your life, the birth of something different from your past. Let them in gradually and gracefully, and give thanks.

Planting seeds requires a time of waiting for the crop to grow. This is not the kind of vacant waiting that a victim does, because by definition a victim avoids her share of preparing and planting. In contrast, a planter is active in the growing and developing process. You cannot see it, but your seeds are taking root beneath your fertile soil. Patience is prospering power. It is the space between letting go, planting, and letting grow. Impatience is the self-centered child within you screaming that you want what you want *now*. Real maturity allows for the natural phenomena to occur at their own pace, no matter what you want. A child grows without realizing it. So do we. We reap our just rewards according to the earth's timing, not our own. This is an enormous lesson.

Since women have historically waited for "their turn" to come, many now misinterpret the meaning of being "liberated" and rush in to combat the will of nature. Some pull aggressively at the roots as soon as they appear. They hunt after the hunting men, making themselves so available that they lose sight of their personas. Rather than take their time, and allow the hand of nature, they visualize love as a fight to get a guy. This does them no good because:

👑 **Gilda-Gram** *What we fight to get, we fight to keep.*

Instead of fighting, some women give up entirely at this point and couple with the first semen specimen who shows. They've fantasized the love songs, the movies, the soaps, the biological time clocks, the myth of happily-ever-after. At the beginning of this book, you read about eight of these women impatient for love, and you added your own story to make nine. These were all women who chose poorly because they didn't know how to choose right. And as different as the women were, all were hurt in the end by hasty choices thought through poorly.

When impatience strikes, be careful to hold to your power and passions. While I was feverishly writing this book, the gardener at my building asked, "Don't you have a *real* job?" I laughed at his comment at first, but I noted some depression later over the slowness of my process. Impatience can touch our vulnerability when others criticize us. I allowed this stranger to hold power over me while I was planting my seeds. Oh, the old External Control force. How poetic that he was a gardener! Patience is the only courage we need. For most women conditioned to wait, in the midst of the misconstrued sense of nineties liberation, patience is a hard thing to come by. Certainly that has been the case for me.

The world is filled with examples of successful people who held to their patience despite criticism and adversity. In both business and love, a person must follow the same five steps of cultivating the soil. Mr. Right-Now can transform to Mr. Right with patience. Let him be. Let him discover he wants you, needs you, loves you. He has to get the notion himself. For you, too, when you're busy plowing your own farmland, busy concentrating on your life, his name suddenly thrums through your veins and echoes down your bones. You can't sleep. You can't eat. You can't think. You can't breathe. It all just happens. You think back to all the personal ads you wrote, when you reduced your charms to the lowest possible word count. You recall your video-dating registrations, when you taped your slickest soundbites. All that effort. For what? Now the earth's mysterious moment has arrived without your having pursued it. While busy fulfilling your private passions, you somehow managed to be "in the building." And there he was.

Reprogramming Your Self-Talk in Your Quiet Time

We think thousands of thoughts each day. The majority of most people's thoughts are repeats of the negative ones we had yesterday. If our self-talk is not positive, we are simply wasting the richness of our lives. Being alone conditions us to wash the tattered habits from our midst without having to impress anyone or ask permission. Being alone allows us to defog our mirrors and finally see our own reflections. Being alone allows us to walk on the sand, look at the waves, and, murmur the title of an instrumental CD by Weinberg and Beck: "Let the Ocean Worry." How freeing!

Talk is said to be cheap, but it's expensive for anyone who continues to think and speak in terms that bring her down. Complete Self-Assessment #26 and vow that you will spend a whole day without one thought of negativity. This self-assessment is a valuable tool because it pushes you to see how you program your life with thoughts that are not always in your best interest. As you are forced to come face-to-face with elements that work against you, you become empowered to make changes and incorporate blessings that work on your behalf.

SELF-ASSESSMENT #26

SELF-TALK PROMISE

I promise myself that I will spend this day without one negative thought. Whenever I am tempted to think bad about myself or someone else, or to tell someone off, I will say, "Cancel." Then I will switch to a more positive and productive use of my time and energy.

Date: _____

RECORD OF TEMPTATIONS, CELEBRATION OF SUCCESSES

- When _____ happened, I was tempted to be negative. Instead I substituted my negative thought with the following positive one: _____.
- When _____ happened, I was tempted to be negative. Instead I substituted my negative thought with the following positive one: _____.
- When _____ happened, I was tempted to be negative. Instead I substituted my negative thought with the following positive one: _____.

> Repeat self-talk positives often. Contrary to the outdated adage "Seeing is believing," reality works in the opposite way: **Believing is seeing**. When you believe something, you will see it manifested.

When they become conscious of their words and thoughts, most people are amazed at what they hear themselves say. Remember Paula, the woman profiled in chapter 6 who preferred to stay with her married lover for eighteen years until he dumped her? Now finally beyond her mourning period, she was ready to accept a number of blind dates from some of her kind friends. But with each new man, she found another thing to turn her off. After keeping track of her self-talk promises, she found that she had often been repeating, "All I attract are losers"; "All men are dogs"; "What's the use of looking for a good man when there are none out there?" When she heard her negative words, she herself was startled. She asked the same kind friends who were setting her up with these men to call her attention to her negative statements when they heard them. It almost became a game for them each time they called "Cancel" at each of Paula's negative thoughts. In fact, this exercise got them also to note their own negativity. Paula began readily to change her phrases to "I might not be attracted to these guys, but someone better is right behind him" and "I'm sure there are some nice guys out there." As soon as she changed her beliefs, she met a guy she enjoyed seeing for the next few months, and then another who had recently been widowed. Both men were nice. Both men were acceptable. And now Paula was at least willing to give both men a chance.

Choosing Whom to Invite into Your Life

Certain issues are directly within your influence. For example, it is time to determine whom you have been inviting into your life. Have they been good for you? Have they pushed your happiness or sadness buttons? Have the new ones been similar to the ones preceding them? In Self-Assessment #27, list whom you have invited, and perhaps continue to invite, into your life. You will place the names of these people into one, two, or all of the categories: Drainers, Maintainers, and Propellers. Some people can take on different roles for us at different times. Your overall objective is to determine if you are missing people in your list who can Maintain and Propel you. As far as the Drainers go, once you see them on your list, you'll know what to do.

WHOM HAVE I BEEN ATTRACTING INTO MY LIFE?

Divide a sheet of paper into the following three columns:

Special Relationships   Friends   Colleagues

In not more than ten minutes, fill the columns with the names of as many people as you can think of. Label each name as one of the following:

DRAINER (someone who saps your energy by trying to keep you down)
MAINTAINER (someone who helps you stay where you are)
PROPELLER (someone who pushes you into new areas and adventures)

- Have you attracted too many Drainers?
- Do you have an adequate number of Maintainers?
- Are you in need of additional Propellers?

Where have the men in your life fit in? Go back to the three columns and list the categories of each of your previous relationships with men as far back as you can remember. Which category is the current man in your life in? Where would you like him to be?

After completing Self-Assessment #27, Maria discovered that her men had consisted of a lot of Drainers, but few Propellers who could prop her up and out when she needed the added boost. She realized these guys instead had brought her down. No wonder she was often depressed. Rebecca recognized that she had a husband who said he supported her work, meeting the description of a Propeller. But in actuality his alleged "support" was really pushy demands that more exemplified a Drainer. Nothing she did was ever good enough to please him. As a result, she found herself under constant stress. Lynda had many Maintainers who just went along with the flow, supported her status quo, and continued to question her upward mobility. No wonder she was miserable that her life was unchanged.

Drainers clearly have got to get the boot because they offer only one-sided caring, all take, no give. But we must balance the Propellers and Maintainers we attract because we cannot always propel forward without sometimes sitting quietly to consider our next move. At times our partner might act as Propeller, then switch to Maintainer. Researchers find that the one ingredient happy couples have in common is their support of each other's passions. When you know your mate is behind your dreams, the positive mood of the partnership motivates you to achieve them. All in all:

👑 **Gilda-Gram** *My relationships should support my self, not sap it.*

A partner's advice may be well taken and may be an offering of additional insight and support. But a woman who is centered, directed by her Internal Control and aware of her feelings and passions, makes herself her own authority. She has the final say as to what to do next.

A woman needs time to get into dry dock, to get out of dry dock, and to proceed back to action at her own pace. She needs to cry as much as she wants, and she also needs to enjoy every tear. (Tears are natural tranquilizers with healing properties. By lowering blood pressure and relaxing muscles, they help reduce a woman's physical and emotional agitation.) She needs to let her inner brat emerge. And go spa-ing, where she can be pampered. And slop around in pants too big, with elasticized waistbands. Only by being home alone can a woman freely explore the magnificence of being manless for a moment, having not a soul to answer to, care about, or care for. With a planned man-o-pause, a woman can separate from the penile petulance that plagued her past. She can bask in her own unedited thoughts. She may choose to regroup rather than regress, or regress rather than regroup. Now her issues and joys are totally hers. Selfishness never felt so good. Enjoying your aloneness is nothing to apologize for.

Even married and partnered women have to separate themselves at regular intervals from their healthy relationships. Otherwise they cannot adjust their changing needs in concert with their growth. When a woman is out of balance, she becomes frustrated, stressed, and angry. Time alone for a woman is crucial so she can take stock of her life, reclaim her peace, and recenter. She needs to take the time to explore her uniqueness and honor her assets. Only by being alone for a period of time can she thrust herself through the dark tunnel and emerge into the light.

Ready to Emerge

So far, we have probed your personal passions, we have asked whom you are attracting, and we've assessed why. Now it is time to delve deeper. Since we have made a case for women to penetrate the mere Externals and value their Internal worth, we are ready to assess who you *really* are inside. This is a very important point, because the only constant in all your relationships is *you*. Yes, you are the *only one* who keeps showing up for each involvement. And you are the one who feels the pain when these involvements don't work out. In Self-Assessment #28, explore your self from inside your soul and discover who you really are without the frills.

SELF-ASSESSMENT #28

WHO AM I, ANYWAY?

Write a description of who you are without using labels such as age, sex, educational background, religion, or occupational accomplishments. Viewing your life from inside your soul, use **positive** *adjectives to describe the* qualities *you possess about your energy, effervescence, and happiness. Examples of some adjectives are clever, kind, responsible, visionary, idealistic, principled . . .*

Was this a difficult task for you? Women especially caught up in their body's Externals find this self-assessment challenging. But the more resistance you had in finding positive adjectives, the more you need to open yourself to new perspectives. It is not because things are fearful that we do not get off the fence. It is because we do not get off the fence that things are fearful. Select and enact a different adjective each day. That's how you'll know your defense is being dismantled.

In Self-Assessment #28 you listed your innermost attributes, the ones devoid of our culture's External standards. Clearly the women who wrote letters to the newspaper running the "Make Me Over" contest in chapter 4 had never done this self-assessment. They were merely—and desperately—needy of improving their Externals. When we look to enhance our Externals before we are comfortable with what we have inside, we are nothing more than mannequins, the plastic bodies men don't even look to get past to see our cleverness or kindness. And the truth is, our feelings of inadequacy about our Externals are often imagined.

Self-Assessment #29 takes a hard look at how you would *ideally* like other people to see your External attributes. Then it has you assess your *real* External self. As we discussed in chapter 4, most women are prone to disappointment with their looks that don't compare with Hollywood. Only by completing this self-assessment will you recognize the irrational disappointment you, too, may possess about your body. For sure, such negativity is projected in the way you relate to men.

WHAT AM I, ANYWAY—IDEALLY AND REALLY?

Draw a picture of your ideal *body as you would like it.*
Comment on the positive and negative qualities of each body part.

Draw a picture of your real *body as you truly appear.*
Comment on the positive and negative qualities of each body part.

Compare your ideal *self with your* real *self.*

- Are you overly critical? If so, why?
- Do you criticize your details or appreciate the big picture?
- Some things can't be changed. Do you accept these as they are?
- What can you realistically change?
- List ten physical aspects of yourself that you are grateful for.

After completing this self-assessment, Suzanne recognized that she had a Dom DeLuise frame with a Cindy Crawford ideal. Reality at first sent her into a tailspin. How could she make peace with the face and body she had been dealt? The list of ten aspects of herself for which she was grateful included her beautiful shoulder-length hair, her perfect white teeth, her flawless hands and fingers, her titillating laugh, and her bold green eyes. For the first time she began to focus on what she possessed rather than on what she lacked. This new target allowed her to project herself at strange places with ease she had never before felt. Suddenly she began to attract men considered "gorgeous" by anyone's standard. This had never happened before. It was the change in her attitude, with her body just naturally following.

Have you come closer to accepting your inner and outer beauty for what it is? You count. You are beautiful. You are valuable. And it's not only about your outer shell. According to the American Chemical Society, the elements in our body taken separately are worth only a depressing $1.25. But when these chemicals work *together*, they produce hormones, proteins, and nucleic acids, bringing the value of our worth to nearly $8 million. (To think we once revered the Six Million Dollar *Man*!) The key here is that all the elements of who we are work *together*. Our determination to ask for what we want, our acceptance of our deserve level, our body language, voice, and words, our ability to style-flex between Taskmaster and Toastmaster, our sturdy Internal Control that modifies all the External pressures—all work in concert to up the value of our *entire package*. Forget the Bionic Woman. Strut your own $8 million self. Like each of the stars in the sky uniquely shining above the earth, you are incomparable. Your glorious qualities inside combine with your radiant external package. Parade your pride because you feel honored to show it off.

Now you're ready for the next step, to uncover your essence. Here, allow your "essence" to mean the combination of your innermost and outermost assets. Complete Self-Assessment #30 and create a trademark that is especially yours.

SELF-ASSESSMENT #30

DISCOVERING MY ESSENCE

Select **one word** *you want others to identify you by. It is your word.*

This word is your unique signature, your personal imprint, your unique trademark.

Feel it. Flaunt it. Be proud of it. It is the new you!

- Close your eyes.
- Visualize the word.
- Smell its ambience.
- Touch its surroundings.
- Hear its sounds.
- Savor its flavor.
- Change your body posture to match your image of the word.
- Breathe deeply with your diaphragm, in and out, and concentrate on the word.
- Write the word boldly on a piece of paper.
- Set the word sailing in the air and watch it fly.

In Self-Assessment #30, Crystal selected the word "elegant." She visualized it, smelled it, touched it, heard its sounds, savored its taste, and changed her body posture to mirror the word. Almost immediately, people noticed that something was different, but they could not pinpoint what it was. Crystal knew. She smiled. Her husband has no idea what has come over her, but he believes he's with a new woman. Not bad after ten years of marriage.

Putting It All Together

You're almost finished . . . but not quite. If this were the usual self-help book, the next most natural step would be to have the reader imagine her ideal man and, through a process of visualization, list his characteristics and have her pray that she will attract him into her life sometime soon. But we're not interested in your ideal man here because our focus is on supporting your best qualities so that you can become your most productive self. When you are the best that you can be, you will attract the right partner because:

👑 **Gilda-Gram** *We attract not who we want but who we are.*

We all know how opposite traits attract, then distract—and eventually repel. Therefore, when it comes to love that endures over time, it is wiser to attract a partner who *shares our essence*. Essence describes who we *are* deep down, beyond our more obvious traits. By identifying and projecting your essence, and by continuing to hone your personal uniqueness, you *become* more attractive. This way, when you dream of that special someone, you have much to offer. Your feet will be firmly on the ground, not flailing aimlessly in the clouds, visualizing someone impossible to manifest.

Now that you have accepted and appreciated all the things you have going for you as a person, begin to keep a "Book of Abundance," listing the events in your life that make you feel wonderful. Each event should be accompanied by its appropriate date. For example, 7/15: "I am grateful for the boss announcing my promotion in front of the entire staff." 7/16: "I am grateful for Jim Conrad asking me to have dinner with him next week." This self-assessment is very important for you to acknowledge and welcome events and people you might have taken for granted in the past. It is also important because when you are of the mind-set of abundance, you will attract others who think similarly. This outlook will also repel men with mentalities of scarcity, poverty, and neediness.

SELF-ASSESSMENT #31

MY BOOK OF ABUNDANCE
Make at least three inscriptions daily.

- Date: _____
  I am grateful for _____ .

- Date: _____
  I am grateful for _____ .

- Date: _____
  I am grateful for _____ .

Ruth had been keeping her Book of Abundance for four weeks. Some of her notations read "I am grateful for the inheritance I received from Aunt Ann"; "I am grateful for the beautiful apartment I live in"; "I am grateful for the love my parents give me"; "I am grateful for the wonderful fiancé I have." At first, like many people, Ruth noticed that she had to jar her consciousness to think of these positive things, which she tended to take for granted. But it also got her to recognize that she was surrounded by many negative people whose External Control she tended to incorporate into her own views of life. This in itself was a revelation. So at first the Book of Abundance served to emphasize her optimism. But then, as she continued to write her inscriptions, she became aware of her fiancé's constant money complaints. She found herself trying to "fix" his negativity with her own feel-good statements. *A page from the overfunctioning woman?* As she continued to write, she also discovered how her boyfriend's morose moods had lowered her entire energy level. The couple was seriously considering marriage during the coming year. He had asked her to sign a prenuptial agreement, which she felt detracted from their romance and also set her up as someone he could not trust. She truly did not care about his money because she had plenty of her own. They were at a standstill. Then the market crashed, and her boyfriend lay in bed, wearing a look of death. He whined, "Ruth, don't you feeling awful about my losing so much money in the market?" Ruth looked at him and said, "Wasn't this the money you wanted me to sign off on in a prenup?" Revisiting her inscriptions from her Book of Abundance, she recognized that this man's mentality of scarcity was too drag-down for her. She was exhausted from trying to uplift his negativity. Soon afterward she broke off their engagement.

We all have positive attributes that we tend to forget about from time to time. The Book of Abundance jolts our mind to remember the things we have going for us. These inscriptions constitute an optimistic attitude about the things we often accept as a matter of course.

....

Gilda-Gram *An attitude of abundance repels a mentality of scarcity.*

....

When we accentuate the positives, we will attract positive men.

Now that you've established *the kind* of man who will most enrich your life, consider what you'll do with him once you get him. In other words, what is your view of commitment? Some women want a man in their lives but not in their beds. Other women want a man in their beds but not in their lives. There are many different combinations of successful relationships. Who is to say what the right one is? You are free to choose whatever suits you. But in order to choose wisely, you must know what your preference is.

In Self-Assessment #32, you will discover what a committed relationship uniquely means to you.

SELF-ASSESSMENT #32

WHAT DO I MEAN BY COMMITMENT?

In the next three seconds, free-associate the words you believe are synonymous with the word "commitment." Do not dwell on any one word for any time. Just jot down each word as it comes into your mind.

What did you discover?

Merna's words for "commitment" were "trap," "manipulation," and "not for me." No wonder she was having difficulty sustaining relationships. Monique's interpretation was "necessary" for the sake of having kids, and she pursued men who were willing and able to comply. Jacqui wrote "a covenant with God," and as an avid churchgoer, she reckoned she'd meet someone at a service. Finally, believe it or not, the teacher we met in chapter 2, Caitlin, was shocked that she had inscribed the word "scary" as a synonym of "commitment." She wondered if it was because her ex-husband had been a drug abuser, gambler, and womanizer. But now, it seemed, the boyfriend to whom she was engaged had sold his house and agreed to move in. *Uh-oh.* No wonder she was so frightened. Now the shoe was on the other foot. As the saying goes, "Be careful what you wish for; you just might get it."

For each of us, commitment has a different meaning. But until we recognize what it is, we may be barking up the wrong tree—and end up with nothing more than splinters.

You've discovered how to make love happen. You learned that it is predicated on who you are. You acknowledge your needs and project them with the spirit that you deserve to have them granted. Once you know that you are the prize, you can commit yourself to yourself. That means establishing well-delineated boundaries, unwavering when they must be firm, but elastic when they need to be stretched. Boundary maintenance allows you to retain your energies for the things that matter to you. They connote a welcome by invitation only. When you pursue your dreams and stick by your borders, you are on your way to finding bliss.

We enhance our bliss by attracting worthy people. That means getting rid of and avoiding the folks unresponsive to the full cycle of giving and taking. Through our body language, voice, and words, we teach men to consider us with respect, and we expect only gracious treatment—which is what we receive. We recognize our inability to control, change, or save another person, and we balance our desire to control our circumstances with our natural kindness and charisma. This is our Power Image, a strong shell with a feminine, soft sell. At last, we have become the total package needed to get the man we want. And there are no subterfuges because our essence is what we had inside us all along, buried as it might have been.

We have risked coming out of hiding. But the risk was constructive. There is a difference between healthy risks and reckless gambles. While gambling is like a throw of the dice, risking is logically designed. It is based on the hard work we invest in ourselves. It is what we deserve to derive after processing the self-assessments. Caitlin, the teacher who feared commitment after her painful divorce, recently told me, "While I was at the doctor, a car blocked me in. I drove onto the sidewalk. I got out. Since my divorce, I have become very capable. I need to remember that." As she overcomes one fear after another, she is regaining her trust in men, and the word "commitment" is not as scary for her now as it once was.

You're convinced you'd like to share your new and daring self with someone terrific. Now that you can get the man you want, you are on your way to keeping him. That requires risks beyond yourself. You have the tools to:

1. Dare to be yourself.
   As you give from the overflow, not from the core, know your power and project it.
2. Dare to be vulnerable.
   Ask for what you need and believe you deserve to get it.
3. Dare to disagree.
   Know how to receive—information you like and information you don't—and feel you have a right to your own values and opinions.
4. Dare to walk away.
   Enjoy being home alone.

Hooking a man was only part of the challenge. Holding him requires that your love and sexual communications be maintained over time. You are now ready to enter part 3 of the "Don't Bet on the Prince!" technology to find out how.

GILDA-GRAMS
FROM CHAPTER 7
Enjoy Being Home Alone

▶ *You are the only person who will never abandon you.*

▶ *If you plan to love someone, recognize he could someday be gone.*

▶ *Love at first sight is lust with potential. But we need time alone to sort it through.*

▶ *At times, it's necessary to be a single bookend.*

▶ *To ignore our past is to repeat our past.*

▶ *Even if you're a couple, you're always a person away from being single.*

▶ *To be a good* we, *first become a good* me.

▶ *My next mistakes will be new mistakes.*

▶ *All good things come to those who plant.*

▶ *What we fight to get, we fight to keep.*

▶ *My relationships should support my self, not sap it.*

▶ *We attract not who we want, but who we* are.

▶ *An attitude of abundance repels a mentality of scarcity.*

PART III

How to Keep the Man You Get

8

Incorporate the Language of Love

👑 **Gilda-Gram** *Fall in* like *before you fall in* love.

In part 2 of this book we outlined the ways to love yourself and thereby become more loving. Finding and projecting your power is the only way to set the hook. It comes from the heart, it is nonmanipulative, it expresses your true self without subterfuge, and it opens the way for a worthy man to return your honesty. But what happens afterward? Our fairy-tale myths never taught us there is life *after* happily-ever-after. As little girls we just assumed the prince would take care of his lady after the book was closed. Unfortunately, current-day reality has taught us that once the courtship is over, men feel comfortable for having won their prize—and they settle in before the TV screen, sometimes for life. Women then lament that the thrill is gone. One wife complained to her husband about his sloppy, unshaven demeanor on weekends. He shot back, "The trouble is you want to continue being romanced." *So, what's so bad about that?* Another wife who finally married after thirty-five years alone dreamed her new husband would feed her bonbons in bed and adorn their cottage with roses. With the reality of his costly child support and his unwillingness to move to the site of her new job, she griped, "I never knew I'd have to continue taking care of myself after marriage. I still feel single."

Truth is, women want the romance to continue as it once was, when they were most adored and pursued. Truth is, once into the relationship, men usually don't feel they must continue what to them had been the romantic charade. Women love love, we love being courted, and we want a man to continue to show us he loves us without prodding. We *know* the Language of Love as we'd like to hear it, but do we *hear* the Language of Love from men committed to using it?

One study claims the average couple spends only seventeen minutes a *week* in face-to-face communication. Another says it's four minutes a *day*. Both agree that whatever paltry time couples do get to talk with each other, the focus usually revolves around household chores, children, and organizational events and not around the relationship. How does a loving pair keep the love boat afloat?

In close relationships, the Language of Love is tuned to the melodic channel that two parties understand. Sometimes there is static; sometimes, without warning, the music changes its rhythm and beat. But the language that works best is the language that the two people share exclusively, with their personal pet names, amid their seductive teasing, incorporating their private jokes, in their special way. The more of a special, playful language a couple has perfected, the better their relationship is. The Japanese have a word for living in harmony: *wa*. *Wa* can be liberally translated to mean a couple getting along through thick and thin. It is based on the three ingredients of Power, Purpose, and Play.

To communicate lovingly, a woman must know *who she is*: **Power**. She must know *what she wants*: **Purpose**. She must know *what to do*: **Play**. If any of these three communication elements are missing, the Language of Love will wane. But when we apply them, we not only *know* who we are, we *express* who we are. This is our Power. We not only *know* what we want, we *express* what we want. This is our Purpose. We not only *know* what to do, we *express* what to do. This is our willingness to Play. As such, Power, Purpose, and Play are *expressions* of our Language of Love. They are based on our capacity to risk honest giving and receiving. Unabashedly, we now dare to be ourselves, we dare to be vulnerable, we dare to disagree, and we dare to walk away if we don't derive what we believe we deserve. We communicate our daring through loving yet unwavering language. We are secure in our risk taking because we are as willing to love as we are willing to lose. We know that life includes losses as well as gains, and a loss does not make us into a loser. Without desperation, but with committed strength, we dare to teach our mate what it is we need and want, then dare to expect and accept only the best treatment from him. Finally, no matter what the outcome, we dare to believe we will always have ourselves. As we communicate these daring roles, we become scintillating to men. One man tiredly traipsed across a continent to take me to dinner one night and said, "You are so different from other women, so refreshing." I was merely applying the "Don't Bet on the Prince!" technology.

Women also become more refreshing to a man when they treat him like something special. That is, they begin each relationship with caring and friendship. They communicate their intention of getting to know a guy before hitting the sack. As Scheherazade showed her Arabian king, the communiqué is "If you stick around, I'll make it worth your while." Currentday translation: "Show me what you've got, and I'll show you what you get." To do that, women have got to lead the way to conversation and build the friendship. An extra bonus is the respect they will get back. Friendships offer feelings of safety. Then the sequence that follows can naturally become:

👑 **Gilda-Gram** *Friends first, lovers later.*

Becoming friends first allows you to:

👑 **Gilda-Gram** *Fall in* like *before you fall in* love.

But falling in *like* mandates our security in knowing who we are. We must feel secure enough to risk expressing our Power.

Expressing Your Power

Whenever a woman discusses taking a risk, I ask, "What's the worst thing that can happen?" Actually, a woman's risk in expressing her Power is not much of a risk at all. What if a man is turned off by it? Simple! Then he's not the man for her. The Power that she entered the relationship with is the Power she takes with her. Nothing ventured, maybe, but a whole lot of insight gained. On to the next possibility.

By now you know that a woman's success at love involves her taking charge of her own destiny. This allows her to determine her own happiness. A woman is responsible for asking the right questions at the start of a relationship, and she must also be willing to receive answers that might not thrill her but that she must nonetheless consider. As she skillfully uses her body language, voice, and words, she applies the S-O-F-A technique to encourage her man's openness. She *selfishly* seeks respect before aiming to be liked and enunciates her boundaries, including her desire to be alone. She acknowledges her man's imperfections and forgives his transgressions, whether she chooses to remain with him or not, for if she is to keep her balance, she must preserve her precious energy. As she balances Taskmaster organization with Toastmaster cheerleading, she is led not by the External Control standards of others, but by her own Internal drives. She is her own person, and she projects that with assuredness. Now she is ready to acknowledge the basic gender differences between herself and her man, to meet these differences head-on, in naked self-disclosure, and to evaluate the language she uses in describing their love and assess what it truly means. No matter what the outcome, she is willing to work on the relationship if that is her goal.

Male Talk vs. Female Talk: Accepting Our Differences

For a couple to engage in successful love language that is uniquely theirs, they must overlook and overcome some of the basic gender language differences. Complete Self-Assessment #33 and see if you know the general variations in communications between the sexes.

SELF-ASSESSMENT #33

MALE /FEMALE COMMUNICATING PATTERNS

Answer **True** *or* **False** *to each of the following statements:*

_____ **1.** Women are more likely than men to get verbal praise.

_____ **2.** Women usually talk more.

_____ **3.** Women are more likely to interrupt men when they speak.

_____ **4.** Women interpret nonverbal cues better than men.

_____ **5.** Women use more polite communications tactics.

_____ **6.** Women are generally touched more.

_____ **7.** Women usually work harder to keep conversations going.

_____ **8.** Women are more likely to ask questions.

_____ **9.** Women often reveal personal information.

CORRECT ANSWERS

1. *False:* Women are less likely than men to get verbal praise. When women do get praise, it is usually for their physical appearance. Men get praised for their achievements.

2. *False:* In one experiment, males and females were asked to describe pictures. The women took three minutes to the men's thirteen. Despite the folklore that women talk more, research shows that in school and at work men are more talkative. Perhaps women do speak more at home where their comfort and security levels rise.

3. *False:* Power doesn't corrupt, it interrupts. In same-sex conversations, interruptions are evenly distributed, but in mixed-sex discussions, men interrupt women more than the other way around.

4. *True:* Anthropologists report that greater nonverbal sensitivity is developed by people who are in subordinate positions so they know how and when to react. They will study the person in control. Women have thus learned to apply their natural intuition and read people for what they perceive them to be.

5. *True:* Men are permitted the use of graphic and coarse language, but women are still encouraged to be ladylike.

6. *True:* Rank has its touching privileges. He who is in power will often reach out and grab. Men may touch women to guide them into a car, to accompany them on the street, to help them on with their coats. Often it is so brief that it's hardly noticed. But at times it can get out of hand.

7. *True:* Research has found that among marrieds, women initiate many more topics than men. Men often kill conversations with their inattentiveness. Women try to keep the music playing, however, by keeping the conversation flowing, for which they are called "talkative."

8. *True:* Women ask questions so they'll be noticed and addressed. They may therefore help men dominate the conversation by prompting them to respond.

9. *True:* Women tend to reveal more about themselves, believing this is the way to keep people interested.

How did you do? Women didn't need Deborah Tannen to tell us that men and women communicate differently. But Tannen did us a big favor because her popularity got men to take note of our differences, to learn some techniques for lessening the discrepancies, and to try harder in making our relationships work.

> *I know that you believe you understand what you think I said, but I am not sure you realize that what you heard is not what I meant.*
>
> —*Anonymous*

There is Male Talk, where a man communicates in bottom-line deals, and there is Female Talk, where a woman communicates in incremental and intricate details. Because of our tendency to unravel a story rather than offer its conclusion first, women have won the rep as blabbers and babblers. But if a woman learns Male Talk, she could present her information differently at first and *be heard*.

Paul and Edyth could not get beyond the usual male/female obstacles in their daily communications. He would return home from work with the typical "How was your day, dear?" question. Edyth would launch into exhausting step-by-step details of who said what to whom and how. Paul could not bear the diatribe and ended up walking away, which hurt Edyth's feelings. He also felt that after working a full day, he needed to chill out by himself with a jog in the park or a beer by the TV, anything but engage in conversation with a talkative wife. In contrast, Edyth's means of regaining closeness with her husband after being separated during the workday was to do precisely what he hated: talk. Men are certainly capable of speech, but they fear intimate monologue from the mouths of women, afraid that they will be chewed out for their failings. For women, it isn't so much the process of talking that they want; it's the chance to be acknowledged that they long for.

After this couple recognized the pattern to their evasion/invasion arguments, they took control. Each partner felt his/her independent Power. So instead of one trying to force the other to use his/her communication style, each jokingly questioned how the recipient wanted to hear a story: Edyth would ask, "Paul, I want to tell you about the Rogers deal we did today. Do you want to hear it in Male Talk or Female Talk?" Usually Paul responded, "Male Talk first." Then he'd ask questions later. Paul, too, would ask the question about whether to conclude a story with its results, which Edyth usually found too cut-and-dried, or whether to pitch the gory details, which his wife preferred. The couple laughed as they respectfully agreed to speak in ways the other could understand. This process eliminated many hurt feelings and stressful arguments that affected other day-to-day aspects of their relating.

👑 **Gilda-Gram** *For stress-reduced communication with your man, use Male Talk first, Female Talk later. Or deals first, details later.*

After the deals/details sequence, another form of Male Talk is seen in the sports metaphor. The natural palaver of Taskmaster men deals with winning and losing, scoring touchdowns, carrying the ball, close calls, going down to the wire, batting a thousand, hitting paydirt, and going into extra innings. Theirs are usually fast-paced monologues, direct and practical, offering "here's what you do" advice and remaining on the surface when it comes to emotions. Talk with friends is enjoyed for its jockeying for status, its repartee, and its camaraderie. Men are often more private, less communicative, and more interested in discussing goals than relationships. Indeed:

👑 **Gilda-Gram** *The four words men hate most are "Let's discuss the relationship."*

So stay away from this topic unless there is something major to discuss. Also keep in mind:

👑 **Gilda-Gram** *Male intimacy is to* commune. *Female intimacy is to* converse.

Female Talk usually centers around precisely what Male Talk does not: emotions, empathy, understanding, and—what else?—relationships. Unlike many men who won't call a woman just to "check in" or say "hi" (unless they are in the courting stages of their romance), women call friends to talk about nothing in particular, but to know that they are not alone, that they can share their thoughts and feelings, and that they feel understood. Talk for women is protection—an emotional condom.

The Need for Emotional Nakedness

Now that we know the natural differences between the sexes, we can more easily rip away our surface masks. When we apply our Power, we can become more real. We can dare to be emotionally naked. When all is said and done, if two people are not 100 percent committed to reveal themselves with candor, there can be no future. Candor requires emotional nakedness, self-disclosure, trusting your partner to accept you as you are. Self-disclosure encompasses three distinct rules.

The Three Rules of Self-Disclosure
1. Self-disclosure occurs little by little, in increments. It requires total trust on the parts of both partners.
2. Self-disclosure occurs in the context of positive interaction. Once trust is violated, self-disclosure will close down.
3. Self-disclosure is symmetrical. When one partner opens up, the other will soon do so as well, though probably with a different degree of openness. Be patient and allow your partner's trust to build.

Whether you are with the love of your life whom you want to hold on to or you are still searching for someone special, complete Self-Assessment #34 to set up a self-disclosing context in which your Language of Love can flow.

SELF-ASSESSMENT #34

CREATING A CONTEXT FOR SELF-DISCLOSURE
1. How do I *envision* myself in this relationship?
2. How does my partner *envision* me in this relationship?
3. How do I feel I should *act* in this relationship?

4. How does my partner feel I should *act* in this relationship?

5. How do I feel I should be *treated* in this relationship?

6. How does my partner feel I should be *treated* in this relationship?

What did you discover? Joan and Danny were a monogamous live-in couple for almost two years. While attending one of their neighbor's parties, Danny began to tell some off-color jokes, which most of the other guests seemed to enjoy. But Joan was upset. To her, Danny, a conservative banker, was usually toned down and quiet. She believed he should uphold his conservative reputation by continuing his usual role even when out socially. When Danny heard Joan's views, he was aghast. He took umbrage over his girlfriend trying to monitor his mouth and life. They got into a heated debate. After completing this self-assessment, Joan understood why. Joan envisioned Danny entirely differently from the way he envisioned himself. From this self-assessment, it was also discovered that he thought she should enact certain characteristics that were not always comfortable for her in social settings. Finally, this exercise revealed that Joan's critical treatment of Danny in front of the partygoers was unacceptable to him, while she did not feel she had done anything wrong. Self-Assessment #34 was the jumping-off point for the couple to rethink their expectations of each other's actions and their treatment of each other. In fact, it has brought them much closer together.

Marjorie had just begun to live with Les after taking a long time to convince him to move in with her. He waited until her older daughter went away to college, so that all they'd have left was the younger girl of thirteen. Both children complained about Marjorie's facade of "phony airs" when Les was around. They also felt confined by their own inability to be themselves, but their pleas to their mother went unheeded. Marjorie was determined to get Les to marry her, and her objective was to portray the perfect woman in a perfect house with perfect children without problems. This change of personality is not unusual for women when they are in a relationship with a man. Remember the women in chapter 2 who were seated at the Chinese restaurant, and how their demeanor changed the moment a man joined them? I have noticed some of the most powerful women melt when in the company of their men. I also noticed how dismally destroyed they became when their relationships disintegrated. Not disclosing our true selves eventually comes to haunt us. Many of these emotionally shattered women confided, "When the relationship broke up, I didn't even know who I was." As we saw in the last chapter, self-disclosure begins when we are without a guy, so that when we are with one, we can come clean honestly. It's so much easier.

Although having gotten the man of her dreams to come this far, Marjorie still felt depressed—so much so, in fact, she attended one of my workshops. After completing Self-Assessment #34, she discovered that she envisioned herself in her relationship as a Barbie doll, feeling that she should act with perfection and feeling that she should be treated with kid gloves. Her partner, however, perceived Marjorie as a woman who was unusually sensitive to his critiques, high-strung in her need to keep a spotless home, and overfunctioning in her desire to please. What pressure! No wonder she was depressed. We do not live in a perfect world, and any woman who tries to perfect her corner of it sets herself up for disappointment. After she recognized what she was doing to herself, Marjorie became real. She balanced her Toastmaster and Taskmaster tendencies and started learning how to communicate honestly. Her relationship has become more natural, and she and Les are planning a less-than-*perfect* wedding.

Each person in a couple could do himself or herself a favor by creating a context for self-disclosure early on. Even if that has not been the case, and a couple well into their relationship is wondering how their Language of Love could improve, the six items on this self-assessment tell them worlds about the communications they may be taking for granted.

The Language You Use Predicts Your Love Future

When we feel our Power, we are willing not only to dare to display our souls but also to lovingly perceive, accept, and compliment our mate's behavior. With 94 percent accuracy, John Gottman from the University of Washington has been able to predict which couples are destined for splitsville just by listening to the language they use to describe their first meetings. Spouses in faltering unions recast their beginnings in a negative light, with language of bad memories, regret, contempt, disillusionment, criticism, and pessimism. They hesitate to tell of their early years with "Oh, I don't remember" or "It was so long ago." They also avoid "we" and "us" terms. In contrast, couples in good relationships describe each other positively, often humorously. They vividly remember their meetings, gently finish each other's sentences, emphasize consensus, and accept kind criticism. Sandra Murray from the Institute for Social Research at the University of Michigan confirms that happy couples see each other's faults through rose-colored glasses, as endearing quirks. So a stubborn husband is interpreted by his wife as an independent thinker. An overprotective mate is seen as simply expressing his care and love. In the end, for being given the benefit of the doubt, these spouses actually take on the positive qualities their wives describe.

Rachel and Art have a wonderful twenty-year marriage with two kids, a dog, a house, two cars, and lots of bills. They frequently recount their blind-date meeting as a fun event, with his walking into her apartment dressed in ridiculously mismatched clothes and her making faces about how foolish he looked. But over the span of the decades they have spent together, Rachel has held on to Art's original garments for their humor. Each person in this couple knows who she/he is. Each person knows his/her Power. Their children see it, their family sees it, their friends see it. This, after all this time together. Who says you can't keep love alive?

On the other hand, Lila describes the first meeting she had with her husband of five years as a disaster. "There I was at my sister's wedding. Thomas was working as bartender. Another man was coming on to me, and Thomas continued to 'protect' me by interrupting our conversation. I couldn't believe his nerve." As anyone might have guessed, Lila is not happy with her union. Alicia similarly described her marriage as a mess. The ceremony was a nightmare, with the guests throwing not raw rice, but cooked rice, because the kitchen had run out of the usual stuff. Alicia was in tears. She thought the sacred ceremony was ruined. Her groom, however, thought it was hilarious. Although she won't predict her future with her husband of three years, she now criticizes matrimony for not being all it's cracked up to be.

Recount the story of your early beginnings with your mate or with your last partner. Complete Self-Assessment #35 and note the language you incorporate. Either predict the future of your current relationship or assess how the language you used might have alerted you to the demise of your last relationship.

SELF-ASSESSMENT #35

THE STORY OF OUR MEETING

Describe the story of how you and your partner met. Include your first impressions and your feelings about him when you first saw him. Do you remember these events as happy? Write from the heart without thinking or analyzing for too long.

Elva knew that she was no longer physically attracted to her husband of fourteen years, but after she read the way she described their meeting—"When I met him, he was the only man who loved me more than he loved his car. He was a fat slob who just fought for me so hard, I finally gave in"—she immediately found a lawyer so she could start a new life. In contrast,

Leslie was unsure of where her live-in lover and she were headed. They had been together for barely two years, and she thought she wanted to finally get married and start a family, but she was ambivalent about him and their entire relationship. She was fearful about his job as a cop, and she didn't like his working nights. But her story read, "When Jeff approached me at that engagement party, his eyes sparkled. He looked so cute in his tuxedo. When he asked me to dance I just melted. I couldn't wait until he kissed me good night." Based on these words, she decided to reconsider her future with Jeff. Did your own description of your romantic beginnings surprise you?

Draw Partnership Boundaries

With all the effort devoted to designing beautiful, fashionable wedding ceremonies, few couples invest in the territorial rights that can make or break their future. When two people know who they are individually, their personal Power sets the stage for how they relate as a pair. One way to prevent problems from arising is to complete the list of Four Partnership Dues and Don'ts. Your Bill of Boundaries guided your *personal* boundaries. Now your Partnership Dues and Don'ts outlines the dues you must pay before constructing your *relationship* boundaries. Both are similar to job descriptions at work, with their delineated role requirements; equally important, they enable lovers to establish the mutual Power terms of their interdependence. Couples can then communicate and uphold these conditions to determine the longevity of their commitment. Completing the next self-assessment is not an option; it's a love mandate.

SELF-ASSESSMENT #36

FOUR PARTNERSHIP DUES AND DON'TS

1. **PERFORMANCE**
   What does a loving partnership look like?
   Loving partners mirror role models of respectful behaviors.
   • Do we behave like loving partners?

2. **ACCOUNTABILITY**
   What does a loving partner do?
   Each loving partner is accountable for doing his/her share.
   • Do we each contribute our share?

3. **FEEDBACK**
   How well am I doing?

> *Loving partners communicate the way they feel.*
> • Do we communicate our feelings?
> ....
> **4. RECOGNITION**
> Do I feel rewarded in this partnership?
> *Each loving partner assesses whether his/her needs are being met.*
> • Does this partnership enhance me?

The Four Partnership Dues and Don'ts outlines power issues that might create untold communication misunderstandings. It removes love from its feminine feelings, right-brain orientation and places it into a masculine logic, left-brain stance. Although it may seem as calculating as a prenuptial agreement, it forces people to recognize the reality that romance can last if each party plays by the agreed-upon rules.

👑 **Gilda-Gram** *Without rules there are no boundaries.*
Without boundaries there is no self.
Without self there is no love.

Dyan and Hal were married for seven years. Throughout their years together they respectfully resolved the usual organizational questions of such things as who would feed the dog, take out the garbage, drive the kids to school, and go to the dry cleaners. Obviously they had successfully mapped out their Performance and Accountability criteria on the Four Partnership Dues and Don'ts. But a new problem was now emerging that caused them to wonder about their marriage's seven-year mark. It seemed that while each had complied with the necessary basics of harmonious living, their Language of Love had dipped in the Feedback and Recognition areas. Dyan completed the self-assessment. In the Feedback area, she found that she longed for Hal to stop what he was doing and simply say, "I love you." In the Recognition arena, she wondered if her marriage was still enhancing her life as it had in the past. Unlike a lot of women fearful of raising these issues with their mate, Dyan dared to be vulnerable about her needs as well as her fears. She sat with Hal over a quiet dinner devoid of kids, showed him the assessment, and told him what she needed. She was comfortable and capable of sharing her emotions because she knew her Power. She told her husband that what she needed to feel enhanced in their partnership was to be told more often of his feelings. She also shared that she needed some time alone to pursue the sculpting that she once loved to do. So good was their communication that Hal immediately acknowledged the links missing in their Language of Love. The two made plans to re-create their old dating patterns, the ones that had originally drawn them together. Both felt better. Neither felt the other had tried to chip away at the other's Power.

Maintaining Your Purpose

At different points in every relationship, it is necessary to take stock of what we have. At assessment time we must ask two basic questions: "What is our purpose in being together?" and "Am I achieving my purpose?" Most people don't consistently assess their relationship in this way, and when a crisis occurs, they cannot imagine how it came to *that*. Of course, most of us would prefer not to ask these two questions because we would rather not rock the boat, however seasick we may feel. But these questions are meant specifically to shake a couple into reality. Continued assessment of a relationship's purpose pushes us to make tiny adjustments in smaller situations so that when major catastrophes occur—and they surely will in life—we can deal with them lovingly without falling apart.

The Power of Praise—Hallelujah!

What is really your Purpose in speaking the Language of Love? Every time we communicate with our guy, our attitude and style cause him to react in one of three ways. He will either feel better, feel worse, or feel no different at all. Obviously, unless we're sadistic, our Purpose in our communication should be to get our man to feel *better* as often as possible. Unfortunately, over time couples tend to take one another for granted, and they treat each other like roommates rather than guests. As women continue to find fault with and negate their men's behavior, the love that had originally bonded two people begins to spiral downward. Helen Gurley Brown's suggestion about writing a love note to the man you love is key. She stresses short, sweet messages, *totally about him*. I agree. Play up the things you love the most, his greatest assets: his smile, his humor, his storytelling, his body. He's your genius with a penis. Make him feel *gooood*. When you do, you will be encouraging his positive communication with you and enhancing the entire relationship. A man may connect with a woman at first because of her physical appeal. But he will *stay* with her because of the way she makes him feel. If a woman's philosophy is not to give her guy compliments and stroke (what she considers to be) his already oversize ego, guess who won't be around for long? The best way to win a man's committed heart is to praise, praise, praise.

By using praise, you will keep the embers burning as you make your man feel better. This may seem obvious, but during heated arguments, it's easy to forget that undercutting, angry language is a surefire way of creating fissures that may be difficult to repair later. Negative words are not aphrodisiacs. No matter what stage of relationship two people enjoy, *each person in a couple needs to feel wanted*. Our desire for positive reinforcement is constant. Look at how much brighter our day becomes when the boss at work offers a simple praise. When praise comes from the person we love, we especially feel elated, recognized, and desirable.

One praise technique in the Language of Love is to offer your partner Honest Positives. These are immediate, genuine, positive statements that tell your man you thank him, you miss him, you love him, in ways you may have forgotten. For example, "Henry, I love watching you walk down the street." Or, "Larry, having sex with you is always so exciting." Or, "Honey, I want to kill you over this issue, but your kisses still turn me on!" Even in the heat of dispute, you can surely find some positive traits of your partner to compliment. In fact, *especially* during heated dispute, if you can jump off the negative platform and into a more positive arena, the entire relationship can flourish. You have already learned how to convert your own negative statements to positive self-talk. Now it's time to offer the same optimism to your man. You are certain of your Power, and now you're ready to cement your Purpose. Keep in mind that your aim is to preserve and enhance your relationship. Since you are already emotionally centered, you can give generously from the overflow without affecting your core.

This is no manipulative gesture. To work successfully, Honest Positives must be true, current, and sincere. Honest Positives work so well that your lover will begin to open up almost instantly. But when that happens, be careful not to rehash long-stored-up grievances just because you suddenly have his attention. Complete Self-Assessment #37 and practice offering Honest Positives on paper before you apply them in real life.

SELF-ASSESSMENT #37

OFFERING HONEST POSITIVES

1. My partner's five most positive traits are:_____
2. Write five Honest Positives you will say to your mate.
   To ensure his attention, begin with his name.

Roberta was having a heated discussion with her husband, Al, about when his children should plan to visit them. Although Al's two kids were already in college, and this couple had a three-year-old of their own, they were usually successful in accommodating both sets of families. But for the weekend Al wanted his older children to visit, Roberta had already made plans for the two of them to get away. This was a vacation that they needed desperately. She had checked the date earlier with her husband and had already lined up a baby-sitter. Now he wanted to change the program because his children were suddenly off from school and this would be an ideal opportunity for them all to be together. After making such intricate arrangements, Roberta was miffed. It brought up all kinds of insecurities for her as she sensed Al's consideration of his first family over his current one. As they were hammering out a new schedule to meet everyone's preferences, Roberta suddenly turned to her husband and said, "I love your hugs . . . and I could use one of them now." This Honest Positive provided an interruptive pattern to their negative words. Al suddenly stopped his attempts at rescheduling to hug his wife. Their voices became softer. They kissed. Roberta dropped her insecure feelings, and Al himself suggested they keep their plans as is, and his older children could visit on their next break from school.

In our culture we seem to be quick to criticize but reluctant to stroke. The rule of thumb has generally been "Ignore his kind actions, but zap his bad ones." At the heart of our caution about freely doling out warm fuzzies is our own fear of getting close, being vulnerable, and getting hurt. So we all seem to find ourselves in the protection business these days. Even intimate partners tend to avoid the very intimacy they crave. Practicing the language of Honest Positives readies us to apply positive reinforcement daily and strengthen the relationship bond. Men want to feel admired, just as we do. When we compliment them, their ears prick up and their chests fill with pride. Of course, if we never offer critiques as well, our communications won't be believed. Researchers Howard Markham and Clifford Notarious have found through their work with couples that "one zinger erases twenty acts of kindness." Most experts agree. Compliments should outweigh criticisms at least by a ratio of five to one, five positives to each negative. Do your compliments and criticisms meet their recommended daily allowance?

Check it out. For one day, keep a Diary of Compliments and Criticisms to assess your usual communications. This will make you aware of altering the negatives if they're debilitating your Language of Love. Complete Self-Assessment #38 and discover what you may not necessarily be aware of.

SELF-ASSESSMENT #38

DIARY OF COMPLIMENTS AND CRITICISMS

Date: ———

In contrast with what we've been taught, flattery gets us *everywhere*. Keep track of the way you communicate your love.

   1. Compliments I gave: _____

   2. Compliments I received: _____

   3. Criticisms I gave: _____

   4. Criticisms I received: _____

If the criticisms you give or get outweigh the compliments you give or get, it's time to change!

After Roberta completed her Diary of Compliments and Criticisms over a period of only one week's time, she recognized that she was more critical of Al than complimentary. She was shocked at her own negative communications. Reminding herself of her Purpose of preserving and elevating their romance, she began consciously to reinforce more of his actions. When we accentuate their positive behaviors, men become more receptive to what we have to say. When they are more receptive to what we have to say, we can continue to sharpen our mutual interaction and our relationship's Purpose. As we intensify our love connection, we are ready for the next test of our Language of Love.

Tuning in to the Appropriate Channel

Each gender has different ways of demonstrating that they are listening. Compared with men, women incorporate more listening noises, or "paralanguage," such as "uh-huh" and "mm-hm." In contrast, men usually sit motionless, probably hearing us but usually displaying little emotional feedback. Most women believe their men suffer from the "Huh, what did you say?" disorder. But your man's reaction may not necessarily mean that he's inattentive or that he's not hearing your every word—or it may. To discover whether your man is inattentive or this is just his listening style, complete Self-Assessment #39.

SELF-ASSESSMENT #39

TEST OF MALE ATTENTION

1. While your man is telling you a story, mirror his listening language by sitting without emotion or paralanguage.
2. Let him continue talking, with you being immobile and silent.

---

3. If your man is like most, he will turn to you in the midst of his monologue and ask, "Are you listening?" (Apparently, not only is he used to your verbal responses, but he depends on them to go on.)

4. When he does ask that question, explain your experiment to him. Tell him you were mirroring his listening behavior back to him. Ask him how that felt.

What happened?

This experiment works every time. When Roberta tried this assessment, Al got to understand firsthand what it meant for him to listen as his wife preferred. If there's any hope for your man to demonstrate his attention, he must first understand how you feel when you speak to a motionless partner. Yes, once again, it's the woman who must bust the communications barriers. But if she doesn't do it, who will?

From the well-known technology of neurolinguistics programming, each of us processes information through a visual, auditory, or feelings channel. Some people are more capable of "style-flexing" quickly from one channel to another, while others concentrate on one dominant channel, or perhaps two, at a time. In order to be heard by anyone, we must speak in the mode our listener understands. To learn to do that, first discover your own listening channel by completing Self-Assessment #40.

SELF-ASSESSMENT #40

MY LISTENING CHANNEL

Discover which listening channel is dominant for you—visual, auditory, or feelings.

Check each item that describes you:

_____ **1.** I like to look at the stars.

_____ **2.** I enjoy getting massages.

_____ **3.** I write goals for myself.

_____ **4.** I talk to myself.

_____ **5.** I am a good listener.

_____ **6.** I enjoy dancing.

_____ **7.** I have difficulty sleeping through noise.

_____ **8.** I touch people when I talk to them.

_____ **9.** My body becomes tense after a bad day.

_____**10.** I enjoy observing people.

_____**11.** I spend much time on my appearance.

_____**12.** I tune in to the sound of people's voices.

Circle the category in which you had the most checks:
VISUAL: 1, 3, 10, 11   AUDITORY: 4, 5, 7, 12   FEELINGS: 2, 6, 8, 9

Now that you've discovered your own listening channel, assess the listening channel of your partner in Self-Assessment #41.

SELF-ASSESSMENT #41

MY PARTNER'S LISTENING CHANNEL

Discover which listening channel your partner uses—visual, auditory, or feelings—to enhance your communication with him.

Check each item that describes your partner:

_____ **1.** He likes to look at the stars.

_____ **2.** He enjoys getting massages.

_____ **3.** He writes goals for himself.

_____ **4.** He talks to himself.

_____ **5.** He is a good listener.

_____ **6.** He enjoys dancing.

_____ **7.** He has difficulty sleeping through noise.

_____ **8.** He touches people when he talks to them.

_____ **9.** His body becomes tense after a bad day.

_____**10.** He enjoys observing people.

_____**11.** He spends much time on his appearance.

_____**12.** He tunes in to the sound of people's voices.

Circle the category in which you had the most checks:
VISUAL: 1, 3, 10, 11   AUDITORY: 4, 5, 7, 12   FEELINGS: 2, 6, 8, 9

After completing both of these self-assessments, you should understand more about the way the two of you listen to each other. Now what do you do? To make sure your information is readily heard, *mirror* or *match* the style of your lover by speaking in the language that he can understand. This assures that your message will be received as you mean it. This technique is called "mirroring" or "matching" your mate's Language of Love.

How to Mirror Your Mate's Channel

- If he says he *sees* your point, respond by *showing* him the bigger picture.
- If he says he *hears* a story about a neighbor, respond with "I'd love to *listen* to that."
- If he tells you he *loves your hair*, respond with "I *feel* great when you compliment me."

People respond to information they are able to understand. It is pointless to speak to your lover in English when all he understands is French. Similarly, it is of no use to speak to him using the visual channel when he is an auditory processor. By tuning in to the language your man understands, you can enhance your Language of Love.

....

👑 **Gilda-Gram** *To clear your communication static, change the channel.*

....

The visual listener speaks through his eyes. He wants to stop and *look* before doing or feeling anything. Do not rush up to him to get too physically close. Communicate gradually, in visual terms. He will then *get the picture* and *brighten* his *outlook* to know you enjoy *seeing* him. Let him *see* what a sensitive person you are. *Show* him how much you can do for him. Ask the visual person, "What do you see?" "How do you picture that?" and "What kind of affair do you see us having?" On an External—but crucial—level, take extra care with your appearance.

The visual listener is disturbed by constant chatter and loud music. He finds it difficult to express his feelings. He prefers face-to-face meetings with you rather than telephone calls. When he's angry he's likely to be silent rather than scream. He is a neat, stylish dresser. He is also a well-organized note taker. He often does not look people in the eyes since he is busy picturing his thoughts while he speaks. He will often look up before telling us that he *sees* our point. While making love, he keeps his eyes closed to feel that we are even closer.

Visual words include *see, look, imagine, reveal, perspective, bright, clear, color, conceptualize, dim, display, draw, eye, illustrate, light, observe, paint, picture, portray, rainbow, recognize, show, view.*

The auditory listener enjoys sounds. He relates better to music than to pictures. He is in tune with the inner logic of words rather than feelings. He paces his life and activities in relation to time, unusually dependent on his watch, as one man put it, "to know how I'm supposed to feel." The auditory man has inner conversations with himself. Never scream at an auditory man. No matter how angry you are with him, try to keep your tones well modulated. Try to match your tone to his in every way. Let him know that you are listening. Ask him, "Can you tell from this?" "Do you hear what I mean?" "How does this sound to you?"

The auditory man prefers in-person or telephone conversations to letters or notes. He spends much time on the phone. He turns on the radio as soon as he enters the car. He loves the sound of voices. When angry, he is quick to let you hear about it. He's articulate and expresses himself well, often enjoying a good debate. He is knowledgeable and enjoys sharing what he knows. He dresses in a sensible, but not fancy, style. He loves concerts and other listening experiences. Auditory men tend to look from side to side before explaining that they *hear* your side of the argument. Their sitting posture also often resembles that of a person who is talking on the phone, with their head resting on their hand.

Auditory words include *hear, listen, ask, tell, say, bang, beat, blare, cheer, echo, explode, groan, howl, loud, melodious, music, noise, pitch, quiet, rhythm, roar, scream, sharp, slap, snap, sound, speak, trumpet, utter, verbalize, whisper, yell.*

The feelings listener wears his heart on his sleeve. Because our culture encourages women, more so than men, to demonstrate their feelings, it is easier for a woman to quickly establish rapport with a feelings man. Feelings men therefore often have more female than male friends.

The feelings man is more concerned with how things feel than with how they look or sound. He enjoys sensual memories: something to touch, smell, and taste. For him to remember you, wear soft, silky, or tactile garments. Use touch whenever possible. Ask, "How do you feel about that?"

The feelings man makes decisions based on whether they *feel* right. He will wait for his feelings to reveal themselves before making important decisions. He prefers comfortable to fashionable clothes. He enjoys talking while performing physical activities. When angry, the feelings person is likely to storm out of the room or pound a table. He is quick to express his emotions physically. He finds it difficult to sit through long meetings. Feelings communicators often look diagonally downward before admitting that they *feel* they are right.

Feelings words include *feel, touch, grasp, catch, catch on, understand, angry, anxious, aroused, bad, behave, bitter, chilling, cold, cool, depression, dirty, dull, emotional, excited, exhausted, glad, good, happy, hard, hate, high, hopeful, hot, hurt, long, nervous, passion, push, rough, rub, sad, scared, sense, sharp, smooth, strong, tense, tired, warm, wet.*

You can encourage trust by mirroring the channel your lover uses. "I love you" is a phrase that is often bandied about too freely; the words "I trust you" might be a better choice. Trust is the deepest ingredient of lasting love. Mirroring your man's language will engender his own trust. Although he won't know why, he will feel that your level of rapport with him is that of a best friend. Men need this feeling to establish and maintain connection.

Pete was an auditory listener who spent hours on the phone gabbing with people with whom he networked for business. When he sat at his desk, he typically leaned his head on one hand, replicating *The Thinker* statue. When he met visual processor Jocelyn, there was great chemistry, he the Taskmaster to her Toastmaster personality. They were locked in sync. At first their different listening styles was a positive source in the relationship, because opposite traits do attract.

One day the couple was invited to visit the country home of a friend of Pete's. As the friend gave Jocelyn directions over the phone, she repeated them aloud while writing them down. Pete half listened as he shaved. In their frenzy to leave, Jocelyn left the directions on the table, but because of the combination of Pete's auditory memory and Jocelyn's ability to visualize her notes, the couple got to their destination without a hitch. And this helped avoid a possible argument. But their relationship began to deteriorate when their different styles became impediments to healing their wounds.

Once Jocelyn had taken the self-assessments included here, she could approach their arguments differently. Consequently, during fights, the couple was beginning to acknowledge their different processing patterns. One thing Jocelyn discovered was that Pete became more incensed when her presence interrupted his oral flow. As an auditory processor, Pete was compelled to let Jocelyn *hear about his points* in the form of a *debate*. But Jocelyn became more upset with Pete's unwillingness to *see her points*. They were quickly getting into name-calling patterns that arose from the frustration behind their language barriers. Something had to be done, or else their relationship was doomed immediately.

Jocelyn removed herself from the room of the argument. She proceeded to another phone line and *called Pete*. Using his more comfortable auditory demeanor, he could at once hear her points without the contamination of her physical presence. Make no mistake, it was Jocelyn who had to learn Pete's auditory mode to be heard. She says holding on to her marriage was worth the effort—at least for as long as she intends to stay. She has internalized the Gilda-Gram: *Choose rather than be chosen*. She is prepared to take her next step with Pete out of strength rather than out of fear. As you can see, Jocelyn continues to grow and develop. In relationships we are *all* works in progress, and the job never ceases.

The language channel we choose can make or break our romantic future. Nadine was seeing a man who upset her by his indirect eye contact. After recognizing him as a visual processor, she understood that as he looked up, rather than at her, he was choosing words to communicate from his visual memory. As soon as she understood, she did not take his lack of eye-alogue personally. Melanie's husband was constantly advising her about what to wear; since her appearance was of less importance to her, she was upset at first. But as soon as she recognized him as a visual processor, she chose this as the perfect arena in which she could satisfy him at a low emotional cost to her. Marilyn couldn't believe the time Dennis spent on the phone in their own home. She thought he should want to enhance his closeness with her. But when she understood him to be an auditory processor, she knew that her man found great solace in conversation, and she loved him enough to support that. Esther was enthusiastic that her new husband often reached out and stroked her arm, hair, face, and hands when they communicated. Having been married before to a cold Prince Charles look-alike, this was a warm and invigorating change. She understood that he was a feelings processor, and was she ever grateful!

Remember, love requires both giving and receiving. We must remember our Purpose in being together. To give and receive passion, we must also offer *com*passion. We must offer our man the same kind of praise we would like to receive from him. We must demonstrate to him how we prefer to be heard. We must speak to him in the language he can readily interpret and accept. Why wouldn't a woman in love want to honor her man this way? To the world, he represents an extension of someone she herself has chosen. That makes him a magnification of her. By esteeming the man she loves, a woman is thereby esteeming herself. No man leaves a woman who regards him with such respect. Besides, when she respects him, he returns the favor in kind.

Announcing Your Willingness to Play

Lighten Up!

Now that Margaret is older and wiser, she admits that one reason each of her two marriages failed was that both husbands refused to Play with her— her first husband in the snow, her second husband in the sand. When we tie the knot, we agree to love, honor, and cherish one another. But the enshrined knot can become a constricting noose if two people don't also agree to have fun. Anthropologists have long noted the importance of Play as the lighter side of gender dynamics. "Neoteny" is the extension of childlike characteristics into adulthood. Play cements closeness and connection. It extends our secret talk into the realm of humor, intimate jokes, and games. While Power and Purpose are needed elements in our Language of Love, these are our more grown-up and serious stabilizers. But there is a void if we don't supplement the serious with more frothy fare. The final element in our Language of Love is our willingness to Play.

👑 **Gilda-Gram** *Play together to stay together.*

With Play, lovers look forward to nonpressured, non-self-conscious togetherness, laughter, and joy.

Play is based on a person's ability to take himself or herself seriously yet accept life lightly and humorously. When two people can find the humor in the strange things that happen, it becomes the glue that keeps the relationship going over time. It is a universal coping mechanism that breaks down anxiety and gives us the necessary distance to put life's insanities in perspective and perhaps on hold. Adults never lose their sense of humor, but adulthood often mandates that we put it aside. Sometimes we forget we ever knew how to Play.

Children laugh over twenty times more a day than adults. One study found that the average number of times per day a preschooler laughs is four hundred, compared to an adult's meager fifteen! Grown-ups now flock to workshops to reclaim their inner child, the part of themselves that once encouraged humor and joy.

Laughter is the language of the angels. *Saturday Review* editor Norman Cousins laughed away a life-threatening disease with Marx Brothers movies and *Candid Camera* episodes. This, after the medical profession assured him he would soon be dead. For sure, humor sharpens the brain. When we laugh, our adrenal glands discharge hormones that make us more alert and improves our memory during stress. Laboratory studies have proved that humor has a significant positive effect on our cardiovascular, respiratory, muscular, and immune systems. Laughter lowers the level of cortisol, a stress hormone, that makes us more prone to illness. It also releases endorphins, natural painkillers that can improve our emotional health. As a total body experience, who would choose *not* to have fun? Actually, many folks.

Bernice met her husband while she was still in college. There was an age difference between them of nearly thirteen years, but both felt their love could survive anything. Their pact was for her to continue her education while he supported her financially until she was through. During Bernice's trying times of exams and term papers, he was also a great source of emotional support. Finally, she graduated. Now in the workforce, at last, she wanted to rekindle the fun she thought she had missed during those long years of studying. Without the stress of her school deadlines, she regained her sense of humor and her desire to play. When she beseeched her husband to engage in outdoor activities with her during the summer and winter weather, he refused. He told her it was unbecoming of a "college graduate" to be so free-spirited. He asked her to "calm down" and act like a "lady." She tried to convince him that Play was a part of her life that she had temporarily put off and now longed to find again. Begrudgingly, one hot summer day, he did drive her to the beach. But when they got there, he told her to walk along the sand for as long as she liked, and he would remain in the car until she'd had her fill. Bernice suddenly did not know who this man was. Hidden by the fact that she was a dependent student, seriously engaged in her studies, she never knew this element important to a lasting relationship was even missing. When she divorced him, she told her friends it was because he would not stroll with her along the beach or stomp with her in the snow, but the reality was that her husband was unable to Play, in the sense of simply enjoying life.

👑 **Gilda-Gram** *If you're too busy to Play, you're too busy.*

And if you're too busy, get a life before your life gets you!

In contrast with people who don't make time to Play, remember Rachel and Art, the lovebirds with the twenty-year marriage who still purr at the sight of each other? While they enjoy the humor of their early romantic beginnings, they now take cooking and dancing classes together. Each can recount the other's days at work as well as the one who lived it. They mutually support each other's upsets about co-workers and friends who have disappointed them. In short, they honor one another and play together, and their twenty years has shown how they intend to stay together. Theirs is a love in progress. It incorporates Power, Purpose, and, of course, a lightheartedness for Play.

To expand the Play aspect of your romance, interpret your Language of Love as a sitcom. Step back from your conflicts, relate to your experiences from a distance, and if you don't like the screen, zap the remote control. Your ability to laugh and Play strengthens your bond of friendship with your partner. Remember, that's where the Language of Love began: friends first, lovers later. Friendship is play that sets the stage for the foreplay yet to come. It is the special tongue that two people instinctively know as their own. It is the consummate language that speaks without speaking. If an ant colony can last for more than twenty years, then there's no reason that a marriage should expire after three or four. Having fun and laughing is the salve that makes the boredom and staleness in a relationship disappear as it builds and strengthens the union over time. Once two people assess their Power, their Purpose, and their willingness to Play, they can use the kind of language that the other can hear, stroke their partner with honest compliments, and look forward to waking up in the same bed for the new day's adventure yet to unfold. The more humor, honor, and goodness we communicate, the quicker the Language of Love will successfully become our more advanced Language of Sex.

 Gilda-Gram *Don't delay Play.*

GILDA-GRAMS
FROM CHAPTER 8
Incorporate the Language of Love

▶ *Friends first, lovers later.*

▶ *Fall in like before you fall in love.*

▶ *For stress-reduced communication with your man, use Male Talk first, Female Talk later. Or deals first, details later.*

▶ *The four words men hate most are "Let's discuss the relationship."*

▶ *Male intimacy is to commune; female intimacy is to converse.*

▶ *Without rules there are no boundaries. Without boundaries there is no self. Without self there is no love.*

▶ *To clear your communication static, change the channel.*

▶ *Play together to stay together.*

▶ *If you're too busy to Play, you're too busy.*

▶ *Don't delay Play.*

9
Apply the Language of Sex

♔ **Gilda-Gram** *Good communication is the best lubrication.*

W e noted how a woman's Language of Love derives from her knowing who she is, knowing what she wants, and knowing what to do. We saw how these basics form the foundation of a woman's Power, Purpose, and willingness to Play. In chapter 8 we discussed how she must express these skills so that whatever she communicates is accepted as she means it. Powerful, Purposeful, and Playful women dare to communicate who they are no matter how the chips may fall. Since they act out of strength rather than out of fear, and since they attract not who they *want* but who they *are*, the men in their lives are as worthy, respectful, and fun loving as they. By setting synchronistic language styles, these women know how to steadily entice their mates. Such is the Language of Love. But it gets even better. The height of ecstasy comes when a woman applies the Language of Sex.

The Three Aspects of the Language of Sex

While the three elements of the Language of Love are based in *verbal* communication, the three aspects of the Language of Sex are based in *carnal*, or bodily, communication. These three aspects are the next steps of Power, Purpose, and Play. They consist of Flirtation, Sensuality, and Sexuality.

When a woman applies the Language of Sex, she will know *what to do*: **Flirt**. She will know *how she feels*: **Sensual**. She will know *who she is*: **Sexual**. As with the three elements of the Language of Love, if any of these three aspects of the Language of Sex are missing, the ability of two bodies to take their verbal communication to the next higher level will be blocked. By *expressing* these aspects, a couple soars to the greatest dimension possible. They can now enhance what has already been built in their verbal communiqués.

These three aspects are sequential and cyclical, because after a period of time everything becomes stale, including our relationships. When we continue to reinvent the excitement that originally brought us together, we change the predictable attraction-seduction-destruction format to ever-flowing arousal. Same lover, *thirsting* flirtation, *throbbing* sensuality, *explosive* sex. To enjoy these moments, the cycle must start and restart as it continues and continues and continues. It begins with the art of flirtation.

Be Willing to Flirt

Flirting is eye-centered teasing, throbbing, and luring foreplay that is totally nonverbal. It requires that a woman know who she is, that she know her Power. When a woman knows her Power, she can boldly beckon her partner with eyes that dance. She can apply the *power stare* with confidence. Eyes reveal what lips conceal. The *look* of love expresses that a woman feels good about herself—good enough, in fact, to risk gambling in the ardor arena. While women say touch is their biggest turn-on, men call sight their most erotic sense. Most men seem to have a direct line between their optic nerves and their genitals. By liberally using eye-alogue for longer than five seconds, a woman can let a man know she is interested without saying a word. Upping her flirtation, she can supplement eye-alogue with a forty-five-degree sideways head tilt, exposing the opposite side of her neck. If she includes the devil-may-care head toss or a hair flip, and if she slowly runs her fingers through her hair, her love interest immediately gets the point.

After lengthy eye-alogue, a woman can incorporate the short, darting glance that eventually becomes fixated on her target. She can lick her lips or pout them slightly. She can expose a flexed palm with the inside of her wrist. When she slides her palm up and down her wineglass, her signals become more than obvious. Finally, she can primp by elegantly smoothing or patting her clothing or fondling some inanimate object. With her Power in tow, she will walk proudly, stomach pulled in, shoulders arched back, and chest thrown out. Flirting is just the first step of the Language of Love.

Flirting sets the stage. It is the glance that gets the guy at the next table to send a drink to yours. It's the look that makes him wonder where you've been hiding. It's the mesmerizing twinkle that lets a husband know he's wanted in the bedroom—now. It's the gaze, the gape, the lusty longing that somehow sends your message . . . all without a word.

When you've flirted beyond recklessness, you are ready for eros-enhancing sensuality. This next step incorporates more senses than just the visual. Now you can expand your primal poses into seductive stripteases with beguiling music. You can video yourself and your lover in instant replays of your most sensual moves. You can incorporate the other senses of touch, taste, and smell as you embrace the world around you. Little by little your circle of inclusion gets greater as you reach beyond the narrower scope.

Express Your Sensuality

Our culture asks, "What's sex without a good penetration?" as it believes good sex entails only the intercourse/orgasm touchdown. Intimacy for men usually emphasizes the *in* of the goal, emphasis on the genitalia (in hopes they'll never fail ya). But it doesn't make sense to go from zero to one hundred in sixty seconds, especially since only 30 percent of women can reach orgasm through intercourse alone without clitoral stimulation. Since men usually derive great pleasure from a turned-on woman, this can ultimately be a problem for men whose sexual confidence is smaller than women think.

Most people tweak and thump so hard that intercourse gets in the way of the important sensual sensations that constitute the deliciousness of the act. For a full body experience, we would have to stretch out our sexuality from one moment to one hour to one week, and then orgasm would not become the only way to reach elation. To really enjoy sex to its fullest, try flirting on Monday, accelerate to kissing on Tuesday, drive to fondling on Wednesday, and keep the juices flowing till Thursday. Sometimes intercourse would be the destination, sometimes it would be the journey itself. Although many men may not admit it openly, they, like women, want to be cared for, revered, tended to, nurtured, and tenderly touched from head to toe. By expanding sex, you enhance the anticipation and the pleasure. Partners who touch each other as if they'll never touch again understand that it's the process, the flirtation, the seduction that counts, more often than the home run. Just as the growth process—not the relationship—should be the goal, so should the buildup—not the orgasm—be the goal. The buildup is the journey. The journey enhances excitement. Excitement is the crux of enjoyment and fun.

It is estimated that the average human body contains 3,500 square inches of skin. Our sensuality can embody each and every one of these square inches. Yet according to the World Health Organization, sexual intercourse occurs more than 100 million times daily around the world. The 910,000 conceptions and 350,000 cases of sexually transmitted disease that result suggest there ought to be some alternatives to sexual satisfaction. Nobody ever died from sexual yearning, and the art of carnal restraint may do a couple good as they build sexual tension over time. Once again, and I'm sorry about this, women must be the ones who are "It" in the game of tag. Since they now know the score, it is the women who must guide their men toward other aspects of the Language of Sex. Actually, this is not so bad after all. Men list one of their greatest turn-ons to be women who are bold and creative in bed. This is your chance to apply your sensual expression in the realm of a rich fantasy repertoire, using all your senses and body parts, not just your genitals. Why not try? The alternative is staying where you've already been. *Bored!*

One form of sexuality that emphasizes this expanded multisensory process is tantric sex. From the Eastern philosophies, it is based on the reasoning that each person is granted only five thousand orgasms. So she or he must preserve each one. Not being orgasm oriented, tantra takes the focus off the genitals and intercourse and substitutes connection of the emotional, spiritual, and physical states. It is cycle energy that mentally forces sex to travel through you, into and out of your partner, and back to you again. By inhaling from the genitals to the heart, the energy is circulated throughout the entire body.

In tantric sex, ultimately, the journey becomes the destination. Appreciation, affection, and attention are emphasized through kissing, caressing, and oral and manual stimulation without dividing love play into foreplay, intercourse, and afterplay. Surprisingly, it is men who say women's biggest sex mistake is not taking or making time for sex, as they had done at the beginning of their romance. Therefore tantric sex not only provides men with the ability to get off the performance hook, but it also generates slow, pleasurable, and relaxed sexuality. Most important, it unifies sex and love.

There are supposedly 2,862 ways to sexually satisfy you and your partner without intercourse. What fun it could be to experiment with at least a few of those. In this way, women could get the time they need to taxi down the runway before takeoff, and men would learn to accept different performance criteria. No one can fail.

Sensuality incorporates all the senses, and each exciting turn-on from one of the five senses can overlap another. Apply a sexy scent that turns your man to Jell-O. Body scent plays a large and seductive role in mate attraction, our sexiest fragrances reflecting our sex hormones. In fact, there are odors at home that can specifically increase penile blood flow between 20 and 40 percent. They are pumpkin pie, doughnuts, licorice, and lavender. You might want to keep these around. Each person also has a unique "smellprint" that smells best to a partner. The Eskimo kiss of nose rubbing is a case of mutual sniffing of bodily scent that takes advantage of these "smellprints."

The Western world has reprogrammed the kiss to become the personal signature of your eroticism. From childhood, the mouth was our primary genital. Without words, it reflects something about our character, our generosity, and how much we want to satisfy a partner. According to one researcher, husbands and wives kiss an average of 5.76 times a day. In a study of people from nineteen countries, three-quarters of women thought kissing more intimate than sex, while, surprisingly, half of the men agreed. Kissing is erotic because of the many nerve endings in the lips. It can incorporate the taste, feel, and breath of each person's energy forces, as well as each person's scent. We'd be wise to get back to the marathon kisses we engaged in at the outset of our relationships to maintain our sensual bond.

Kissing is a tasty turn-on that also involves touch. Touching involves strokes and caresses that can drive a partner crazy. When we touch our partner, we can sense his hot spots. Some of these spots have more nerve endings than others, and they therefore register more sensation. While the spine and the upper arm are the least sensitive, the tongue tip, fingertips, and the tip of the nose (Eskimo style) are our three greatest touch centers. With a little flicking, licking, sucking, squeezing, blowing, and biting, your pleasure ratio can soar. Remember to expand his erogenous zone from his toes, to his scrotum, to his hands, to his ears, to his full 3,500 square inches of loving.

Don't forget the sexy sounds of sighing, bed creaking, lovers' heartbeats, and seductive music. These intonations affect hormone release, brain wave activity, heart rate, and the body's electrical energy. Lavish him with Honest Positives, especially about his performance. Offer praise without appraisal. Mentally masturbate his ego. A woman needs cognitive stimulation before clitoral stimulation, and that's why we crave compliments. By the same token, we must remember to allow our orgasms to be obvious and demonstrative *audiogasms* so our man knows without a doubt he's turned us to butter. When a man strays, he blames not only his woman's loss of attractiveness, but her loss of attention to *him*. Men love a turned-on woman, one they know they've single-handedly sent to ecstasy. Let your man know you're there for him in mind *and* body. And let your body talk through all your senses.

Enjoy Your Sexuality

The *Journal of Personality and Social Psychology* found that women with a positive view of their sexuality have more fulfilling love relationships. This is understandable when we consider that sexuality is an expression of sensuality, and sensuality expresses our willingness to probe our senses for excitement. To enjoy your sexuality to its fullest, you must own your power in bed. Since you already know how to project a Power Image while you're vertical, all you need to do now is switch the same skills into the horizontal position. But first, in the upright position, take off your clothes. Stand in front of a mirror. Say aloud, "I am a sexual person"; "I love my beautiful body"; "I know how to give a man pleasure"; "I deserve to receive pleasure myself"; "I enjoy showing my partner how to please me in bed." Feel the pride of your unique beauty. Smile as you run your hand along your personal pleasure spots.

Sex is not as much about the sexual act itself as it is about the way a woman views her body and her freedom to use it. Despite the many taboos with which we have been raised and the silent double standard that still exists when it comes to women and men, every woman must feel that she has a right to enjoy sex. She need not apologize. She is proud of her body, so she is happy to tell her partner how she *deserves* to be turned on.

Sex is a couple's language of mutual ecstasy. Exciting sex extends their ordinary communication into a higher realm. For this freedom to become excitement, a woman must discard the ancient myths and old wives' tales. She must get rid of her inhibitions and fears. She must be willing to lose control.

Clear Your Sexual Myths and Act on Sexual Truths

For many people, sex is a mystery that consists of lewd fantasies and dull marital myths. How much of what you know about sex is based on fact? Check your own sexual awareness by completing Self-Assessment #42. You may be surprised about what you *don't know*. Once you gain the knowledge you need, you can reach sexual harmony as your sex life becomes hotter than ever. Knowing about your own body, as well as your partner's, allows you greater freedom to experiment and enjoy the fruits of lovemaking you never imagined possible.

SELF-ASSESSMENT #42

OF LIBIDOS, FANTASIES, AND ORGASMS

Answer **True** *or* **False** *to each of the following statements:*

_____**1.** Without an erection, a man can't ejaculate.

_____ **2.** Almost everyone, single or married, masturbates.

_____**3.** A good marriage can survive problematic sex.

_____**4.** In the beginning of a relationship, people often don't feel comfortable sharing their sexual preferences. As the relationship unfolds, lack of sexual communication often remains the same.

_____**5.** Unlike women, men are ready to make love anytime, anywhere.

_____**6.** When a partner initiates sex, it always means that she/he desires her/his partner.

_____**7.** Women reach orgasm most easily in the missionary position.

_____**8.** Men and women have an equal number of erogenous zones.

CORRECT ANSWERS

1. *False:* Even a limp and partially erect penis can ejaculate.

2. *True:* People of all ages masturbate. Couples in new, sexually charged relationships masturbate as they fantasize about their partner when they are apart. Marrieds masturbate to balance their different sexual needs and appetites.

3. *True:* A good marriage is the key word here. The presence of a problem does not mean the absence of sexual satisfaction. A loving and committed relationship involves sexual compromises that partners are happy to make to accommodate each other.

4. *True:* In the first, fragile stages of a relationship, trust and sexual forthrightness are rare. But later on, couples are reticent to discuss sexual concerns for fear of being seen as manipulative, deceptive, and dishonest when they first began. They also worry about threatening their partner's security. It seems that there is never a good time to discuss these sensitive issues, so old habits remain hard to break.

5. *False:* Like women, men have horny spells as well as lulls. Although, anthropologically, most women are more discriminating than most men, the myth that men need only to find any woman and a place puts additional pressure on them to perform.

6. *False:* People make love for all sorts of reasons: to get intimacy, to be touched and held, to escape intimacy through sex, to release tension, to figuratively screw someone. During the REM cycle of sleep, men can have as many as five erections, each lasting thirty to forty-five minutes. While these are not necessarily related to sexual desire, they can still be put to good use.

7. *False:* Although many women enjoy a man's take-charge top-penetration position, the majority find that being on top provides good clitoral stimulation against the man's pubic bone. Being on top also allows her to control the rhythm and pace of the experience. Men rate a woman's being on top as a favorite position, followed by sex from behind.

8. *True:* The human body has many areas that tremble and tingle from tantalizing touch. By departing from the notion of genitalia as the sole source of satisfaction, a couple can awaken many new and titillating avenues of excitement.

How did you do? What did you discover that you did not know before? Sexuality is a forbidden topic in a lot of circles, as many people remain reluctant to discuss their problems even with their private physician. When sexual truths are hidden, myths and misinterpretations preside. But this does not have to occur when two people know and apply the beautiful Language of Sex.

Nevertheless, sexual myths remain pervasive. For instance, much of our fascination with sex lies in the "use it or lose it" myth which tells us that males hit their sexual peak near adolescence, and females reach theirs somewhat thereafter. Based on this supposition of chronological demise, everyone over thirty would be sexually despondent. There is truth that as we age, so do our biological parts, genitals included. But new research suggests that the simplest way for a man to stave off impotence is to keep having erections on a regular basis, because a flaccid penis is probably the least well oxygenated organ in the body. It is also suggested that an orgasm a day keeps the prostate surgeon away.

The same recommendation holds true for women advised to get regular "lubes and oil changes," because weekly sex doubles a woman's estrogen level, promotes fertility, reduces stress, helps prevent cardiovascular disease, burns 100–250 calories an hour, and promotes longer life. A study at South Illinois School of Medicine further found that a third of female migraine sufferers felt better after making love, with pain relief directly linked to orgasm intensity. Also, good sex induces good sleep as the body's hormones and neurochemicals are balanced in such a way that the brain shuts down after the earth has moved. Even Freud prescribed three orgasms a week. Recent studies have also shown that breast cancer survivors who experience orgasm—whether through masturbation or lovemaking—recover more quickly than those who do not. So if sex is so good *for our health*, why don't we desire it more? Why is it that the number one sexual complaint brought to therapists by committed couples is lack of desire?

Are You Bed Dead?

How great is your level of desire? Complete Self-Assessment #43 and measure your desire quotient to determine your propensity for ecstasy with your mate.

SELF-ASSESSMENT #43

TESTING OUR DESIRE QUOTIENT

Answer **True** *or* **False** *for each of the following statements:*

_____ **1.** Our bodies enter into uninhibited and creative combustion.

_____ **2.** I allow myself to let go in bed.

_____ **3.** We touch and kiss and flirt even when we're not having sex.

_____ **4.** When sexual problems arise, we discuss them.

_____ **5.** He listens to me, he is sensitive to my needs, and
I feel safe with him.

_____ **6.** We are emotionally naked, and I make myself sexually available to him.

_____ **7.** We enjoy experimenting with new techniques, toys, and erotic massage.

_____ **8.** We make time for red-hot romping even with our busy schedules.

_____ **9.** We do not feel sexual pressure to perform.

_____ **10.** We concentrate as much on foreplay as we do on afterplay; it's the whole experience that counts.

SCORING KEY

Count your number of T's:

8–10 T's = High Desire Quotient: **Hot to Trot**

4–7 T's = Mediocre Desire Quotient: **Turn Your Sugar into Spice**

0–3 T's = Low Desire Quotient: **Bed Dead**

Our problems in the area of desire often lie between our ears, not between our legs. If your desire quotient was high, you probably know how to apply the three aspects of the Language of Sex. However, if your desire quotient was mediocre or low, you need to get some sexual fine-tuning. For starters, close your lips, close your legs. Open your ears, open your heart. Believe in your own sexuality.

👑 **Gilda-Gram** *There is a sex goddess in every woman— and she is you.*

Your natural sexuality need only be unleashed.

Are You Aged to Perfection?

No adolescent could possibly offer the life lessons a baby boomer has already come to know. Yet today's aging adult has so confused genital prime with sexual prime that the parts that need to work often close too soon for renovation or, worse, for life. In record numbers, the "not-tonight, dear" curse is afflicting men where it used to be reserved solely for women. Yes, as a man ages, he requires more time between orgasms. At seventeen years old, he may be ready again in just seven *minutes*, but a fifty-year-old may require eight to twenty-four *hours*. Many men have problems dealing with their bodily changes. In reality, for most healthy adults, sexuality can continue throughout a lifetime.

With men's increased pressure to perform at their Taskmaster best, the need to provide the lights, action, atmosphere, foreplay, and now afterplay makes sex another chore in need of accomplishment. When the promised performance doesn't pan out, there can be disaster. Remember "Puss-in-Boots" Krista? When she and her benefactor finally did get together sexually, he found, to his alleged amazement, that he couldn't get an erection. What an embarrassment for him after hours of promises of great sex over the phone, a whole continent away. While he was struggling, he admitted having just begun taking medication for high cholesterol. So, freaked out over his inability under the sheets, he careened out of bed like a gazelle to look at the pills' packet insert to see if "impotence" was a possible side effect. He was disappointed to learn that the side effects made no reference to his fear . . . and there went the rest of the night, along with any hope for a relationship.

A study at Virginia Polytechnic Institute found that not being able to perform well sexually is one of man's greatest phobias (while a woman's top fears are unattractiveness and winding up a bag lady!). Women are surely coming into their own, and it now seems that just when they want it more, their partners want it less. Men's fear of not measuring up to a woman's expectations is called MISS: Male Insecurity Sexual Syndrome (otherwise translated to "Sorry, I've Got a Headache").

Truth be told, although our genital prime will come and go, most people never reach their sexual potential. Sex at twenty is ego oriented. Sex at thirty is purposeful. But sex at forty and beyond can be calming, peaceful, and connected. Those who come close to sexual prime are usually in the last age range. Finally, what they always did all night long now takes them all night long to do. Who'd complain about that?

The expectation factor that leads people to believe they will no longer be of any sexual use often becomes a self-fulfilling prophecy. Men expect not to be able to rise to the occasion; women expect to be drier than a doornail. He feels unmanly; she feels unattractive. These, the worst of each gender's fears. Because of our anxiety over failing, many couples simply quit trying. Sexless marriages are more common in our culture than we might suspect. A survey of six thousand marriages found that one out of six was not intimate. When our partner can't perform, we women as the relationship police blame ourselves: Will I be able to get him to have an erection? Am I attractive enough? Will I lubricate? Will I have an orgasm? Will I have an orgasm quickly enough? How many orgasms will I have? By itself, sex is not the most important factor in a relationship. But when placed in the context of a relationship's ups and downs, it can take on overwhelming significance. While we must learn not to *overfocus* on our sex lives, we also must remember we should expect a healthy one—and know how to command it.

Dear Dr. Gilda:
I guess I'm being selfish, but I've been dissatisfied sexually for
so long. You are probably asking, "Is your relationship based
on sex?" No, it isn't, but it does play a small role, and when
dissatisfaction comes into play, it seems as if sex accounts for
a lot.

Asking for sexual satiation is not selfish. Sex is a need to be satisfied, just as we need to eat and quench our thirst. We all have the right and, in fact, the obligation to ask for what we need. If we don't ask, we end up cheating ourselves. If we cheat ourselves, the primary person in our relationship, how can we possibly be available for our lover?

Not everyone wants to eat the same foods at the same hour. Like food, the range of our sexual appetites is very broad based, and our perceptions of what is earth-shattering is just as different. In Woody Allen's *Annie Hall*, the camera switches back and forth between Allen and Diane Keaton speaking to their separate shrinks about their lovemaking frequency:

He: "Hardly ever. Maybe three times a week."
She: "Constantly. I'd say three times a week."

No two people will always agree on what is satisfying. But one thing is for certain: when we feel comfortable with ourselves, we can freely ask our partners for what we need. If we instead feel more comfortable telling our friends or therapist about what we are *not getting*, our lover never gets to know our needs. Then we miss our just desserts.

The Language of Sex requires that you slow down, sharpen your senses, think seductively, and invite spontaneity. Begin with flirting, evolve to sensuality, and tease to sexuality when you're primed. The Language of Sex expresses the Language of Love. Make it a full body adventure. Let it last. But most of all, remember that going from flirtation to sensuality to sexuality takes time. Unless you have a bus to catch, slow down. Savor every moment.

The Need for Time

Time is an important factor in establishing a deep and lasting bond. While passion can hit quickly and fade just as fast, commitment requires the building of intimacy over time. The *McGill Report on Male Intimacy* lists five elements that determine how well two people will bond emotionally: time spent together, shared experiences, depth of interpersonal communication, exclusivity, and concern for one another. Note that this is a report on male intimacy. And it's just another sign that men want the same things women do. A recent survey suggests that people who ended up marrying knew their partner longer before having sex than couples in short-term re-lationships—whether they had met at a bar, a party, school, or work. In time, a couple has the opportunity to develop a deep friendship that goes on long after the first romantic swoons. Friendship is the basis of sexual freedom. It allows two people to reveal their vulnerable as well as their silly sides with-out self-consciousness. In short, they can truly be themselves. Even if their sexual attraction is not strong at first, it could eventually develop as a pair's emotional intimacy deepens. "Friends first, lovers later" sets the founda-tion for mutual caring. When this sequence is applied, sex gets better over time.

👑 **Gilda-Gram** *Horizontal loving is enhanced when vertical caring is intact.*

How do we maintain a loving and appropriate partnership? Don't sepa-rate sex and love. In many ways, the relationships of the couples we ob-serve while growing up direct our adult experiences. If one or both partners learned to separate love and sex, sex may serve as a substitute for the emotional intimacy they lack in marriage—even when they are divorc-ing. That is why some couples continue to have sex after they split. How-ever, this kind of activity can never make up for the lack of committed intimacy, which is probably the reason the couple separated in the first place. But the good news about human behavior is that if any of our sexual habits no longer serve us, we can alter them. While we know we can never alter someone else's habits, we can certainly change our own because:

👑 **Gilda-Gram** *How we love is* learned, *not* inherited. *What we* learn *can also be* unlearned.

In popular culture, sex is the showcase for love. In an effort to put it in its proper perspective, some organizations such as the National Chastity Association recommend celibacy before marriage so that premarital sex won't get in the way of romance. And if becoming a "retrovirgin" is tough to swallow, you should know that a new brand of Christian romance novels takes place in the marriage setting and unwinds with *prayer,* not drink or nudity, to teach the ropes of abstinence to the single and pure. This philos-ophy apparently holds that the shelf life of virginity has no expiration date. For those concerned about the rise of STDs, this "put your hormones on hold" doctrine may be a safe and satisfying way to go. In any case, most people in our culture would agree that there are two separate types of sex: casual sex and committed sex.

Casual Sex vs. Committed Sex

Dear Dr. Gilda:
I am insane over a fabulous guy at my college. He is pursued
by lots of other girls and he knows it. We are becoming friends.
I would love for us to have a relationship. My friends say I
should stay away from him because he has a reputation for
using girls. Can they just be jealous? Should I sleep with him
anyway? I want him bad!!

This woman says she wants a *relationship*, but she's willing to *give it away* to some gorgeous, popular hunk-in-a-hurry because she imagines they have already become "friends." The handwriting is certainly on the computer screen here. I tell her she's setting herself up for hurt and disappointment and that in order to possibly win this guy's heart—if it's even worth winning—she should set herself apart from the others and *take her time*. If it's really a relationship she wants, she won't find it by jumping into the sack so soon, especially since that's what he's constantly being offered already.

When singles begin dating, they often feel pressured to choose between the two most important questions in their new sexual world: "How much?" and "How soon?" If they haven't fully thought this issue through, they may end up writing letters like this one, which is similar to hundreds of others I receive just like it:

Dear Dr. Gilda:
There's a man I've liked for two years. We've been having sex
now for a couple of months. The problem is, he doesn't want to
commit. I enjoy being with him, and I don't want to ask for a
commitment because I don't want to scare him off. I've never
loved anyone as much as I do him. Everything about him is
perfect. We're perfect for each other. Please help.

It's amazing what some women consider "perfect." If this woman is hurting, this "relationship" is far from "perfect." How long is she willing to go on not communicating her needs in this affair? Is it worth putting her needs on the back burner so as not to "scare him off"? Every woman involved in a similar situation must decide what is most important to her—satisfying her desires or fulfilling his. Surely, at first, casual sex is the only thing open to singles, while committed sex is more for the seriously monogamous. But these are not absolute distinctions. Committed partners can and should have sex for fun with each other, while the casual sex of single partners may develop into committed love. But—and this is a big one—

if singles do choose to engage in casual sex, they must (1) accept it exactly for what it is, and (2) be honest with themselves and admit that if it remains purely casual, they can live with it as is. Unfortunately, most women hope that the man they mess with will *change* into a committed partner. Uh-oh, that word again.

All in all, the thing we seek most in a committed sex partner is not a hot Lothario who keeps us guessing, but a caring companion who is steadily by our side. While men say they primarily seek physical attractiveness for *casual* sex, for their long-term commitments they prefer honest, faithful, warm women to the traits that meet the eye. Women want someone who is generous, honest, and has a sense of humor. Someone with similar values and interests who is sensitive to their needs. Someone to just hit the sack with for the night and hug and hold whether the sex is good, bad, or nonexistent. Someone to offer sensuality as much as he offers sex. Because our potential partner does not come with the *Good Housekeeping* Seal of Approval, we're on our own to figure out his appropriateness *for us*.

In time, and with patience, casual sex could transform into committed sex. But that means we must put off immediate gratification with Mr. Right Now, however needy our groin. That's a tall order. It depends on what a woman wants. If she wants commitment, she must recognize that even in this age of equality, many men still differentiate between the good girl and the bad girl. In their minds, the good girl does not sleep with a man too early, otherwise he assumes she's sleeping with many others as well, and there goes the respect. Women, too, were often taught in childhood that girls who like sex are "sluts," and sexy women are compliant bimbos. To offset these hackneyed stereotypes, we must enjoy our daily life with all our passions until someone worthy appears on the scene. When he does, we can slowly begin to build a friendship for the future. This process cannot be rushed, because there will be the usual testing and trusting and pushing and pulling. Each step may require another negotiation. With each negotiation, we learn something new about ourselves. Therein lies the greatest objective of life—to learn and grow, not solely to become part of a pair.

A Tale of Two Titillations

Wendy and Scott had been married for six years. For this couple, there was nothing sexier than their monogamy. They were happily attending their close friend's dinner party, where the margaritas were flowing and the crowd of people was laughing heartily. This couple exuded infectious love and respect for each other, and even at this late stage of their relationship, at every dinner party they attended, onlookers were amazed that to this couple, merely passing the salt seemed like foreplay. They found it difficult to keep from touching one another every chance they got. While sitting by the fireplace and chatting with the other couples, they innocently picked up a large book of photographs to browse together. Of all things, it was a copy of Madonna's book, *Sex*, with its explicit sexual acts and poses. As they looked at the photos, their combined temperatures rose enough to heat the entire house. They were overwhelmingly driven to excuse themselves to go upstairs, where they converted their teasing into playful cavorting. Although they never engaged in intercourse, the titillation of the forbidden fruit with the party downstairs made them feel like spontaneous sexual outlaws. It was certainly one of the most erotic experiences the couple ever recalled. Intimacy based on trust is founded on what we've processed in our minds, our hearts, our souls, not just our plugs and outlets.

👑 Gilda-Gram *Intimacy depends more on our willingness to trust than on our skill at sex.*

On the other hand, Kimberly and Aaron were a couple of singles who had had a different kind of sexual interaction. On a sleepy Sunday morning, Aaron invited Kim over to his place for a jog in the park. They had not had sex before, but during their two previous casual dates, they had enjoyed some evenings of exciting and passionate petting. This would be the third-date test point of the three-date singles rule. Kimberly intuited that Aaron's offer of "jogging" was a euphemistic invitation for sex. In her heart, she believed they were well matched, she a fun-loving Toastmaster, he an organized Taskmaster. She sensed that he desperately needed a laugh out of life, which her flamboyant yet nurturing personality was happy to provide. All people come together to accentuate, balance out, and/or mask parts of their private selves. Both Kim and Aaron seemed to thrive on their differences. On this summer day, she didn't know if she was more horny than ready to be intimate with this guy, but not having been held by a man for some time, she felt a strong urge to find out. So strong is the need to be touched that many women land in bed when that had not been their primary intention.

When she appeared at his door, she was surprised to find that, despite ample time between his inviting phone call and her arrival, Aaron had not yet even gotten showered and shaved. Not at all like a fastidious anal character. She knew that had the roles been reversed, she would have pampered herself for hours in preparation for what was to follow. Not at all like a freewheeling oral character. Actually, when she arrived, Aaron was busy exercising (for his bad back), which caused him to drip with perspiration on this hot summer day. He told her he wanted to complete his workout, would she mind? At once she gleaned that this was not going to be your typical days-of-wine-and-roses seduction. With experience in the realm of being ravished, Kimberly found Aaron's behavior quite curious. But she was a spirited adventure seeker, so she wanted to see how this man's propensity for loving would unfold.

The woman waited in the living room, exploring her man's choice of music and books, which she felt would reveal more about him. She was aware that he asked few questions about her and her life, even about the important article she was writing for a famous magazine, which he knew she was slaving over. He admitted that at thirty-two, he was not in love now nor had he ever been in love before. But he showed great emotion for his small children, so she reasoned that as time went on, his heart might open for the love of the right woman. In short, *he would change*. Notice how a woman with the best intentions misleads herself in the *hopes* of being loved.

When Aaron was finished exercising, he called to Kimberly from the bedroom. As a responsible little foot soldier, she marched on command into the bedroom where he pulled her passionately to him and kissed her so hard, she wanted to disrobe then and there despite the sweat. Yep, she was horny all right, and this man somehow brought out the seductive side of her that she usually kept under wraps. But she told Aaron that his beard was so rough, it hurt her face. He offered to shower and shave so that he would not cut her up. How kind and considerate this man is, she decided.

When he emerged from his bathroom, he kissed her with baby-fine skin. She had always enjoyed the succulence of his juicy kisses. As they began to get into what Kimberly had believed was the real reason for her coming, Aaron said mechanically, "I can't perform oral sex on you now because I've just shaved, and your hair down there will irritate my skin. So don't think I'm rejecting you." Spoken like a true analytical anal—or was it *storm trooper*? She had spotted allergy creams in his place for every rash known to mankind. But she also flashed to his complaints of aches and pains throughout his body, his constant lack of sleep, his upset with his thinning hair, his concern about his weight gain of five pounds, his caution when jogging for fear of knee damage, and his terror over possibly losing the job he worked so hard to get. Yes, this guy did have his hypochondriacal quirks.

Since oral sex was a part of sexuality Kim enjoyed and had looked forward to, she thought, Why didn't he tell me about this rash stuff before he cleaned up his face? For sure, on this occasion, Aaron had no intention of offering lip service. Talk about ice cubes on a hot fire! Obviously he had been down this road before, no pun intended. Obviously he had been accused of rejection in the past by some former partner(s), and he wanted to stave off an "incident" with Kim. So this was his excuse not to provide cunnilingus, although he surely enjoyed fellatio on him.

Thinking that she didn't know Aaron well enough, Kim never asked him directly why he had not told her about his allergy problem before he shaved. This is what happens when singles have sex too soon: *I'm good enough for him to partake of my body, but I'm not good enough for him to tell me things straight*. In all fairness, Aaron may have been suffering from a case of first-time jitters that served to mar his potential for open communication. In any case, from there the scene progressively deteriorated.

These were two people with possibility. They were a pair launching into intimacy for the first time, undoubtedly too soon. Twenty years ago Masters and Johnson said that 50 percent of American couples don't communicate what they'd like to enjoy together. Nothing much has changed over the decades. At the beginnings of intimacy, partners need to ask about each other's preferences. Aaron never asked Kimberly what she liked in bed, and she was too uncomfortable to assert her personal tastes. It was only date three, after all. If they hadn't rushed into this, maybe they would have felt freer to communicate their preferences. Meanwhile Kim wondered why she wasn't bold enough to speak her mind. Where was the *Cosmo* girl she thought she had become?

During their scurrying under the sheets, he kissed her softly as they touched. *Oh, those kisses!* His good looks and firm body got her sexually oiled. Then Aaron asked her to give him a backrub. She worked steadily, but he became critical that her hands on his pecs were not following his specs. *Oh, these Taskmaster's rules!* He directed her to knead his skin "as she would knead bread," he said. (What in the world did she know about bread making? she thought.) *Where was this Taskmaster's owner's manual?* After she tried her darnedest to please him in the way he requested, she thrust herself facedown on the bed from exhaustion. He gave her back a few strokes, but then complained, "Hey, *I* was the one who wanted the backrub." They engaged in some other brief sexual aerobics, and while this was going on he kissed her, which she enjoyed. *Oh, those kisses!* This guy definitely turned her on. But his body refused to cooperate in the way he wanted. The warrior blamed his inability to maintain an erection on his need for a condom. Now the ode to his eminence became the lament of his limpness!

In sex, the lowest common denominator rules. At the beginning it is the woman who gatekeeps the fortress and decides the ifs and whens of a couple's sexual union. Once it occurs, however, it's the man whose real or imagined fears determine its continuation and outcome. With all the pulling, tugging, rubbing, and hugging—with no outcome—Kim questioned her own desirability, her attractiveness, her cellulite. (*Hey, girls, the latest findings suggest a high correlation between cellulite and a woman's sexual potential. Go figure!*) Aaron didn't give up, and finally, alas, his member complied. Bodily fluid without emotion. Ejaculation without orgasm. Orgasm as a full body sensation allows a man to retain his erection. It has the potential of joining sex with love and can last a full twenty to thirty minutes. Ejaculation alone involves emission, expulsion, and exit. It is based solely on sexual gratification and lasts about a minute. Aaron never knew what he missed by separating love and sex. For Kimberly, it seemed close enough, perhaps . . . but no cigar. What did she do? She faked an orgasm.

Since the female orgasm inspires bonding, most women who have not built trust into their relationship before having sex fear being hurt. So, like Kim, they will protect themselves by fabricating the extent of their ecstasy. Like fake diamonds, fake fur, and fake leather, the big *faux O* has become a part of many women's sexual repertoire. Often they want to build a man's ego without letting on they feel too insecure to let go. A *Glamour* magazine study found that 98 percent of female respondents faked orgasm without their partners ever knowing. In the well-publicized "Sex in America" survey conducted by the National Opinion Research Center, 44 percent of men said their partners always climaxed, but only 29 percent of the women said they did. Actually, for a man to tell if a woman has faked an orgasm, he'd need the right equipment and an expert to determine her blood pressure, heart rate, brain activity, and vaginal contractions. In this case, Aaron didn't notice or even care. The average amount of time a woman needs to go from arousal to climax is thirteen to fifteen minutes, while it takes a man just three to five. In other words, it takes a woman three to four times longer than a man to be sexually aroused, but most men don't get the clitoral translation. In record time, playmate and primate both satisfied the same person—him.

It was over. A card-carrying member of the Germs "R" Us club, Aaron darted into the bathroom to remove his condom and shower *again*. In an effort to be close, Kim joined him. While beneath the streaming water, Kimberly asked Aaron to hold her. Although he complied superficially, he quickly disengaged his body from hers. She felt emotionally abandoned. He was careful not to suds up his private parts so he wouldn't break out from the soap. She found it miraculous that he hadn't also complained about an allergy to the latex condom that strikes 5 percent of Americans. Although, without that, he could be dead meat.

When dry, the couple returned to bed, where Kim thought that, at last, they could cuddle. This period of après-sex is known as "afterplay." After both partners ideally feel satiated, this resolution phase is for caressing, cuddling, holding, and sleeping, all of which could bring them to the final stage of emotional unity. Kim felt she still needed the connection she originally sought. Aaron put on a video of a movie he had taped earlier and proceeded to turn his back on her, while, without asking, he assumed they would watch the film together. Aaron kept his dense back to Kimberly for almost two hours. You know, the back that needed to be kneaded.

When she left, it had already become dark. Although she had just spent the day in bed with a man she felt tremendous chemistry with, Kim felt empty and lonely. This guy who was initially hot to trot was now an emotional refrigerator. Dispassionately shut down. Not an unusual scene for sex between singles, as *Seinfeld*'s Elaine explains to a friend. She notes that something happens to men after they have sex. It is as though they need to flee the scene of an accident. They use the excuse of having to get up early. Suddenly they all become farmers!

The fever had broken. Poor judgment, bad timing, wrong partner. Or maybe the sex thing simply happened too soon in their interchange. Now Kimberly wondered why she had even bothered; was she delusional? She thought that all she had wanted was a pleasant buffet of sharing. Too bad Aaron was out to lunch.

Sexual Communication Must Be Honest Communication

👑 **Gilda-Gram** *The Language of Sex speaks volumes about things a couple won't discuss.*

As Kim would concur, a recent survey found that 55 percent of women said that sex without love was not enjoyable. While it is true that a woman must open herself up physically to let a man enter, a man must open himself up emotionally to be known. Who needs what, and when, can present problems for an emerging relationship. A woman needs love to find comfort in sex, while a man needs sex to find comfort in love. Especially for women, openness is required. It is an offshoot of committed sex. This honest communication can also prevent the unsung worries over aging and drying.

👑 **Gilda-Gram** *Good communication is the best lubrication.*

When two people are honest, no one engages in an activity before she or he is ready. Because women tend to become closer through conversation, their communication can prime their sexual appetite. The same is true for men who are evolved. (Another reason for women to choose their prince wisely.) In even the best of unions, as time goes on, there will be sexual ups and downs. Couples who can freely discuss their sexual issues don't need a sex therapist. They know to communicate their concerns on neutral territory, not in the bedroom, so that they don't contaminate the sheets. Their ability to openly work things through on their own becomes their special brand of K-Y jelly.

Kimberly was not sexually honest. Taking on much too passive a role in their interchange, she never requested what she wanted Aaron to give her. She had waited for him to ask—which never happened. The idea that a woman must take charge of her sexuality, even if she's in a committed relationship, existed as early as the nineteenth century. In an 1876 marriage manual, a Mrs. E. B. Duffey cautioned a woman to

> *give or withhold her favors according to her own best judgment, uninfluenced either by fear or over-persuasion. A man has no "marital rights" in this respect, except to take what is granted to him freely and lovingly. Passion must come . . . accompanied not only with love, but with the tender graces of kindness and consideration. . . .*

That was over a century ago, and women today still voice their longing for a kind and considerate lover. Studies reveal that today's women are more sexual than at any other time in history. And a female's sexual appetite triggers her partner's desire because:

👑 **Gilda-Gram** *A turned-on woman is an aphrodisiac.*

But a woman's willingness to engage in intercourse is only one side of her sexual expression. She should also be involved in her self-caring. Most women want to feel protected in knowing a partner won't hustle to the wind after they've hustled them to bed. So when your hormones are humming, and you suddenly have amnesia about using the word "No," stave off the possibility of hurt with this general rule of thumb:

👑 **Gilda-Gram** *Don't get naked until you feel safe.*

But the question remains about how to integrate our sexual needs with our desires for all-encompassing love. Many single women lie to themselves, as well as to their partners, that they are up for casual sex. Secretly most hope it will evolve into more. One study found that adults lie an average of thirteen times a week, or at least that's what they admit to. Little white sexual lies often punctuate even the best relationships, whether the people are married, single, or in between. Men lie about listening to women; women lie that sex was grand. While we may seem able to get away with many of these untruths for a while, eventually push does come to shove, and the beans do get spilled in bed.

The overall Language of Sex does not lie in the long run because it can't. It is a visceral kind of communiqué, and it says things about us carnally that we're too shy to reveal about ourselves in words. For example, one woman's partner wanted her to bring him to the height of ecstasy, just short of orgasm, then he would send her home so that he could masturbate alone and not display a loss of control *in front of a woman*. Another woman rejected lambskin condoms not because they are not as safe as latex, but because she is a vegetarian who would *never consider taking animal products* into her body. Still another encouraged her three-year-old daughter to sleep between her husband and herself because she *really couldn't stand being touched by the man she was married to*. Yet another woman continued to sleep with a man she believed was bisexual, and even cheating on her with another woman, simply because "for now, it's better than being alone, and maybe he'll eventually come around."

Some people use the Language of Sex because they are afraid of the Language of Love, which suggests the Language of Commitment and Intimacy. Intimacy demands honesty. It involves participating, not spectatoring. It avoids emotional freeze-outs. It averts shutting down. When we are involved, we are vulnerable—and subject to our mate's taking advantage of our hearts. When we trust a man, we are more willing to take that chance.

Is It Intimacy or Formality?

We have just seen the difference between two couples. Wendy and Scott were an integrated, involved pair. As with the question of whether our individual control force is Internal or External, each person has the capacity to choose between *Self-Validated Intimacy* and *Other-Validated Formality*. Self-Validated Intimacy involves your willingness to self-disclose who you honestly are. No subterfuges. You'll accept the consequences of your self-disclosure, whatever they may be. You feel your Power, and it is obvious. It is this coming to terms with who you are as a person that lays the foundation for what you can bring to your authentic sexual self. Like Internal Control, Self-Validated Intimacy begins not with a woman's partner, but with herself.

♛ **Gilda-Gram** *For a successful sexual union, each partner must have a clear sexual identity.*

If Kimberly had incorporated a strong sense of Self-Validated Intimacy during her brief courtship with Aaron, she would probably never have agreed to go out with such an egocentric man on a second date. He was not Self-*Validated*. He was Self-*Involved* and suffering from what I call *ESD: Emotional Shut-Down*. ESD men can demonstrate their emotions for things that are safe, for example, anger at a business meeting, love for their children, attentiveness to a client. But they are carefully protected when it comes to showing affection toward a woman. In an effort to find validation of his worth, as many men do, Aaron sought it through sex. And he most likely always separated the act from the deep emotion of love. While opposites do attract, and Kim's Toastmaster personality felt safe in the arms of Aaron's Taskmaster, we also choose people with traits similar to ours, which serve as the basis for getting along. Actually, it is not surprising that Kimberly, too, suffered from ESD. Three years after a long, troubled relationship, she was just emerging from her mourning. That was one reason she was unable to spot the Aaron type of character. Many people, both married and single, search outside themselves when they don't know enough to find their Power and Purpose within. As we know, External Control just doesn't cut it. Similarly, Other-Validated Formality is a cheap shot at love.

Even if Kimberly had allowed her better judgment to get lost in her choice of a second date, if she had incorporated a strong sense of Self-Validated Intimacy, she would not have allowed her sexual yearning to direct her to enter an affair before she was ready. But even if she decided to indulge anyway, she would not have questioned her own desirability and attractiveness when Aaron's apparatus nose-dived. Finally, with a strong sense of Self-Validated Intimacy, she would have backed out of bed when Aaron's back turned on her.

Obviously Kimberly and Aaron hadn't spent enough time together to know if they were even compatible. Yet each looked to the other for fulfillment. Such Other-Validated Formality may work in the short run, where mind and body are separated and the aim is merely to get a Jiffy Lube. But it can never transform into a loving, long-term relationship, because if we have not allowed ourselves to be known by our partner, we will lack the security we need for self-revelation.

When a couple is willing to wait for intimacy, they take their time in getting to know each other. This way, when they are ready, they can honestly share their preferences in acknowledging that each of them may want to be satisfied differently. In time, partners can sharpen their sexuality with the help of, and in the presence of, the one they love. Ultimately, a Self-Validated woman is in charge of her own feelings and her own sexual gratification. Similarly, Self-Validated men are not ESD personality types. They know their physiology, feel free to communicate it to their partner, and trust that their women will do their best to partake in the pleasure. In the same vein, Self-Validated women don't blame their partner for not "giving them" an orgasm. They know that, like their personal Power and their zealous Purpose, their orgasm is both their right and responsibility. They know how their body is best satisfied, and they openly share that with their partner and trust that he will gladly help them fulfill their passions. Wendy and Scott both exuded Self-Validated Intimacy. That is the reason they were able to continue to explore the freedom and enjoyment of each other's bodies after a few marital years with all life's ups and downs. For them, unlike many other couples they knew, marriage was not domestic incarceration, but a legalized playpen in which to bountifully romp and rollick. And like a fine wine, their romping and rollicking *improved* over time.

What happened in Kimberly's mind to make her believe she was ready to consummate this courtship? It was glaringly obvious that Aaron's life didn't have room for anyone other than himself, his work, and his ailments. Kim was indeed delusional to think this man would transform into a knight in shining ardor with her offering of a sexual Band-Aid. Maybe we see these turnarounds in the movies, but in real life as we know it, it usually doesn't happen that way—that is, unless the *man himself* finds a need to change. Those of us in the self-help business have seen those miracles happen occasionally. But from the woman's self-care standpoint, it is vital she "let go and let grow" the seeds she has already planted. No matter what the outcome with a prince, she must forever remember that she always has herself.

Is It Sex out of Need or Sex out of Want?

Kimberly knew that she was sexually ripe, a natural function of being alive. There was physical chemistry with Aaron, but no emotional connection and no Language of Love working to help set up trust. Kim knew that she longed for a man's touch. "Skin hunger" is a real physiological need. But for Kim, any man might have sufficed to fill that void. The problem is that sometimes our sexual hunger motivates us to desire out of *need*, rather than out of *want*. As we discussed in chapter 3, *needs* are "must-haves" to survive, while *wants* are "prefer-to-haves" to feel good. No healthy woman desires out of a need to survive. If she does, she is obsessed, and obsession is about her own ego, not about wanting a shared, interdependent life with a man. Desire out of *need* can be empty. It falsely promises to make us whole. It's the notion that one bookend is useless and cannot stand alone. Since desire out of need has us desperately searching merely for another body for satisfaction, it sets us up to be discarded after we have served our purpose.

If it was sexual satiation Kimberly craved, the customary expedient for that malady is masturbation. Babies masturbate from the first months of life. In fact, boys and girls can have orgasms before they are even seven years old. By masturbating, a woman can manipulate her brain into thinking her body is beautiful. She won't go blind or grow hair on her palms. The satisfaction derived from masturbation is a random act of kindness a woman bestows upon herself. After masturbation, a woman could feel liked, loved, and wanted—all without demonstrating neediness and imagining intimacy where none exists.

Masturbation has gained increased popularity with the use of helpful aids. Now that we've discarded our Barbies, grown-ups are cruising adult toy stores devoted to selling pleasure props. In a survey of Americans who use "sexual enhancement products," it was found that the average vibrator-wielding female is a monogamous white mother who is Christian, college educated, and in her thirties. She conservatively votes Republican and has a family income of over $40,000. She owns one or two vibrators and uses them while both masturbating herself and while making love with her partner. So much for thinking nice girls *don't*.

Most women prefer to be loved long-term rather than be conquered and abandoned. A woman's painful regrets after a disappointing interlude like Kimberly's is the stuff that country music is made of. But there's no use having guilt after the fact. All a woman can do is dry her morning-after tears and get on with her life, acting smarter with the next guy who's waiting in the wings. The ideal is to have desire out of *want*, where a woman and her partner can be emotionally independent and satiated *before* pairing up. This way, whatever they become together is an enhancement of what each of them already is alone. They can spend some real time learning about each other and establishing trust. They can appreciate one another as people without agonizing about potential that may not be there. When they finally do engage in sex, they can meld their tired bodies into one with truth and caring. There is the feeling that when they awake, there will be the constancy of their partner's concern. It is this feeling that most women attempt to manufacture in their short-term sexual unions. It is the lack of this feeling that makes for sadness after a woman has realized the reality of rejection.

Desire out of *want* requires a strong foundation that always begins with the individual herself. She must know who she is, what she's about, and she must be openly willing to share this knowledge.

👑 Gilda-Gram *Sex is not an act we* do; *it is an expression of who we* are.

Of course there are differences in the sexual styles within each of the categories of casual sex and committed sex. Not everyone involved in casual sex is oriented toward lust and desire out of *need*. Sometimes they simply want a secluded niche to scratch their itch. Similarly, not everyone in the committed sex category operates from the standpoint of trust and desire out of *want*. Sometimes they need to scratch the same itch as the casual sex seekers. Overall, these categories are generalizations based on the findings of women as a group. Of the two, which would you prefer?

CASUAL SEX	COMMITTED SEX
Other-Validated *Formality*	Self-Validated *Intimacy*
Lust	Trust
Chemistry	Connection
Desire out of *need*	Desire out of *want*
Short-term tryst	Long-term lovemaking
Questioning of self	Acceptance of self
Self-conscious body image and performance	Freedom and flexibility
Physical release	Tender affection

You've identified where you would like to be. If you're like most women, it's no contest. The preference is for a committed involvement so as not to end up identifying with the sadness of Kimberly or commiserating with the disenchantment of *Seinfeld*'s Elaine. Determine where you are. If there is a discrepancy between where you'd like to be and where you now find yourself, it's time to change your behavior. Just remember that communication is the basis of lubrication. The Language of Sex is predicated on your ability to express your Power, your Purpose, and your willingness to Play. It extends into Flirtation, Sensuality, and Sexuality. All these steps take time, and time builds the needed trust for committed sex. The Language of Sex cannot successfully be achieved during a one-night stand. Above all else, your mission is to grow. When you express yourself and bet on yourself, you are more attractive to a worthy man. If you're truly enjoying your own life for what it is, what's your rush?

GILDA-GRAMS
FROM CHAPTER 9
Apply the Language of Sex

▶ *There is a sex goddess in every woman—
and she is you.*

▶ *Horizontal loving is enhanced when vertical
caring is intact.*

▶ *How we love is* learned, *not* inherited.
What we learn *can also be* unlearned.

▶ *Intimacy depends more on our willingness
to trust than on our skill at sex.*

▶ *The Language of Sex speaks volumes about
things a couple won't discuss.*

▶ *Good communication is the best lubrication.*

▶ *A turned-on woman is an aphrodisiac.*

▶ *Don't get naked until you feel safe.*

▶ *For a successful sexual union, each partner
must have a clear sexual identity.*

▶ *Sex is not an act we* do, *it is an expression
of who we* are.

CONCLUSION

Be a Worthy Partner and You'll Have a Worthy Partner

👑 **Gilda-Gram** *If he's mine, I can't lose him. If he's not, I don't want him.*

ook at the ten lead-in Gilda-Grams in this book. They have been selected specifically to form the basis of the "Don't Bet on the Prince!" technology. When a woman accepts and repeats these Gilda-Grams, and completes and analyzes the self-assessments, she will know how to succeed in love by betting on herself.

The lead-in Gilda-Grams are:
- Ask "I am *who*?" before saying "I do."
- Make yourself the prize before you prize a partner.
- Commit to yourself instead of waiting for a prince to commit to you.
- What we believe we deserve is what we receive.
- We alone create our destiny.
- We will never be loved if we can't risk being disliked.
- The art of receiving begins by giving to yourself.
- We attract not who we want, but who we *are*.
- Fall in *like* before falling in *love*.
- Good communication is the best lubrication.
- If he's mine, I can't lose him. If he's not, I don't want him.

Throughout this book we discussed how women have traditionally bet on some fictitious prince to take care of us and make our lives better. While we were betting against all odds that the prince would continually be there for us, the prince was betting on a prince of another kind—often his career—to sweep him off his feet and take care of him and us and the kids forever. When neither the man-as-savior nor the company-as-benefactor keep those alleged promises to stay by our side happily ever after, both genders feel cheated. Women are dismayed when their men dump them and display fears and foibles. Men are crestfallen when their companies pink-slip them from the arena they thought was eternally theirs. For both genders, then, another form of existence starts to unfold. This new state touts only one person to put our faith in—the one we see in the mirror each morning when we brush our teeth.

The trouble is that most of us resist betting solely on ourselves. "I just want someone who will make me happy" is the constant theme I hear from women young and old who never realize that no one can make them happy but themselves. We seem to feel unworthy, incapable, uncertain of our assets as they stand alone. Somewhere in our upbringing, we surmised that men are brighter, better educated, and more aware of what to do next. Yet as a former management consultant to male entrepreneurs, I noted one thing the successful ones all had in common: they totally believed in themselves. Those who did not remained *Wanna-Be's*, while the positive belief systems of the others propelled them to outstanding *Will-Be* outcomes. I learned that what we ultimately get from life is determined by what we believe we *deserve*. I applied this finding to love and loving. When I studied the women who partnered with worthy men, they were no more beautiful, brilliant, or successful than any of the rest of us. But they demonstrated the same obvious ingredient as the successful entrepreneurs: they believed they *deserved* to get their guy. So I came upon my concept of *deserve level* as the basis for a woman's success in hooking, hugging, and holding a man.

Next, I recognized that so many of us were stuck in a "nice girl" mentality, unable or unwilling to speak our minds for fear we wouldn't be *liked*. We are so fearful of being abandoned that we wholesale our Power to the men in charge and become (milque)Toastmasters. To be liked, we count everyone's needs before our own and become extraordinary Overfunctioners. When we recognize that we are accepting, and thereby *teaching*, men to walk all over us, some of us misuse our Power and become demanding Taskmasters in order to get our discarded needs met by force. We are angry, and angry women are ugly. But real Power is not controlling power; it is balance from within. Nonetheless, we struggle and strain and depend on men's External stroking rather than operate from the Internal knowledge of our self-worth. How can we get men's respect if we don't believe we are worthy of it? Observing this, I developed the means for women to star in their own commercial. At last a woman's worth would be not only accepted but projected as well. Once she understands her strong core, she can give from whatever she has remaining without depleting what she herself needs to survive. In this way, a woman can enjoy her natural nurturing at no cost.

These alterations in a woman's behavior require that she be adamant about taking care of herself. She must leave men who have hurt her and not hang in in hopes they'll change. Her right to say "No" is also a responsibility to her own self-care, and once she exercises it, she will garner respect, a less frivolous response than the liking she had originally set out to get. She now knows who she is, and when she communicates it, she is ready to receive what she believes she deserves. Such receiving requires forgiving the people around her on whom she has expended undue energy by blaming them. She lets go of the blockages and lets in the love she knows is forthcoming. As she receives this love, she becomes a more receptive and perceptive listener to her mate. Feeling understood and cared for himself, he in turn supports her need for time alone to pursue activities she is passionate about. In her Power, she outlines her relationship boundaries from the start so that her love can grow without major misunderstandings. Knowing that the only way to love a man is to realize he may someday be gone, she recognizes that even as a couple, she is always just a person away from singlehood. With this philosophy, should her relationship disintegrate, she pursues her Purpose all the more so she can heal more quickly.

The "Don't Bet on the Prince!" woman dares to be herself—vulnerable, disagreeable, and willing to walk away should her needs and wants become unmet. She hooks and hugs the *right* man. Now she needs to hold him. She undertakes the Language of Love from strength, not from fear. This cements the relationship she has found with the worthy man she's longed for. Together they enjoy lasting, committed sex. The bond only thickens. She expresses herself as a sex goddess, a goddess of love, a goddess of goodness, a goddess of manifesting her future exactly as she wants. Using her Power, her Purpose, and her willingness to Play, she chooses, rather than waits to be chosen. She now gets to negotiate her life without the help of a man's magic wand. She is totally in control. She *deserves* what she's gotten, especially because she's achieved it on her own. And her worthy man appreciates her for having lived her life as independent and self-sufficient.

Betting on yourself takes careful planning. Remember Ina from chapter 4, the woman who had to tell her husband's ex not to call their home? Remember how that act won her the title "bitch"? After completing the self-assessments, she recognized that she had been giving away too much of her Power to Max over a period of many years. Like many women, she had moved into his apartment when they first married, exchanged the activities she loved for his, and had nothing left of the woman she had once been. She had become a Cheshire Catwoman, her lines of uniqueness erased except for her Toastmaster smile. Things had to change. For starters, she got her driver's license. As it had been for Caitlin, whose husband did not want her to learn to drive, a driver's license became Ina's first declaration of independence. Next, she decided to attend her own family's Christmas celebration, rather than the one held by Max's nasty family. For the first time, she asked Max to compromise on her behalf. Before completing these self-assessments, she had never *asked* Max to do anything for her. We know that if we don't ask, we don't get. Asking for what she now believed she deserved was an entirely new behavior. She was no longer Miss Nice Girl. Although Max was financially well-off, Ina reemerged in the publishing industry, the career she had left before her baby was due. She now exercised her Power and pursued her Purpose. Her happier attitude made a difference in her marriage. Max began to change his perception of his milquetoast wife to that of a woman who controlled her own life. He stopped taking her for granted. Together they allocated a lot of their spare time to Play. Respect returned to their marriage, and their connection is now stronger than it's ever been.

Our friend Christine, too, has made some life changes. She realizes that, like the rest of us, she's a work in progress, and life's journey toward growth is never completed. Motivated by the awareness she reaped from completing the self-assessments, she has recognized that she now wants to build on her innate Power, Purpose, and willingness to Play. She has begun volunteering at the battered women's shelter where she had spent a night escaping from Howard. She sees in these women a lot of the dependence on men she has experienced herself. They discuss their need to be liked and to be loved and their willingness to accept poor treatment in exchange for a warm male body by their side. They are all slowly reassessing their values and building independent lives. They have formed the first "Don't Bet on the Prince!" Support Center. It's a start.

But of all the women we've met, Kimberly is especially inspiring. After she left Aaron that last evening, she decided not to engage in sex again with anyone until she had a committed partner. She went out on many dates, most of whom wanted to make love, and to all of whom she renamed herself a "retrovirgin." No man lit her fire. She often thought of Aaron. She had gotten to know him somewhat before that fateful sexual fiasco. She sensed his dichotomous fear of a woman controlling his life yet his strong desire to have a permanent relationship. She still desired him. Yes, perhaps she was delusional. Blame it on the oxytocin, that relationship superglue that turns a woman to Silly Putty after sex. She knew she'd never call him, but she could not get him out of her mind. She just sensed something . . . yet she was determined to let it go.

Then, one night, at a glamorous party, there he was. When she saw him, her legs wobbled. She felt the same spark she had experienced months earlier. He greeted her affectionately, yet the memory of his Taskmaster control and bedroom chill raised a flag of caution. Yes, her florid flamboyance contrasting his button-down conservatism tugged at her heartstrings again. Opposites certainly do attract. Throughout the evening, he stared at her and touched her often. It seemed as if he had been body-pierced by Cupid's bow. Another man at the party interested in Kim was also being attentive. Now in a position to comparison-shop, Kim was sure of the chemistry she felt for Aaron.

Although he asked to spend that night with her, this time Kim preferred to wait until she trusted him more before offering her body again. He called during the week. They spent hours on the phone over the course of several nights. Yes, there was definitely a connection between them. He invited her to spend the weekend with him. But when she learned that he was having houseguests, she declined. A "Don't Bet on the Prince!" woman wants to get to know a man better without being part of a chorus line. He asked if she would meet him at his apartment when his friends left. She agreed.

She drove thirty-five minutes to his house on Sunday night. Her body moistened in anticipation of seeing him alone for the first time in months. But once again, her hopes for unity with this man were dashed. When she arrived at his apartment, he was having a temper tantrum about the work he had to do for Monday. He was overwrought. He was nasty. She tried to convey that the majority of heart attacks in our culture occur at 9:00 A.M. Monday mornings, falling into her old "fix-it" pattern. But she was also genuinely concerned about this man.

Unfortunately, he never heard. He criticized her suggestions. He put her down. She tried to ignore his foul mood, saying "Come to bed with me." Going back on her covenant with herself, she admitted that he could have had her in bed in a moment.

Instead Aaron replied, "I don't want to be ordered around." She tried again: "Please come to bed with me?" She knew that another man would have ripped her clothes off without another word. What a waste! To Aaron, Kim had obviously become the vision of his controlling mother, and he was at once transformed into a reacting, rebellious little boy. He turned his back on her again, although this time figuratively, for what she vowed would be the last time. Hardly the control freak she was now accused of being, Kimberly did take control—that is, of these negative surroundings.

She flashed to similar circumstances when she had remained in a bad situation in hopes of turning things around, fixated on overfunctioning for a man's vulgarity. But she was smarter now. Love is not supposed to hurt. *Get up, get out!* she thought. She refused to be ignored and criticized, especially after making the trip to see Aaron. Kimberly put on her coat and walked out. Without apology, he let her go. This incident certainly did allow Kim to know Aaron better. She suddenly saw him as a man without conscience. Some years later, she thought, when his daughter grows up, he'll be furious if a guy treats her this way. But today, with Kimberly, he was without remorse. She walked to her car, drove home, spiritually wished him love and healing, and went dancing at a local club. Aaron needed her, she knew, but she also knew that *she did not need him—or this*. For the first time in her life, she realized she could not save a man. Aaron's epiphany would undoubtedly require some crisis. Crises are blessings. They push us over the fence and get us to view life from a different blade of grass. They make us grow. Maybe there would someday be a miracle for Aaron, but Kim would not wait around to find out. She manifested the miracle of her own growth as she realized that her happiness was not just a prince away, but only as far as she *dared* to dream.

There are many combinations of couples like Kim and Aaron. Most of us, at one time or another, have remained too long in situations that sapped us. Ultimately there is only one way to find a worthy partner. It is to *be* a worthy partner, to know when something is not serving you—and move on. Bet on yourself and enjoy your life and all its offerings. When the next Charming Prince saunters past you, you will not be pressured to be swept away too soon. You will take your time to establish the friendship you need for committed, lasting love. You will understand that the rules are yours, and you can change them when and if you wish. If you are already with a less-than-Charming-Prince, seek your passions first and allow him to seek his. Either your relationship will be enhanced or you will find a better one waiting in the wings.

When you bet on yourself, your life is wonderful. You can afford to be graciously calm. While your composure piques a hunter's desire, you can stand aside and watch what is about to unfold take its natural course. Your mantra is golden:

👑 **Gilda-Gram** *If he's mine, I can't lose him. If he's not, I don't want him.*

You have found the self for whom you've searched so long. No one can take that from you. You finally love the person you are. And you are awesome. Enjoy!

> *Sometimes, a journey to another place*
> *puts us where we've started.*
> *But our insights now have somehow changed.*
> *Suddenly, we have only to open our eyes*
> *to find our Power, our Purpose, our willingness to Play*
> *. . . and they have been there all along.*
> *Now we finally know.*

GILDA-GRAMS

FROM CONCLUSION

▶ *If he's mine, I can't lose him. If he's not, I don't want him.*

ABOUT THE AUTHOR

Dr. Gilda Carle has been an educator throughout her career and has taught elementary and junior high school in New York City's South Bronx. She has worked as a management consultant, training executives in Fortune 500 companies, and as a spokesperson for Hallmark's Shoebox Greetings, emphasizing the need for humor in relationships. As the "Love Doc," she has responded to the many letters sent to her on MTV Online. She now teaches the psychology of communication at New York's Mercy College and speaks regularly to audiences throughout the world. She holds a Ph.D. from New York University.

Best known as a television personality and talk show therapist, Dr. Gilda offers advice on love, sex, and relationships on *Sally Jessy Raphaël* and other popular television and radio shows worldwide. The in-house therapist for *Soap Opera Digest*, Dr. Gilda is often featured in national publications, and she has a monthly column in *'Teen* magazine. She lives in New York.